CW00918589

THE WARRIOR QUEEN

THE WARRIOR QUEEN

The Life And Legend of Æthelflæd, Daughter of Alfred the Great

Joanna Arman

To my grandmother Patricia Arman-Smith:
February 1920–April 2016
Another formidable lady, fondly remembered. I know she would have loved to read this book.

First published 2017

Amberley Publishing
The Hill, Stroud
Gloucestershire, GL5 4EP

www.amberley-books.com

ISBN 978 1 4456 6204 6 (hardback)
ISBN 978 1 4456 6205 3 (ebook)

British Library Cataloguing in Publication Data.
A catalogue record for this book is available from the British Library.

Typesetting and Origination by Amberley Publishing
Printed in the UK.

CONTENTS

LIST OF ABBREVIATIONS

Anglo-Saxon Chronicles Michael Swanton trans. and ed. *The Anglo-Saxon Chronicles* (London, 1996).

Annals of Ireland Fragmentary Annals of Ireland, translated by Joan Newlon Radner, Electronic edition compiled by Beatrix Färber, Maxim Fomin, Emer Purcell, CELT: Corpus of Electronic Texts Edition, University College Cork, 2004, 2008, http://www.ucc.ie/celt

Æthelweard A. Campbell, ed. *The Chronicle of Æthelweard* (London, 1962).

Bede Bede, The Ecclesiastical History of the English People, ed. and trans. Judith McClure and Roger Collins (Oxford University Press: Oxford, 1994).

EHD Dorothy Whitelock ed., *English Historical Documents Volume 1: c500-1042*, Second Edition (London, 1979).

Judith 'Judith' in Richard Hamer ed. *A Choice of Anglo-Saxon Verse* (London, 1972), p. 135–157. Cited by lines and page number.

JW: vol. 2 *The Chronicle of John of Worcester: Volume II: The Annals 450–1066*, ed. and trans. R. R. Darlington and P. McGurk (Oxford, 1995). Cited by (modern) page number.

WM: GRA William of Malmesbury, *Gesta Regum Anglorum: The History of the English Kings, Volume 1*, ed. and trans. R. A. B. Mynors, R. M. Thomson and M. Winterbottom (Oxford, 1998). Cited by page of modern translation.

WM: HN William of Malmesbury, *The Historia Novella*: *The New History*, trans. K. R. Potter (London, 1955).

Worcester Charter 'Document 99: Arrangements about the building of fortifications in Worcester (about 889–899)' in Whitelock ed. *English Historical Documents Volume 1: c. 500-1042* (London, 1979), p. 540-1.

A NOTE

I have chosen to use the original spellings for many of the names in this book as often as possible, using the Anglo-Saxon diphthong Aesc or Ash, rendered as Æ and pronounced as something between and A and an E. So the name of my main subject and her husband are all spelled with this letter, as they would originally have been. There are so many variant versions and spellings of Æthelflæd's name that this seemed the most sensible option.

However, I have used the modern spelling for other names and words, such as Alfred (rather than Ælfred), because this is the version that is most commonly used today, and most people are used to it.

Some may object to my use of the term 'Vikings' to apply to the Scandinavians who came over to Britain in the eighth and ninth centuries, as this was never an ethnic description and was not generally used for them at the time – really, it was a job description, meaning something like pirate. I have chosen to use this term because it is so well known and will be easily understood by readers.

Where appropriate, I have tried to use the correct term, 'Danes', to refer to the men of Denmark who settled in Britain from the tenth century but, as will become obvious, not all of the Northmen whom Alfred and his children encountered were from Denmark: some came from Norway and had settled in Ireland, but were then expelled and ended up in England and Wales. Calling them Vikings was easier than calling them Hiberno-Norsemen, or Hiberno-Scandinavians.

For this, and any other oversight, I beg the informed reader's forbearance.

GLOSSARY OF NAMES

Although the Anglo-Saxons did not use surnames, some first names were common, especially among royal families and the aristocracy. This list of figures mentioned in this book sharing the same or similar names has been included to make it easier for readers to distinguish between them. The nicknames given to some of the historians and chroniclers are also given in inverted commas.

Archbishop Æthelred Archbishop of Canterbury 870–888. The prelate is reported to have often been in opposition to King Alfred during the first decade of his reign, until the attack on Chippenham on Twelfth Night in 878.

King Æthelred King of Wessex 865–872. Fourth son of King Æthelwulf, and older brother of Alfred the Great. Paternal uncle of Æthelflæd, who died when she was an infant. According to Asser, he made an agreement with Alfred, settling the succession of the kingdom on the children of whichever of them lived the longest. In the event, this was Alfred.

Æthelred 'Mucel' Mercian ealdorman, father of Ealswith, father-in-law of Alfred the Great and grandfather of Æthelflæd. Believed to have been of ancient Mercian royal stock, and possibly a descendant of the famous King Offa.

Æthelred, 'Lord of the Mercians' Ruler of Mercia *c.* 879/80–911. Husband of Lady Æthelflæd from *c.* 886 until his death in 911. His title, ealdorman or Lord of Mercia, reflected his subordinate status to King Alfred. He was, however, described as king in sources from outside Wessex and from after Alfred's reign. His origins are uncertain, but he was almost certainly of royal or noble stock, and possibly a native of Gloucestershire, where he chose to make his capital.

Æthelstan Died 855. Eldest son of King Æthelwulf of Wessex and eldest brother of Alfred. He never became King of Wessex as he predeceased his father by several years, but was for a time recognized as 'king' over Essex, Kent, Sussex and Surrey. As this territory was subsumed into the Kingdom of Wessex, he was probably more like a sub-king under his father. It is likely that there was a considerable gap in age between him and his youngest brothers, who were probably very young when he died.

King Æthelstan Born *c.* 893–895. Son of King Edward 'the Elder' of Wessex, and nephew of Æthelflæd. He was sent to her court in Mercia, to be raised by her and her husband. Despite his possibly illegitimate birth, he was accepted as King of Mercia after the death of his father in 924 and became King of Wessex following the death of his eldest half-brother the following year. He would ultimately become the first officially recognised king of all England, ruling from 927 until his death in 939.

Æthelweard Youngest son of Alfred and Ealswith, and youngest of Æthelflæd's two brothers. He was destined for a career in the Church, like one of his older sisters, and was educated accordingly. He died in 920.

Æthelweard Chronicler and distant descendant of King Æthelred. He held the office of ealdorman 'of the Western Provinces' from 975 to 998. More importantly he wrote a chronicle allegedly based on a lost version of the *Anglo-Saxon Chronicle*. His chronicle mentioned exploits of Lord Æthelred of Mercia that do not appear anywhere else.

King Æthelwulf King of Wessex 839–858. Father of Alfred, and maternal grandfather of Æthelflæd. His father, the warlord Egbert, had gained control of Wessex in the early years of the ninth century. (Wessex was then a smaller kingdom, only later expanding to include much of the South of England including Kent and Sussex.) According to tradition, Egbert was exiled during the time of Offa with the connivance of King Beorhtric of Wessex, son-in-law of Offa and husband of the notorious Eadburh. According to another tradition recounted by Asser, King Beorhtric died when he was poisoned by his wife, who was intending to kill one of his men, but is it possible he may have actually been killed fighting against Egbert.

Æthelwulf Son of the Mercian ealdorman Æthelred 'Mucel', brother of Ealswith wife of Alfred, maternal uncle of Æthelflæd. Whether he was older or younger than his sister is unknown. He appears in Mercian charters from 884 and into the late 890s, so he was a member of the Mercian court and died *c.* 901, the year before his sister. Given this date, his niece may have known him and worked with him for nearly fifteen years.

Ealswith (also spelled Ealhswith) Wife of Alfred, daughter of Æthelred 'Mucel' and mother of Æthelflæd. Although married to a king, she never carried the title or rank of queen, and never had a coronation because the West Saxons did not have queens as a result of the incident with the proverbially wicked queen Eadburh. Ealswith died in 902, having retired to a nunnery after Alfred's death, and was buried next to him in the now lost building of the New Minster, Winchester.

Æthelswith Elder and only known sister of Alfred. Aunt of Æthelflæd; married King Burgred of Mercia, *c.* 853. Mercia did not have the same rule as Wessex, and so she was recognised as queen. She is not known to have had any children, and eventually followed her husband into Italy as a pilgrim exile, where she died in a religious house in 888. She is believed to have left behind the gold ring engraved with her name.

Ragnar (Lothbrok) Legendary Danish warrior. Said to have been the father of Ubba, Ivar 'the Boneless' and Halfdan, some of the leaders of the Great Heathen Army. His existence and exploits are only known from poetry, sagas and legendary sources, mostly dating from centuries after his supposed death, so his very existence is doubtful. One of the most famous stories about him says he met his death by being thrown into a snake pit by Ælle, King of Northumbria.

Ragnall King of the so called 'Fair Foreigners' and 'Dark Foreigners', grandson of Ivar 'the Boneless'. Unlike his great-grandfather, Ragnall was a very real historical figure, a Viking of Irish extraction who was among those evicted from Dublin in 902, with whom Æthelflæd and her brother were in conflict for much of the early tenth century. Ragnall seized York, defeated the King of Scots and his allies at the Battle of Corbridge in 918 and became King of York in 919, the year after the men of the city had promised to submit to Æthelflæd. This promise was cut short by her death in 918, and Ragnall eventually submitted to her brother Edward shortly before his own death.

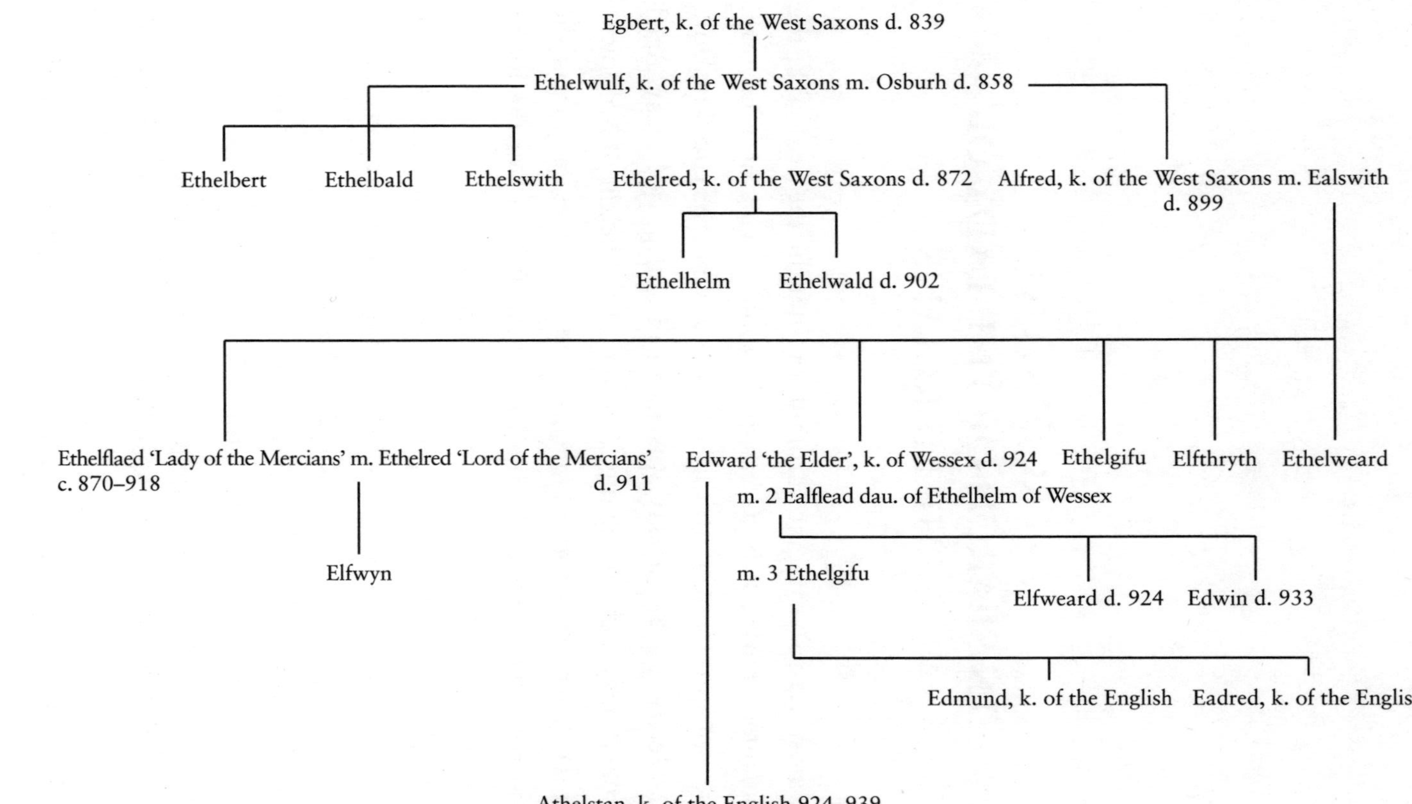

Egbert, k. of the West Saxons d. 839
Ethelwulf, k. of the West Saxons m. Osburh d. 858
Ethelbert
Ethelbald
Ethelswith
Ethelred, k. of the West Saxons d. 872
Alfred, k. of the West Saxons m. Ealswith d. 899
Ethelhelm
Ethelwald d. 902
Ethelflaed 'Lady of the Mercians' m. Ethelred 'Lord of the Mercians' d. 911
c. 870–918
Edward 'the Elder', k. of Wessex d. 924
Ethelgifu
Elfthryth
Ethelweard
m. 2 Ealflead dau. of Ethelhelm of Wessex
Elfwyn
m. 3 Ethelgifu
Elfweard d. 924
Edwin d. 933
Edmund, k. of the English
Eadred, k. of the English
Athelstan, k. of the English 924–939

INTRODUCTION
IN SEARCH OF THE LADY OF THE MERCIANS

Almost 1,100 years ago, around 12 June in the year 918, the daughter of Alfred the Great died. While staying at Tamworth, the ancient capital of the equally ancient Saxon kingdom of Mercia, the royal lady was taken ill and passed away. Aged around forty-eight at the time, she was at the height of her power. In the ten years before her death, with the forces of Mercia she had reclaimed, or secured the submission of, most of the towns and cities of Mercia that had been held by the Vikings since the closing decades of the previous century. In a final political coup, her influence had reached the formerly great kingdom of Northumbria where the Vikings of York had been preparing to offer her their submission.

This remarkable woman, named Æthelflæd and known to her people as the 'Lady of the Mercians', was the undisputed mistress of most of what is now England north of the Thames and south of York. Her power would not last a year beyond her death, with her daughter seized by her brother Edward 'the Elder', King of

Wessex. Although he would do much to consolidate her territorial gains – and his son, Æthelstan, would become the first officially recognized King of England – it would be over 600 years before another woman would rule England or any part of the country in her own right.[1]

In the 1,000 years after her death, the reputation of the Lady of the Mercians would wax and wane; new legends, heroes and heroines would arise. However, there would always remain a grain of interest in the lives and careers of the West Saxon dynasty who were credited with forming and establishing the English nation in the late ninth and earth tenth century. In the Elizabethan age Æthelflæd was scarcely mentioned, her Iron Age counterpart Boudicca being more favoured, probably for the characteristic she shared with Elizabeth I: her famous red hair. The obscurity continued into the early modern period, until the rise of the Victorian flair for all things medieval.

So it was that, less than 100 years ago, in the year 1918, the Lady of the Mercians attracted sufficient interest for a statue of her to be raised outside Tamworth to mark the anniversary of her death. (Similar statues of her father had been raised in Wantage and Winchester to mark the anniversary of his death and his ascension to the throne.) The statue was a somewhat romantic representation typical of the time, but nevertheless it is a useful representation of the ambiguous nature of Æthelflæd's life and career. The right arm of the statue rests on the shoulder of a young boy, almost certainly her nephew Æthelstan, yet the other hand rests on the hilt of a sword. She is nurturing and motherly, looking down tenderly at the boy who was virtually her adoptive son, but simultaneously is prepared to defend her kingdom and her people as a woman in the 'traditionally masculine sphere of warfare'.[2] Up until recently, the average person in the street would not even recognise the name Æthelflæd, and if asked about her father might know of him only from the story of the burned cakes. There has been a rise in her profile recently due to popular literature, most notably Bernard Cornwell's series *The Warrior Chronicles*.[3] If the Lady of the Mercians is known at all it is therefore most likely in the guise of a warrior queen, a notion attractive in the modern age. In artistic and fictional representations, she is often cast as a sword-wielding, armour-clad medieval equivalent of Boudicca. It is ironic indeed that Boudicca is much more famous when a comparison is made between what is known and believed about the two women.

Everything we know about Boudicca comes from Roman sources written many years after her death. Also, in spite of her status as a popular hero representing the struggle of plucky Brits against Roman oppressors, Boudicca was ultimately defeated. Her army's sacking of Colchester and London, their guerrilla raids and skirmishes against Roman outposts and military units were their main achievements. Boudicca may have rallied her people, and been a serious threat to Roman control in the early decades of their occupation, but the only serious battle she fought proved to be a resounding victory for her enemies, resulting in more than 350 years of Roman rule.

With Æthelflæd there are two notable differences. First, we have a contemporary, or near-contemporary, account of her reign and achievements in the form of the Mercian Register, which consists of a number of passages spread across various manuscripts of the *Anglo-Saxon Chronicle*. Secondly, if the records are to be believed (and a degree of dramatic hyperbole cannot be ruled out), Æthelflæd was almost never defeated by her foes on the battlefield. Furthermore, where Boudicca and her British horde burned Roman cities, Æthelflæd and her countrymen re-established Roman towns, and even built some of their own from scratch. The towns of Warwick, Runcorn and Stafford owe their existence, in whole or part, to her.

Boudicca was a mother whose career (we are told) tragically ended when she took her own life to avoid shameful captivity. Æthelflæd too was a mother, with one biological and one adopted child, and died of natural causes at the height of her power. Yet this was far from the end of the story, as she was the only ruling woman in English history to have been succeeded by her daughter – and a few years later by Æthelstan, the nephew and adoptive son who had been raised at her court.

In literature and fiction, Æthelflæd is often cast as the archetypal warrior queen, but also as a frustrated wife trapped in a loveless arranged marriage who seeks romantic fulfilment elsewhere. In the case of Bernard Cornwell's *Warrior Chronicles*, it is Uhtred, the Saxon-born Northumbrian lord raised by Danes, who becomes her lover. Her husband, Lord Æthelred, by extension, is often cast in a negative light as a callous, unwanted and even abusive husband.

Leaving aside the tropes of romantic fiction, and the mythologising of past ages, is it possible to learn something of the real Æthelflæd? We do not have a full-length biography of her like the *Life of Alfred*, which was written for her father by the Welsh monk Asser. As a consequence, the contemporary sources have little to say about her childhood and early life. When she enters the historical record in the *Anglo-Saxon Chronicle*, it is as an adult in her forties, and she is dead within a few years. Such is the nature of this source, with its terse narrative style, reporting major events with only brief entries. It is little wonder that 'other contemporary sources' are included with the best-known modern edition of Asser's *Life of Alfred* – to truly get to know him, and learn about his life and career, it is sometimes necessary to read between the lines and consult other available sources, such as charters, legal codes and writings from neighbouring kingdoms. Thus, to see the bigger picture of Alfred's life it is necessary to look at the wider context of his times, and his relations with his family and contemporaries. It is only sensible to assume that the same applies to his daughter.

She too was a product of her times. Her life was dominated by the conflict with the Danish and Norwegian Vikings. Her father's kingdom was the last to stand alone against their onslaught, and it is possible that her uncle, King Æthelred, died as a result of a military engagement against them. In this sense, it was the war with the Danes that made Alfred king and placed his family on the political and military stage. Æthelflæd was probably born only a year or so before her father succeeded the throne of Wessex, and she would have been raised at his court. For this reason, it is possible to discover something about how she spent the first sixteen or so years of her life from examining the actions and movements of her family, who must have shared many experiences with their patriarch. For instance, Alfred's wife and children almost certainly accompanied him into his famous exile in the Somerset marshes. At the time Æthelflæd would have been around seven or eight years old – old enough to remember that desperate time when all seemed lost, and to remember her father's legendary victory at Edington, when his great enemy Guthrum was defeated and he won back his kingdom. She would not, of course, have fought in the battle, but she would certainly have known about it, and it had a very real impact on her family. In the years following the battle she would have been educated alongside her older siblings, and it is hard to believe that a young girl of keen intelligence and ability (these features would be displayed later in her life) would not have observed her father, and learned from him the rudiments of rule and statecraft.

Though in her childhood she was a daughter of Wessex, the connections with Mercia ran deep in her family. Her own mother, Ealswith, was a Mercian of noble (some even say royal) lineage. Her aunt had been married to Burgred, a man considered to be the last fully independent king of Mercia before the Danish takeover of parts of the kingdom. At the age of fifteen or sixteen she was married to Æthelred, 'Lord of the Mercians' and erstwhile ally of her father, who she may already have met sometime before. Æthelflæd would spend the rest of her life in Mercia, with the exception of some military campaigns and visits to neighbouring kingdoms as co-ruler and consort for her husband. In Mercia, she may well have continued her tutelage as a political leader alongside her husband and the nobles of Mercia.[4]

When she emerges into the full light of history in the opening years of the tenth century, it is as an active and assertive political figure, whose counsel and assistance is sought by her people in time of conflict. Soon afterwards, her husband's death is reported – in the year 911. It is then that she appears as the leader of Mercia, leading attacks on Danish-held towns and establishing her own fortified settlements. Clearly, something almost unprecedented had happened: the Mercians had chosen this capable woman to be their ruler, in preference to a male relative or submitting the King of Wessex. Her apprenticeship in

Mercia (and even in Wessex) must have shown then that she was fit to rule and to lead, and the faith of the Mercians proved to be well placed in the seven years of her personal rule.

The Mercian Register, a short subsection within the *Anglo-Saxon Chronicle* that was begun under her father, accounts for her career as a round of military engagements and sieges, with towns being established. On the basis of its record, it is tempting to see her as the archetypal warrior queen – a sword-wielding Amazon leading her war band into Danish territory and personally fending off attacks on her kingdom. Yet the realities of the time reveal that rulers had to be more than just successful warriors. How did Æthelflæd fulfil the expectations of her role, and command the loyalty of her people? How did she survive, let alone achieve victory in a world so fraught with treachery, danger and intrigue, when ruling was often a recipe for a short life?

Also, how is it that that Æthelflæd was one of only a handful of medieval women who took on the role of a man, but did so entirely without incurring the censure or wrath of male commentators? Henry of Huntingdon, the eleventh-century canon of Lincoln, was particularly enamoured of Æthelflæd, saying that she would have been praised as king and hailing her as more famous than Caesar. Other chroniclers of the following two centuries were also apt to praise the Lady of the Mercians for her bravery and courage, as well as her moral virtue. I will argue that one famous twelfth-century clerical chronicler, William of Malmesbury, used her as a moral exemplar for his own generation, in which another formidable woman was involved in a struggle for power: the Empress Matilda. Through his writings, and those of his successors, Æthelflæd would enjoy a historical afterlife that lasts to our own day; but like her father, she would also become a legendary figure onto whom later generations could project their own priorities, attitudes and expectations.

It is in the process of answering the questions posed above that a new picture of Æthelflæd emerges, more complex than that found in any individual chronicle, record or novel. She emerges as a woman who was by turns pious and ruthless, an astute politician and a patron of learning – a warlord, a mother and a wife. Her life and legacy may defy many modern expectations and preconceptions about women in the Viking age (and the medieval period more generally), as well as what they could achieve.

I

SONS OF THE WOLF

She was not born to rule. In fact, the infant Æthelflæd was probably of very little importance, another girl born into the royal family of an insignificant corner of 'Dark Age' Britain. Perhaps this is why there are no accounts of her childhood in the sources of the time. This was not necessarily a deliberate oversight, as there are few accounts of the early years of any significant women, or indeed men, in the first millennium after Christ. They usually emerge into the full light of history only as adults, blazing across a poorly documented and tumultuous era like flares across the evening sky, only to disappear as soon as they came, mere footnotes in some grand work of history whose writer saw fit only to mention them for their contributions or reputation (or sometimes the lack of it).

At the time of her birth, Æthelflæd's father was an *atheling* of the Kingdom of Wessex. The simplest definition of this term would be 'prince', although there is actually a lot more to it than that. Really it could mean anyone of noble birth who could potentially claim the throne. At the time of his own birth in 849 it was not expected that Alfred would ever be king (as he was the youngest of five sons of King Æthelwulf of Wessex), and it has been proposed that he may have been considered for a career in the Church.[1] In his later life, Alfred would interpret the trip to Rome that he made when he was four or five years old as the first confirmation of his destiny. Alfred's biographer Asser would claim some forty years later (likely using the king as his source) that the Pope anointed the child Alfred for kingship. Such a story seems unlikely, as the Pope would have been informed Alfred was a younger son, one of several 'spares' to one of the many royal families of Europe. It is also possible that Alfred went to Rome with his brother Æthelred, and that the Pope would not have seen any need to interfere in West Saxon politics by favouring one brother over another.[2] So what was actually going on, and what events really conspired to make Alfred the ruler of the last kingdom to hold out against the Viking onslaught, and Æthelflæd the daughter of the king?

Before Alfred reached the age of sixteen, three of his four older brothers were dead. The sources do not elaborate on the cause of their deaths. It is entirely possible that there was a large gap in age between Alfred and his eldest siblings. Æthelstan, the fist son of Æthelwulf, had predeceased their father by several years, dying sometime around 851. Given the gap in ages, it is entirely possible that the eldest two of Alfred's three remaining brothers, Æthelbald and Æthelberht, died of natural causes, of some unspecified disease or as a result of combat injuries. This was, after all, a time when living to the age of fifty was a notable achievement. None of the eldest three brothers of Alfred were known to have had any children, leaving a more level playing field for the two youngest remaining sons of Æthelwulf.

Alfred seems have been closest in age to his one surviving brother, Æthelred, who became king of Wessex in 865. Both brothers, now in their late teens, decided that it was time to marry. The connections of their family with Mercia were strong. Their elder sister Æthelswith was married to Burgred, the king of Mercia, probably when both her brothers had been very young children. There is a tradition that Æthelred married a Welsh woman, but his wife appears in a charter with the name Wulfthryth, which is not a Welsh name. It is possible that she was instead from Mercia. By the end of his six-year reign, it is known that King Æthelred of Wessex and his wife had produced two surviving sons, Æthelhelm and Æthelwold.[3]

Alfred married a Mercian lady of noble birth in 867 or 868. Her name was Ealswith, and she was the daughter of Æthelred Mucel, a man described in the *Life of Alfred* as an 'ealdorman of the Gaini'. It is commonly believed that the 'Gaini' were an ancient Saxon tribal group after which the town of Gainsborough in Lincolnshire was named.[4] His wife seems to have been one Eadburg, a Mercian noblewoman who survived him by some years. It is possible that they met when Alfred and his brother went to the aid of King Burgred of Mercia in 867. At the time their Mercian brother-in-law was struggling against the Great Heathen Army, then under the leadership of Ivar 'the Boneless', one of three sons of the legendary Ragnar Lothbrok. The Danes were shored up at Nottingham and Burgred was attempting to lay siege to the city. His attempt was unsuccessful. The Saxon forces were simply not equipped to take Nottingham at the time, and many soldiers seem to have left in order to return to their homes to bring in the harvest. Eventually, Burgred resorted to the time-honoured technique for getting rid of Vikings: he paid them to leave. From 867 onwards, the Great Army was able to proceed though Mercia on their way to East Anglia and Northumbria unmolested. The Mercians had bought themselves a form of safety, at least for a time.

Æthelred, Alfred and his new bride returned to Wessex the following year, and after this time it appears that the young man, who was now an *atheling* of Wessex, began to flex his political muscles. Alfred's will, and the account given in the *Life of Alfred*, tells a story of smooth succession and harmonious relations within the family and dynasty of which Alfred became the head by various accidents of nature. The later part of the narrative, as has already been stated, can probably be believed – there is no reason to believe that Alfred's eldest brothers died of anything other than natural causes. Yet the relationship with what remained of his extended family may have been more strained in the closing years of the 860s.

Pauline Stafford argued that relations between Alfred and his brother may have become strained after they returned to Wessex. Ealswith had bought her husband important lands and connections. Perhaps more importantly, she may well have had royal as well as noble Mercian blood. She has been identified as a possible descendant of Coenwulf, a king of Mercia in the early part of the ninth century, whose line had been deposed by none other than the father of Burgred.[5] Examining the evidence of charters, it is argued that the marriage of Alfred to the descendant of 'an older and side-lined' Mercian dynasty, and his actions following the marriage, may not have gone down well with the rest of his family.[6] Alfred, now the only other surviving son of Æthelwulf, seems to have started to assert himself, wishing for his brother to recognise his position as an heir to the throne. He now had land and wealth of his own, and had made a considered marriage to a Mercian lady of distinguished birth. Now he had friends in Mercia, as well as prominence in Wessex. In short, he had become an important man in both kingdoms at a time when Mercia was in trouble. What was to stop him making a bid for power if something were to happen?

Perhaps it is no coincidence that Æthelred appears alongside his sister and brother-in-law in charters during the closing years of the 860s. Was he reasserting his allegiance to the established Mercian royal family whose queen was, after all, his sister? His own wife was also elevated to the status of queen (or at least she was accorded this title in a charter), and even if Alfred was the nearest adult heir in Wessex, Æthelred may have sought to ensure that his sons were provided for, and their royal birth remembered. When they grew up, they could, after all, replace their uncle Alfred as his successors.[7]

Ultimately, events were to overtake the interconnected royal dynasties of Mercia and Wessex, and upset any future plans they may have been devising. The Viking armies that had arrived in 865 had taken Northumbria, and in 869 East Anglia fell with the death of King Edmund. Mercia had not been officially conquered, but it was pliant and did not oppose Danish forces. Only Wessex had thus far escaped the advance of the Great Heathen Army. The kingdom had been raided, but there had been no serious attempt made to capture or hold onto any West Saxon territory. All that was to change in the winter of 870/71. Ivar and his brother Ubba were no longer in charge of the Viking forces, and both largely disappear from the record after the conquest of East Anglia. The army was now under the leadership of Halfdan; they set their sights on Wessex. The history of the fateful year reads as an almost continual round of battles and skirmishes. The *Anglo-Saxon Chronicle* reports the first engagement was around 10 miles away from Reading in Berkshire, where they were defeated by an ealdorman named Æthelwulf. His elation at victory was not to last long, for only four days later there was another battle, in Reading itself, in which the combined armies of the ealdorman, King Æthelred and Alfred were defeated by the Vikings, and Æthelwulf was killed. Only four days after Reading came the legendary victory for the royal brothers at Ashdown, in which two combined Viking armies were supposedly defeated and several jarls killed alongside one of the leaders of the army by the name of Bagsecg. One story, which speaks of Alfred fighting the Vikings while the king remained in his tent at prayer, is found later in the *Life of Alfred*.[8] The *Anglo-Saxon Chronicle*, however, does not present the battle as anything less than a joint effort with the two brothers in full cooperation, probably as part of a strategic initiative that might even have been agreed upon before the battle. Despite the setback at Ashdown, the Vikings were not finished, and less than two weeks later Alfred and his brother suffered yet another defeat at Basing, near Basingstoke. The two sides had fought throughout the winter, but still more was to come. Two months after Basing, probably in late March 871, the brothers again came upon the Vikings at a place called Meretun, near the town of Wilton in Wilshire. The *Chronicle* account tells us that at first the Saxons succeeded in pushing back their foes, but by the end of the day the Vikings were the masters of the field. Once again the West Saxons had been defeated, and this time a bishop had been killed. The cost of Meretun would ultimately prove even higher, however, as only a few weeks later the death of King Æthelred is recorded. It is widely believed that he died of wounds sustained in the battle, perhaps from an infection. The fourth son of Æthelwulf was dead, and finally Alfred was the last king standing in the last kingdom.[9]

There has recently been some suggestion that Alfred was a usurper, taking the throne that rightfully belonged to his brother's sons. In the later Middle Ages, when succession to the throne of England was usually determined by primogeniture, there might be some basis for such a claim, but it is less likely in the complex world of early medieval Britain. Simply put, there was no one single system or rule governing the succession to the throne of Wessex – or indeed Northumbria, East Anglia or any of the other kingdoms of the Anglo-Saxon age. Technically, any claimant could become king if he got the support of the *witan* or council. Adult heirs with leadership and military experience usually won out over underage children in these leadership contests. Æthelflæd was probably little more than a toddler, and her cousins not much older, whereas Alfred was a seasoned warrior in his twenties who had fought alongside his brother and the men of Wessex in the military engagements of 871, and he had even helped lead forces to victory at Ashdown. He was, purely and simply, the most qualified and convenient candidate to rule in a time of uncertainty. More fighting was the come, this time in Wilton, before the year was out until finally both sides came to a rapprochement. It may seem strange that the Norsemen were prepared to talk after they had won several battles and skirmishes, but their West Saxon opponents had proved determined opponents, and ultimately the Vikings had not come away with much loot or any significant territorial gains in the campaigns of 871. Both sides had lost, and in the end Alfred, like his brother-in-law three years before him, paid the Vikings to leave his kingdom. In autumn 871, they finally withdrew to London.[10] Wessex had bought peace for a time, but the price would prove to be high.

2

THE GREAT HEATHEN ARMY 871–DECEMBER 877

> ... never before has appeared such a terror in Britain as we have now suffered from a pagan race, nor was it thought that such an inroad from the sea could be made ... can it not be expected that from North there will come upon our nation retribution of blood?
>
> Alcuin, letter to King Æthelred of Northumbria

The precise date of Æthelflæd's birth is unknown. It is generally accepted that her parents were married early in 868, and that she was the firstborn child of their marriage. This means the earliest possible date of birth is sometime late in that year, or early the following year. Many historians, however, favour a date of some point in the first half of the 870s.[1] I have chosen to settle upon the year 870, or early in the year 871 at the latest.

Asser recorded that Alfred was first struck by a sudden unidentified debilitating illness at his wedding feast, an illness that continued to plague him at intervals throughout his life.[2] It is generally held that this was Crohn's disease, a chronic condition involving inflammation of the intestines that can go into remission for long periods and has such symptoms as chronic pain, fever and fatigue. Alfred was still perfectly able to father children, as he had no fewer than five including Æthelflæd, as well as some who died in infancy. If Æthelflæd was born by 870, she would already have had two male cousins, the sons of her uncle King Æthelred. Despite the complexities of the ancient British systems of succession, males usually came before females, and so the daughter of Alfred would have been far down the line of succession, if she was counted at all. The lack of surnames in the Anglo-Saxon age resulted in some rather interesting naming patterns for children. All of Alfred's known siblings had names beginning with the prefix 'Æthel', which denoted royalty or nobility. Alfred chose to keep up this tradition with most of his children (except for his eldest son, who was named Edward), but the name Æthelflæd seems to have been an unusual and original choice, and she was not named after any extended family members or recent ancestors. The name seems to have been a typical compound of two elements: 'Æthel', meaning noble, and 'flæad', the meaning of which is less clear. Michael Wood suggested that her name meant 'noble beauty', although the second element could also mean something like 'flood', or something flowing over, so her name might actually mean something like 'overflowing with nobility'.[3]

It is almost impossible to know the precise details of the earliest years of Æthelflæd's early years in the 870s as the records simply do not mention her; it is not known for certain where she was born. Don Stansbury suggested that it may have been at Chippenham, where a royal palace existed in Alfred's day. His sister Æthelswith had been married there some fifteen years before his own marriage, and the residence seems to have been favoured by the sons of Æthelwulf.[4] So it is possible that Ealswith was based there at the time of her first child's birth, but there were many other royal residences throughout Wessex. The kingdom by that time encompassed most of England south of the Thames, from Somerset to Kent. Given the dearth of sources covering her early years, it is necessary to examine what was happening to her parents and her people at the time; to examine events and circumstances that indirectly involved or affected her, or would do so in the future.

The Coming of the Danes

The English of the late ninth century were no strangers to the Vikings. Their first recorded raid was in 793 on the monastery of Lindisfarne, although there may have been some raids before that. From that time, it almost became an established pattern that the Vikings would come, raid and leave in the winter. In the eighth century the raids were an inconvenience, and for some a deadly menace. The clerics spoke of the judgement of God. Yet at the time, the Vikings were not a major political threat to the English kingdoms, whose rulers and nobles were more often than not fighting among themselves.

The Danes, however, were a different matter; they did not come simply as raiders. Really, the Danes first made excursions into Wessex in the 830s, some fourteen years before Alfred's birth. His grandfather, Egbert, won a victory against them at a place called Hingston Down in modern-day Cornwall.[5] In 850, a Danish army wintered for the first time on the Isle of Thanet. From the 830s onwards the forces were getting larger, coming with more ships, and were able to attack large settlements such as Canterbury, but their activities were still ultimately raids. It was in 865 that all that was to change when the notorious 'Great Heathen Army' arrived (once again using Thanet as their base), but this time they came not only to raid, but to conquer – something the rulers of the Anglo-Saxon kingdoms were to learn when their attempts to pay or fight them off proved unsuccessful. Often, they would leave for a time, only to establish themselves in another kingdom, and a branch of the army would return under a new leader.

After coming to terms with Alfred and agreeing to leave Wessex during 872, the Great Heathen Army took steps to consolidate their gains. First of all, a revolt was put down in Northumbria in which King Egbert, a supposed puppet installed by the Danes, was overthrown. Then, the army under Halfdan moved into Mercia where they established a base at Repton in the winter of 873/74. The kingdoms of Northumbria and East Anglia had fallen to them in the five years since their last incursion, and this time Mercia would receive no assistance from Wessex. Unable to overcome them, King Burgred and his wife were deposed and driven into exile, and he died the following year. His wife lived out the rest of her days in a nunnery. With Burgred's departure, there would never again be an officially recognised and independent King of Mercia. Perhaps then, Alfred had done well to find allies outside the established royal family. They would soon prove vitally important to him, and determine the course of his daughter's life. After Burgred's departure, the Danes installed another supposed 'puppet' king, Ceolwulf, a shadowy figure whose life and career has recently been debated by historians.

In recent decades, there has been an attempt to rehabilitate the Vikings and to emphasise the non-violent and sophisticated aspects of their culture. Some have even gone as far as to say that there is little archaeological evidence for pillaging and burning, and that the fearsome reputation that the Vikings earned from these activities is undeserved, largely resulting from exaggeration by churchmen. While it is undeniable that the Vikings were superb sailors, courageous adventurers who discovered new lands, and that they produced some incredible works of art, the violent aspects of their culture cannot be entirely discounted. In the words of John Haywood, peaceful settlement was usually preceded by violent conquest.[6] Indeed, the ninth and tenth centuries were beset by violence generally, with the evidence suggesting that the clergy in particular bore the brunt of the violence from the Viking raids, and they had a very real impact British culture for centuries to come.

For instance, in the eighth century Britain had been home to some of the greatest scholars in Europe, including the Venerable Bede and Alcuin of York (740–804), a leading figure in the revival of learning and scholarship fostered in Emperor Charlemagne's court known as the Carolingian Renaissance. One hundred years after Alcuin lamented the sacking of Lindisfarne in 793, it was remarked that few clerics could be found in the entire country who knew their Latin well enough to understand the services that they conducted. That this decline in learning and scholarship happened to come at the same time as the Viking raids cannot have been a simple coincidence. While there was probably no large-scale decimation of the English population, the constant threat of raids, and destruction of property and abduction, must have taken their toll. Quite simply, raiding and the attended activities, including the taking and trading of slaves, were mainstays of the Scandinavian economy. Coming from a land with few natural resources, going 'a Viking' may have been the only way to make a living for many people.

In Wessex the King's policy of paying off the Danes was also having an impact, and would prove not only unpopular but nearly fatal in the long term. Alfred could not produce the amounts involved from his own estates, and so the 'enormous financial burden' had to be raised from the people of Wessex and from church estates. It may come as something of a surprise to us to learn that there were some in the church who never forgave the King of Wessex, and considered him a despoiler of their lands for generations afterwards.[7] Alfred and his contemporaries must have realised that paying Danegeld could only be a temporary solution, especially after 874 when Danes who had been paid to leave one kingdom would simply move to consolidate their gains elsewhere, but would eventually return. However, the first payment of 872 had bought a few precious years of peace. Alfred's actions during the years between 872 and 878 are rather obscure. He does not seem to have expended much time and effort to prepare his kingdom to resist further Viking attacks, something he seems to have regretted in the hindsight of his later years. He does seem to have made some effort to prop up the economy by 'restoring the silver content of West Saxon coinage'. This was not necessarily done for the good of the economy, but perhaps to 'increase the value of monetary exactions that he extracted from his subjects'.[8] Elsewhere, he was granting land to at least one of his *thegns*, who later sold the same parcel of land to another with the king's consent – the charters covering these land transactions reveal the presence of a number of important men from Kent, some of whom were later made ealdormen. Perhaps Alfred was trying to shore up support in the eastern reaches of his kingdom.

In his personal life, Alfred probably divided his time between his estates and dealt with the day-to-day business of kingship, such as presiding over land transactions, alongside occasionally indulging his well-known passion for hunting. It is known at least two of Æthelflæd's surviving siblings were born before 875, her eldest brother Edward (who would later become king of Wessex after Alfred), and one of two sisters named Æthelgifu. Considering the difficulty of determining the dates of birth of royal children at this time due to lack of recorded details, it is possible that all four of her siblings may have been born by the middle of the decade, including another sister, and finally the youngest, a second brother named Æthelweard. Æthelflæd would have been five years old, or older, in these years – old enough to remember the events of the time, and the birth of her youngest siblings.

Other than occasional visits to the royal vill or residence where the family was based, it is likely that Æthelflæd seldom saw her father; he was too busy with warfare and the business of ruling. As a girl, she would almost certainly not have been given the training in arms and martial pursuits that were part of the traditional education of male children, and probably spent much of her time in female company with her mother and other noblewomen or a nurse and female attendants.[9] This is not to say that there was no opportunity for good old-fashioned fun, though. Through the years, there has developed the idea that medieval children were either treated as small adults or were largely ignored as child mortality rates were so high, but recent examinations of the evidence have revealed this was not the case. It is certainly true that many children died before they reached their teens, but this does not mean parents through the ages were indifferent or lacking in natural care and affection towards them. The study of history often reveals that despite cultural, social or ideological differences, the men and women of the past were largely the same as us. It is sometimes hard to relate to those who lived 1,000 years ago, but they had feelings and emotions; they loved, laughed and felt pain and joy like the rest of us. There is a poignant passage in one of the many translations Alfred made in his later life where the king compared the loss of a child with the lowest depths of human sorrow, and we know of other sources that are candid about the sadness and sorrow of parents in such tragic circumstances. Alfred may have been speaking from experience. He and Ealswith had lost at least one child, including a son who would have been named Edmund, in infancy.

The children of the Anglo-Saxon age who survived beyond babyhood certainly enjoyed playing just as children do today. While Christine Fell argued that there is no specific evidence of children's toys in the archaeological record, it has been argued elsewhere that this lack may be a result of interpretation, or that they simply have not survived. Simple playthings like ragdolls have existed in some form for millennia, and may well have been just as popular and well loved by little girls (without meaning to engage in gender stereotyping) in the past as they are today. These could have been constructed very easily from materials available around the home, such as fabric or wood, and maybe stuffed with straw or anything else that was to hand. It is pleasant to imagine the little princess Æthelflæd and her sisters practising and honing their sewing skills by making miniature clothes for their favourite dolls from offcuts or spare rags. Board games have been discovered in adult Viking burials, and it is not unlikely that children might have played with them as well. Perhaps adults taught their inquisitive little ones the rudiments of such games. As has been suggested, children might well have played with objects not intended for play.

This makes perfect sense, considering how parents and caregivers today sometimes have to warn active children that objects they might pick up around the home are 'not toys'.

There are occasional clues in literature about other activities that children and young people enjoyed. The Lives of Saint Cuthbert and Saint Guthlac refer to children wrestling and playing athletic games in the street. Bede recounts the story of a bishop who despaired at a young charge who was desperate to put his horse to the test by racing one of his peers. The cleric eventually relented, only for the lad to be seriously injured when he fell off, just as he had feared. Even with the Viking threat looming (and as she grew up she must have been aware of it), Æthelflæd was, to the best of our knowledge, a normal and healthy child who must have enjoyed playing outdoors with her siblings and other noble children.

There has been an interesting suggestion that Æthelflæd was sent to the Mercian court to be fostered with her aunt, Queen Æthelswith. Fosterage was a common practice in the Anglo-Saxon age. It usually involved sending a child away at around the age of seven to another family, the royal court or an ecclesiastical institution to be educated and prepared for adulthood. It was a type of 'elite apprenticeship' or 'prep school' where noble children received the training they needed to prepare them for their roles in adult life, as well as making important contacts and relationships with their peers. Fosterage also helped nurture important alliances for the grown-ups involved and created extra kin for the child, who could come to form a closer bond to his foster family than his birth family.[10]

Alfred, according to his biographer, was not sent away for fosterage, and there is no direct evidence that Æthelflæd was, but it has been inferred by a reference in Asser to the fact that her brother Edward and younger sister were 'always raised' at the West Saxon court. If she was sent to Mercia, she would have been very young for a fosterling – no more than six, but probably younger – when King Burgred of Mercia was forced to leave his kingdom and bring any fosterage arrangements to an abrupt end. To be sent away for fosterage at such an early age does seem unusual, especially for a female child. Girls could be given to the Church as infants, which has been counted as a form of 'fosterage', but they were usually child oblates who had effectively been gifts to the Church and remained in abbeys and convents for the rest of their lives. Perhaps she was simply entrusted to the care of a nurse or other female attendants as an infant and they mostly resided at one particular palace or royal vill instead of following the mobile court in its circuit from one property to another.[11]

Another suggestion is that Æthelswith actually came to stay in Wessex for a time after her husband's deposition. The *Anglo-Saxon Chronicle* does not directly say that she went to Rome with her husband in 874, although this is generally assumed. The next time she is mentioned in that source is fourteen years later, when she died herself on the way to Rome as a pilgrim. It is often stated that she accompanied her husband to the city sacred to Christianity, and became a nun before her death. This probably was indeed the case, but there may be room for some speculation that she did not leave straight away, and could have returned to her homeland. As a childless widow she would not have been seen to pose any threat to the royal family, and she had been married for twenty-one years so was probably well into her thirties. If she did enjoy a brief sojourn in Wessex she may well have spent time with her young niece, and told her of the kingdom of Mercia as well as recounting her time as queen. Æthelflæd may have been impressed by the position and title that Mercian queens were entitled to, compared with her own mother's standing. As a young child, she could not have known the great destiny that awaited her there.[12]

In contrast to her sister-in-law, Ealswith, Alfred's wife was not given the title of the queen of Wessex. The wives of kings in that land rarely ever were, and instead they carried the more eponymous title of 'King's Wife'. It was said by Asser that none of the kings of Wessex in Alfred's day allowed their wives to carry the title and responsibility of queen. Even the conservative Welsh monk, who was never sparing in praise for his subject, considered the practice a strange departure from the normal custom of the Germanic peoples. The explanation for it was a story about a previous royal consort, one Eadburh, who had been the daughter of the famous Mercian King Offa. According to the story, Eadburh had been a paragon of evil, and had accidentally poisoned her husband, King Beorhtric, when she had been trying to kill one of his nobles, Ealdorman Borr, and was subsequently driven from the country.

It has been suggested that this story was some kind of calumny spread by the ancestors of Alfred against the consort of a king from a rival line and a descendant of Offa, who had driven Alfred's grandfather Egbert into exile. Egbert would ultimately defeat the Mercians in battle, and it has been suggested that the real cause of Beorhtric's death may have been a battle against him. If the new king of Wessex had indeed killed Beorhtric in battle, and his wife had fled, perhaps taking a large amount of treasure with her, it may have been in his interest to blacken her reputation. Yet there is no record of any children from the marriage, so there was no cause to discredit any potential heir, and it does seem unusual that common practice would have been made on the basis of what was essentially a lie. Surely someone would have known if the former king had died in battle instead of dropping dead at a feast from poison? Regardless of the historical basis of West Saxon tradition, not every king paid much attention to it. Alfred's eldest brother had insisted on having his Frankish wife Judith consecrated as queen, and it is possible that his brother Æthelred's wife may also have been recognised as queen. Alfred, for whatever reason, chose not to accord Æthelflæd's mother this title, and her name does not appear on any charters, unlike those of other royal and noble ladies of the time.

This does not mean she did not play an important role at court, in the household or in the rearing of her children. The Anglo-Saxons do not seem to have had any objection to teaching female children to read and write at least, but not all members of the elite classes had any use for such skills, which they probably considered to be the preserve of clerics. At five or six, Æthelflæd was probably too young to begin her formal education under a tutor, and her siblings certainly would have been. As with being fostered, seven seems to have been the normal age when such activities commenced.

Ultimately, as before, the events of the ongoing conflict would overtake the family. The Danes returned in 876 when Guthrum seized Wareham in Dorset, his forces having marched through Wessex unopposed and seemingly unnoticed. Alfred was unable to dislodge them by laying siege to the town when it became known to him that a huge Viking fleet was tacking along the coast of Wessex on its way to join Guthrum. Months before, a small group of seven ships had been routed, but this one was much larger, reportedly comprising over 100 vessels.

Once again, the time had come for negotiation. The king of Wessex opted to try and buy off his adversary with payment of the (by now notorious) Danegeld, but this time he wanted more solid assurances that the Danish lord would actually keep his word and leave. So at Wareham the agreement was struck, and in a style that would later become customary, hostages were exchanged. On this occasion, however, the king of Wessex took the unusual step of making Guthrum take his oath on a sacred ring. This object has been identified as the ring of Thor, 'a large gold armband worn on the chieftain's arm', and an object which the Vikings themselves would have sworn oaths upon.[13] Asser seems to have wanted to gloss over this incident and said that Guthrum had sworn on Christian relics, but that does not seem plausible. Clearly Alfred realised an oath sworn to a god his adversaries did not believe in would not be considered binding, so perhaps he was appealing to the sense of honour that existed in their religion – working on their terms, so to speak. Ultimately, his efforts proved fruitless. Guthrum did not keep his promise to leave Wessex via Wareham. However, nature was to intervene on the side of the West Saxons when the Danish lord moved on to Exeter with his army (according to the sources, stealing away under cover of darkness). Any hopes they may have had to establish a permanent foothold in Wessex were stalled by the loss of 120 ships in a storm or severe bout of fog off the coast of Swanage. These were the same ships that had been making their way along the Wessex coast. It seems very likely that they were part of a large-scale invasion fleet.

Following the storm, Alfred and his men gave chase in much the same manner as they had done five years before, and encamped outside Exeter. Even though Alfred seems to have refused to attack the town to dislodge the Danes, it would appear that the Saxons were at an advantage. They were able to keep their army provisioned while the Danes were cut off from supplies, having only those they had gathered before Alfred came. So once again the two armies came to terms. Perhaps on this occasion the negotiations were even initiated by Guthrum, whose hopes of an imminent invasion had been lost with the ships that went down in Swanage. The scales were certainly tipped in favour of the Saxons.[14] The Danes gave hostages (and Alfred does not seem to have given any in return), once again made oaths, and this time kept to them. After having been in Wessex for more than a year, capturing two towns and raiding land in Hampshire and Wiltshire, Guthrum's forces finally departed in August 877. They did not go far, only travelling as far north as Gloucester. When back in Mercia, Guthrum decided to carry through on a deal he had apparently made some time before with the new king of Mercia, Ceolwulf, to divide the kingdom between the Anglo-Saxons and the Danes, keeping much of the western part of the kingdom while the east was divided between the leaders of the Danes.

Back in Wessex, Alfred had once again managed to persuade his enemies to leave by any means necessary, but it would appear that his people were beginning to lose faith in their king. In 877, the same year that the Guthrum's army were shored up in Wessex, the Archbishop of Canterbury had written to the Pope complaining about the king's practice of paying off the Danes. The cleric seems to have been particularly riled that the king was using income from Church lands to raise the funds necessary. The nobility may also have grown disgruntled with the repeated, and ultimately unsuccessful, attempts at a peaceful settlement with the Danes, who just kept coming back. It would appear that the notable men of Wessex became disillusioned with their king, and may have played a role in the events that were to take place over the following months.

3

PATH OF THE EXILE
JANUARY 878–MAY 880

'Often the solitary man enjoys
The Grace and Mercy of the Lord, although
Careworn he long has had to stir by hand
The ice cold sea along the waterways,
Travel the exile's path; fate is relentless.'

The Wanderer

When Alfred chose to settle in for Christmas in 878, Guthrum's army was less than 50 miles away in Gloucester. They had withdrawn from Wessex, but barely. Perhaps Alfred realised this and chose to spend the festival with his court at the estate near the border with Mercia. Chippenham was a burh, a fortified settlement (the word is actually the origin of the modern place names ending in -borough or -bury), so he may have considered it a place of safety, secure enough to keep an eye on the borders of his realm while being alert to any attacks from the north. By Alfred's day, the average burh would have consisted of a ditch in front of an earth rampart, topped with a wall (this was usually wooden, but could be constructed in whole or part of stone or masonry). Often the walls would be equipped with a fighting platform, to give defenders the advantage of height. There would be a gate, and perhaps a guard tower of some description. Burhs usually would have effectively been walled, self-contained villages or small towns, communal affairs that could provide a home to many people and the necessary amenities, such as a church and room to keep livestock.[1] The royal palace at Chippenham had extra protection because of its location 'on a rise on the land' that was located in a small meander of the River Avon, so it was surrounded on three sides by water, and the region was heavily forested. By land, it may have been accessible only by a bridge (or by coming through the forest). The location suggests it was probably a popular hunting ground, but also a good place to hide away from marauding Danes.[2]

Theoretically, at least, it should not have been easy for the inhabitants of a properly manned and defended royal vill like Chippenham to have been taken by surprise. So why was the king forced to flee for his life on Twelfth Night in the first days of 868? The sources record that the king was attacked by the treacherous Danes at his estate at Chippenham. The *Anglo-Saxon Chronicle* records that they 'stole out' of Gloucester to Chippenham 'by stealth'.[3] It has been depicted as a surprise attack on a court totally unprepared and engaged in the drunken revelry traditionally associated with medieval festivities. Yet in recent years, historians have suggested there may have been something more going on. Far from drinking and revelling, Alfred may have been gathered with his household and nobles to discuss business when they decided to depose him. It has already been mentioned how there had been friction between the king and the Archbishop of Canterbury in the early part of the decade, and while it may seem surprising that the nobles of the kingdom would suddenly turn on their apparently capable young ruler, he was not so capable at the time. Alfred had not achieved a decisive victory against the Danes. Instead the two sides had been caught up in an almost constant war of attrition, with some respite only being achieved when the Danes were paid off for another few months or years. Alfred had only just 'managed to keep hold of his Kingdom by a mixture of energy, luck and bribery'.[4] Paul Hill proposed a possible scenario, in which Guthrum had been aware of the disaffection among members of the witan and had exploited it, entering into negotiations with them. He left Gloucester for Chippenham and the conspirators 'had no choice but to reveal themselves', and entered the king's hall to let him know that they had effectively rejected him. It is possible that some people had already submitted or agreed to submit to the Danish leader. Perhaps they had in mind a similar situation to that which had occurred in Mercia – that Guthrum would choose a new king to rule in his stead, or might even take power himself. Perhaps they even had in mind a son of Æthelred, or even handing over the kingdom to Guthrum himself.[5]

It might even be possible to identify the persons who were involved from names that disappear from the king's charters after 878. The names of Cuthred of Hampshire, Ælfstan of Dorset, Mucel, Eadwulf and one Mildred (a male rather than a female name as it is today) do not appear in official records after 878. Only one person is actually explicitly named as a traitor in later accounts, and his name was Wulfhere, an ealdorman who held lands in Wiltshire. His lands were granted by Edward the Elder, Alfred's eldest son and ultimate successor to one Æthelwulf, having been confiscated from or abandoned by the former because he had 'deserted the king'. So Alfred, it would appear, was effectively deposed by the important men of his own court and kingdom in the bleak midwinter with the Danes ready to enter Chippenham. It has been speculated that the gates might even have been left open for them.[6]

Another theory is that the king was forewarned of a conspiracy to hand him over to the Danes and had just enough time to flee. Both circumstances may be possible. Any plan to hand him over to the Danes could not realistically have resulted in anything other than his death, but what if, as with his Mercian brother-in-law before him, the nobles at Chippenham hoped he would simply abdicate and leave the country to live out his days quietly in a religious house? Perhaps they hoped that their new master Guthrum might place one of them on the throne.

Whatever happened at Chippenham, it is known that Alfred left with only a few select members of his household (probably including a handful of soldiers or armed thegns) and almost certainly his young family. None of the near-contemporary chronicles record that Ealswith and the children went with him from Chippenham into exile, but it is generally accepted that they did; their fate would not have been good if they had been left behind. It is likely that they made their escape by fleeing into the forest that bordered the royal vill, which eventually merged into Selwood Forest, which today spans the borders of Somerset, Wiltshire and Berkshire. For nearly three months, and all the way through the bitter winter, Alfred and his followers lived as fugitives, tramping slowly though the western part of the kingdom. Possibly his wife and young children did not follow him in these wanderings, and after the departure from Chippenham were left in some place of safety, perhaps at the home of a nobleman or at a minster or church.

Asser's *Life of Alfred* and the *Anglo-Saxon Chronicle*, written retrospectively in later decades, give a rudimentary account of this time. From them and other evidence, we can deduce that the royal party made their way to and through 'woody and marshy places' on the Somerset levels. This area, covering much of the west and east of the modern county in south-western England, today consists of flatland reclaimed for farming, as well as wetlands. In Alfred's day the whole area would have been a flooded marsh, punctuated with lightly wooded islands and probably beds of reeds and long grasses. At the same time, Guthrum was trying to consolidate his position in Wessex, taking control of the royal vills around Chippenham and establishing bases. In an ironic reversal of fortune, it was Alfred who decided to 'go Viking' on Guthrum in the early months of 878 by mounting a series of raids against the enemy who sought to flush him out.[7]

Asser recorded how Guthrum's forces proceeded through Wiltshire and the surrounding counties 'by force of arms ... forcing many men ... to sail overseas ... and nearly all the inhabitants of the kingdom having submitted to their authority'. It is doubtful that the Danes simply went through Wessex raiding, but it seems that they also set up bases in various places. In an ironic reversal of fortune, during the first half of 878 it was Alfred and his men who became the raiders, and the Danes who became their pursuers. Asser again records that they were in dire straits, living on what they could 'forage from frequent raids, both on the Vikings and even from their own people who had submitted to them'.[8] These 'raids' seem to have consisted of deadly hit-and-run attacks on small Danish parties, or nocturnal attacks in which provisions were stolen. Alfred may not simply have been stealing to live. He was, even inadvertently, sending out a strong message to the people of Wessex and their rulers. The last son of Æthelwulf may have lost his throne, but he was not dead and gone, nor was he without support. He was continuing the war on a small scale, and in some sense taking revenge on those who had sided with his enemies.

As before, however, Guthrum was not expecting to work alone and was expecting aid from his allies by sea. It came in the form of an army led by Ubba, supposedly the last surviving son of the legendary Ragnar Lothbrok. They landed on a beach near Lynmouth, in the county of Devon. The progress of the army would have been disastrous for Alfred, who would have been 'trapped between Guthrum's patrols ... and the new Viking army'. Such an outcome cannot have seemed unlikely, as the only resistance Ubba met came from a local lord named Odda and a small force allegedly consisting mainly of farmers and peasants. Wisely seeing that an all-out battle would result in defeat, they withdrew to the top of the ancient ramparts of Cynuit, which has been identified as the Iron Age hill fort on Countisbury Hill, a ridge which towers over the beaches near Lynmouth from a height of 850 feet today. Taking the bait, or perhaps unable to resist engaging with an upstart Saxon lording presumptuous enough to get in his way, Ubba 'ordered his men to besiege the hill', counting on the defenders soon running out of supplies.[9] He did not have long to wait. According to tradition, Odda and his band came down from their ramparts early in the morning and took the Danes by surprise to win a stunning victory in which Ubba and hundreds of his men were reportedly killed. The ealdorman also reportedly achieved a symbolic victory by capturing Ubba's famous raven banner. This was something like a totem, depicting the slaughter bird believed to be sacred to the Norse god Odin. It was also believed that the banner would flutter in the wind before battle if the god had decided to grant victory to his devotees, but would hang limp if defeat was imminent. We do not know if there was a strong wind that day.

The engagement at Cynuit was to change the fortunes of the fugitive king. Shortly afterwards, King Alfred and his band made a more permanent base around modern-day Athelney, a hilly promontory covering no more than 2 acres, as well as some of the surrounding islets. Today Athelney is a prominent hill, and the name means 'Isle of the Prince' in Old English, hinting at the original topography of the region. Extensive flooding in 2013 allowed for some idea of what the area would have been like in the late ninth century, with the hill alone rising above the water. The royal party had been wandering for nearly three months before establishing themselves at Athelney, sometime around 23 March 878. Alfred probably did not choose the location by accident. He knew the region, which was home to wild deer and other game, and he and his family would probably have hunted there in his youth, and he was to find support there when he was joined by Æthelnoth, the ealdorman of Somerset. The location was also useful. Although located and effectively hidden among the 'torturous streams' and 'black mists' in the heart of the Somerset levels, Athelney was far from the middle of nowhere. 'A network of Roman roads and trackways ... skirted the marshes', allowing the king and his followers to strike out 'tirelessly and relentlessly' against their enemies.[10] Their ranks were now boosted by the ealdorman of Dorset, though they probably numbered no more than a hundred or so men. Of course, if it was possible to establish a base around the area and to use the local roads for travel and transport, it was also possible to be attacked. There is no evidence in the sources of Danish incursions to Athelney (although it's possible that any such attacks might have been ignored or overlooked), although the eleventh-century observer William of Malmesbury suggested that Athelney was only accessible by boat. Unlike in the past, Alfred does not seem to have wasted time during the hiatus in warfare. A hill near to Athelney known as the Mump, which stands 75 feet above modern ground level and was then an island, was used as a lookout post, and archaeological excavations have uncovered evidence of metalworking there. Clearly Alfred and his men were taking the trouble to equip and prepare themselves to face the enemy.[11]

Most of the myths and legends about Alfred that have endured to this day relate to his time on Athelney. Many are well known, such as the tale that the inattentive and distracted king allowed cakes to burn while staying in a peasant woman's hut. Rather like the tale of the cave and the spider, for the fourteenth-century Scottish king Robert the Bruce it was a tale that came to define King Alfred; indeed it is sometimes all he is remembered for today. Although they are not historically accurate or verifiable, and may seem far-fetched to modern people, the stories about the exploits of Alfred during his months in exile can reveal something about his beliefs and motivations as well as the culture and times in which he lived. In the surviving corpus of Anglo-Saxon poetic literature, there are no fewer than two poems that feature exiled warriors lamenting their fate. These are *The Wanderer* and *The Seafarer* and are preserved in *The Exeter Book*, one of four medieval manuscripts in which most of the surviving texts are contained. *The Exeter Book* dates from the eleventh century, although many of the poems are believed to be of much earlier origin. Perhaps King Alfred identified with the plight of these literary exiles wondering in the wilderness, and he found solace and wisdom in such lines as:

> ... and all the kingdom
> of earth is fraught with hardship, the decree
> Of fate alters beneath the heavens.
> Here property and friendship pass away...
> ... blessed is he who keeps his faith; a man
> Must never been too keen to reveal
> His cares unless he knows already how
> To bring about a cure by his own vigour.[12]

Nor was Alfred the first exiled king. In the seventh century the first great Christian king of Northumbria, Oswald Iding, had spent much of his youth in exile in Ireland and Scotland, ending up on the Isle of Iona, where he converted to Christianity before reclaiming his kingdom from other claimants and the aggressive ravages of a neighbouring king. Like Oswald before him, Alfred was noted for his devotion to Christianity (it had, after all, been nearly 300 years since Oswald and his fellows had bought the faith to the Saxon people), and in his later years he would show a strong belief in his own destiny. Many years later, various observers would claim that Alfred was visited by their favoured saints and patrons, from Saint Neot (a late ninth-century Cornish monk) to Cuthbert, the bishop of Lindisfarne in the seventh century who gave him encouragement and predictions of victory. For later observers, such anecdotes about the pious king, driven into dire straits by his pagan foes and turncoat Christians, probably made for good, instructive tales. Even modern storytellers have found good fodder during the period of exile, not just for Alfred but also for his daughter. In one modern work of fiction, the young Æthelflæd spots a group of Danes while wondering in the woods, and runs off to tell her father so that he can avert a possible attack.

Realistically, in the late spring of 778 Alfred probably only had one goal in mind, though a truly lofty one: to win back his kingdom. Guerrilla warfare and raiding could not go on indefinitely. Alfred needed a major victory, one that would tilt the balance back in his favour. His chances improved after Odda's triumph, for now various nobles and thegns were prepared to communicate with him and even directly come and join the exiled king. According to Asser, before he had been on Athelney three months, in early May Alfred and his retainers travelled to a place called Egbert's Stone, a place that is difficult to identify today – Asser says it was on the 'eastern side of Selwood Forest'. The location seems to have been useful, for we are told there came there 'all the inhabitants of Somerset and Wiltshire, and all the inhabitants of Hampshire, joined up with him, receiving him as if one restored to life'.[13] The meeting was almost certainly prearranged rather than spontaneous, and those who met up with the king probably already knew he was still alive, but it does say something for the planning and preparation that had been going on in the previous months. This preparation was necessary, for the young king was preparing for the greatest battle of his life.

4

RETURN OF THE KING
MAY 878

There have been numerous accounts of the great military engagement that followed only a day or two after the meeting at Egbert's Stone. Like many of the other events of this time, it has also gone down in history as monumental, almost legendary. Asser recounted how

> the next day when the morning dawned he (Alfred) moved his forces to a place called Edington, and fighting fiercely with a compact shield-wall against the entire Viking army, he persevered resolutely for a long time, at length he gained victory by God's will. He destroyed the Vikings with a great slaughter.[1]

Asser's account is frustratingly short. For a more detailed picture of what took place, we need to look to other sources. Edoardo Albert provided such an account in his biography of Alfred. It would appear that the gathering of the Saxon army had not gone undetected. Guthrum had scouts and patrols, who told him of 'men ... moving, slipping down trackways and into the forest', and now informed him that Alfred had emerged from his hiding place and was moving towards the place from which he had fled five months before. He was returning to Chippenham 'with an army at his back'.[2] Guthrum, who was undeniably a good commander, prepared to meet his adversary, marching his army out of their fortified burh and on to Bratton Castle, an Iron Age hill fort on Salisbury plain – once again, an example of early medieval armies making advantageous use of ancient earthworks.

Guthrum's position was well thought out. Alfred, although he had the advantage of numbers with around 4,000 men, would have to fight uphill. Yet Bratton Castle was not just a hill; it occupied a ridge ringed by ditches, allowing Guthrum to funnel Alfred's forces into a narrow formation, which would not allow them to outflank him. The king of Wessex took his men up nonetheless, realising the battle would be reduced to nothing more than 'a brutal shoving match'[3] – such had been the nature of many battles in Britain for centuries. Despite what has been portrayed on television, the Saxons and Vikings both used similar weapons and equipment, such as large, rounded shields with metal bosses that would be held in front and interlocked with the rest to form a wall. Protruding from this wall would have been spears (much more common than swords, which were an expensive, high-status weapon), looking like the spines of a porcupine. Alfred's soldiers of the lower orders might not even have had spears, but brought with them farming implements. When the shield walls met, the action of the battle would have consisted of hacking and stabbing, with any weapons available, at gaps in the enemy shield wall, or men who had lost their shields and fallen. One particularly nasty weapon was a spear with protrusions that allowed its user to hook shields and move them aside.

The battle lasted a long time. It real terms this may only have been a few hours: in brutal hand-to-hand fighting, before mechanised weapons, men tired quickly from the life-and-death struggle. In this instance, Alfred's numerical advantage pressed home as the Danish ranks began to tire. So many battles of this time proved to be conflicts of will as well as strength and manpower. They could be lost, the men abandoning ranks to break and run, or pursue a fleeing enemy only for that enemy to take advantage of the gap in their lines. This seems to have happened to the Danes at Chippenham, and when holes opened in their ranks, the men of Wessex quickly filled them, cutting down the men behind the first line as well as the wounded and the stragglers. In the end, Guthrum's forces simply ran. Guthrum, his commanders and his household warriors would have tried to reach horses; ordinary soldiers would have had no horses and simply fled on foot. They ran back towards to the safety of Chippenham.[4]

Now that they were certain Guthrum's men had indeed given up, and that their rout was not simply a ruse or a trick to draw their enemies from their line, Alfred's men were allowed to give chase. Once again Asser elaborated on what happened next. The king 'pursued those who fled as far as the stronghold, hacking them down, he seized everything he found outside … men (whom he killed immediately), horses and cattle – and boldly made camp in front of the Viking stronghold with all his army'.[5] The standoff lasted two weeks, with Alfred, in an ironic twist of fate, laying siege and the enemy holed up in his own royal vill. The king was ruthless, cutting off all supplies and, as mentioned, seized all livestock to starve out his enemies. After two weeks, the enemy capitulated and came to terms. This time, apparently, there was to be no political wrangling or a payoff to make the Vikings leave. The Danish army offered to leave the kingdom once and for all, and offered Alfred as many hostages as he wanted. The final act, however, marked the surrender after Edington and was different from the rest, for Guthrum agreed to accept baptism and became a Christian.

Modern historians almost universally agree that the battle of Edington was the most decisive of Alfred's reign, far more important than that at Ashdown or his grandfather's victory at Hingston Down. For over five months the king of Wessex had struggled to survive in the hinterlands of his kingdom. He had built up his army from nothing. For years the fighting had been a close-run thing, brutal and attritional, only stopping when the parties had worn each other out with casualties, fighting and siege, and one party decided to pay off the other for a temporary respite. Betrayal, defeat, failure and broken promises had caused the last entirely independent king in Anglo-Saxon England to lose his kingdom, but he had made a spectacular comeback.[6]

The period after the battle of Edington is somewhat better documented then the first seven years of Alfred's reign, and the first eight of his daughter's life. The reasons for this become apparent when one examines the later years of King Alfred's reign, which played host the famous educational reforms and the time when the *Anglo-Saxon Chronicle* and the *Life of Alfred* began to be composed. But those events were still in the future in the late spring of 878, after the momentous victory at Edington. Alfred had regained his kingdom and seemingly vanquished his enemies. Now he wanted to consolidate his victory, and he was not prepared to do that by simply paying the Danes to go away as he had in the past.

With the destruction of Ubba's forces at Cynuit and the victory at Edington, the previously deposed and unwanted king was in a position of power and could force Guthrum to agree to his terms. Three weeks after the battle, Guthrum and the members of his household undertook baptism in a church at a small estate called Aller, which was not far from Alfred's marsh refuge at Athelney. It may be asked why Guthrum was prepared to accept the Christian rite when he had never shown any inclination to do so in the past, and why Alfred apparently placed so much importance on it. Vikings had been baptised before, and it had not stopped them breaking any oaths or agreements they had made and going back to raiding and making war on their Christian patrons.[7]

Alfred could have killed Guthrum – perhaps there were even some in his household who argued ought to have done so – but by doing such a thing he would have created a power vacuum, which could have been filled by any ambitious warrior who might decide to regroup and launch a fresh attack. Perhaps, as in 871, the Danish and English armies had simply been worn out by years of fighting. What was more, the Danish army was scattered between Chippenham and Cirencester further to the north, and the hostages Alfred had taken might well have included important survivors from the army that Guthrum was not prepared to sacrifice. Alfred thus probably regarded his foe as sufficiently harnessed.

Guthrum's baptism might well have been as much of a political act as a religious one. Alfred and his erstwhile ally Ealdorman Æthelnoth of Somerset became his godfathers at the ceremony, which brought Guthrum into the fellowship of Christian kings and nobles. His name was changed to Æthelstan and he was shortly to be installed as the new Christian king of East Anglia.

Here again Alfred seems to have revealed himself as an astute political player, for there was a surviving Saxon claimant to the East Anglian throne, none other than the brother of the martyred Edmund who had been living in exile in Wessex. The king of Wessex made no attempt to restore him to the throne, instead opting to install his new godson. Alongside Guthrum there were also baptised thirty men of his household (probably household warriors), a wise move that was perhaps designed to ensure that the Danish lord had the support of his men. The ceremony was followed by several days of feasting and festivities. Alfred had his wish, and had symbolically and religiously asserted his dominion over the Dane, but allowing him to become king of a neighbouring territory was also intended to show that he was prepared to work with Guthrum provided he did not turn on him and attack him again. Of course, one of the other terms of the surrender had been a complete withdrawal of all Guthrum's forces from Wessex. It took them several months to do so, but eventually in October of 878 they withdrew to Cirencester, not far over the border into Mercia, and eventually into Guthrum's new kingdom of East Anglia.

Not long afterwards, the last king of Mercia disappeared – quite literally. Ceolwulf II, the supposed 'unwise King's thegn' and puppet of the Vikings, disappears from the historical record sometime between 879 and 880. The *Anglo-Saxon Chronicle* does not record his death – nor do any of the other Alfredian sources – so what ultimately happened to him is unknown, but it is generally supposed that he either died or was deposed. An agreement between Alfred and Guthrum, which is usually dated to 880, carved up Mercia to create two separate kingdoms, one under English rule (and subject to Alfred) and the other ruled by the Danes; this became known as the

Danelaw. Alfred and Guthrum were essentially 'dividing the spoils'. Thus, to some observers, the disappearance of Ceolwulf appears to have been suspiciously convenient. Some have even gone so far as to suggest that the Mercian king's demise may have come about as part of a sinister conspiracy in which Guthrum and Alfred colluded to get rid of a mutual rival. Indeed, after the king of Mercia's demise the Mercians were essentially forced into a closer alliance with Alfred to protect themselves from further Viking incursions.[8]

Ceolwulf is certainly an enigma. There are only two references to him in the *Anglo-Saxon Chronicle*, one recording how he became king of Mercia in 874 and using the derogatory designation given above. The other records how the 'Great Heathen Army' divided the kingdom between them in 877, and 'some they gave to Ceolwulf'.[9] He did not, apparently, object to this division, which does seem to interestingly foreshadow Alfred and Guthrum's later agreement. The last king of Mercia may have been something more than a passive puppet of the Danes. It has been suggested that he may have been of royal blood, and a member of an ancient dynasty that had ruled the kingdom in the early ninth century. All these rulers had alliterative names beginning with C, something that was common in Anglo-Saxon naming patterns, leading them to have been dubbed the 'C dynasty'. Evidence from charters and coins suggests that he was operating as the independent king of Mercia (or at least of the northern and western parts that were not parcelled out among the Vikings), performing normal roles like granting land, and that he was accepted as king by his people.[10]

He does seem to have devoted a lot of time and energy to fighting the Welsh. *The Annales Cambriae*, or Annals of Wales, were composed in the later part of the tenth century, but like many such early medieval chronicles some of the information may date from before that time and they record events from earlier centuries. Among other things, the *Annales Cambriae* and the Irish annals record a battle fought in 877 between Rhodri Mawr, the king of Gwyneth (a powerful kingdom in north-west Wales) and 'the Saxons' led by Ceolwulf. In this battle Rhodri was said to have been slain alongside one of his sons, named Gwraid.[11] Three years later another battle was recorded as having been fought at Conwy, in which revenge was wrought 'by the help of God' upon the English for the death of King Rhodri. It is usually held that the English opponents in the battle were actually led by Æthelred, the later 'Lord of the Mercians', but the wording of the entry does raise one intriguing alternative. This is that the 'revenge' for the death of the great Welsh king actually may have involved not just a victory against the English, but also the killing of the man who was held responsible for having slain the great Welsh king – none other than Ceolwulf of Mercia.[12] Is this what happened to the last man to have been recognised as the king of the Mercians? It cannot be known for certain, but it is perhaps not impossible that the Saxon commentators might have ignored or overlooked what they saw as the ignominious end of a Danish collaborator at the hands of his Christian neighbours.

In place of Ceolwulf there emerged the future husband of Æthelflæd, another nobleman bearing the ever-popular name of Æthelred. He would become known in West Saxon sources as the lord or ealdorman of the Mercians. Like his immediate predecessor, his origins are unknown. Chapter six will provide a more detailed examination of his origins and his relationship with his future wife. He would go on to become another long-term ally of Alfred, fighting alongside him during campaigns in the 880s and 890s, when fresh Viking armies entered Wessex under new leaders.

Back in Wessex, Alfred decided that the time had come to rebuild his kingdom. In his later years, he would come to consider the early part of the 870s as time he had unwisely wasted. Later tradition, and some modern writers, would have it that Alfred began to plan and imagine the rebuilding of his kingdom during his months in exile. It is not impossible. What we *do* know is that Alfred learned from his past mistakes and had realised that something needed to change by 880. At this point he began the process of fortifying his kingdom to allow his people to effectively defend themselves. Yet there was more to his plans than a shake-up of the defence system. What Alfred had in mind was a system of social and cultural revival and reform.[13]

5

DAUGHTER OF WESSEX 880–886

Now that Alfred had his kingdom back, he would have recalled his family from where he had left them after the meeting at Egbert's Stone. They had probably stayed on at Athelney during this time, but now returned to resume their lives in Wessex. After Guthrum's baptism, King Alfred's strategy took on a new course. Before he had paid the Danes to go away; now he had effectively set up and sponsored his former enemy as king of East Anglia, in spite of the fact that a brother of the martyred King Edmund was still very much alive, and may even have been present at the West Saxon court. The former Danish leader's new position, as mentioned, protected Wessex from Viking attacks from the east.

The Building of the Boroughs

Alfred decided that more was needed than to simply place his trust in his erstwhile enemy. Thus it was from the early 880s that one of Alfred's most famous actions began: the reform of the defensive system and the establishment of the burhs or boroughs. These were a series of fortified settlements that criss-crossed the kingdom of Wessex at regular intervals. Some were built from scratch; others made use of existing structures such as Iron Age hill forts or Roman ramparts, or were added to existing towns.

Asser has this to say on the matter when lauding Alfred's achievements towards the end of the king's life:

> And what of the cities and towns to be rebuilt and of others to be constructed when there were previously none ... and what of the royal halls and chambers marvellously constructed of stone and wood at his command? And what of the royal residences of masonry, moved from their old position and splendidly reconstructed at more appropriate places by his royal command?[1]

Of course fortifications had been constructed before, and there is evidence of them earlier in the Anglo-Saxon period, as early as the seventh and even the eighth century. These were usually fairly simple structures, consisting of earthworks topped by palisades. In some cases, royal or noble estates had been fortified in this way. (Such fortifications are believed to have been denoted by the suffix 'tun' in place names.) Chippenham may have been a fortified royal settlement on these lines.[2]

Alfred's new project involved constructing a different kind of fortification with each burh designed to be a place of refuge as well as residence. Asser's reference to cities and towns implied large-scale settlements. By the standards of the time, a large-scale settlement would have had a population of several hundred – at the very most a few thousand. Many burhs were originally intended to 'provide shelter for people and livestock during Viking raids, as well as channelling their movements, blocking fords and other strategic points, and generally making it more difficult for invading armies to manoeuvre across the country'.[3] A document known as the *Burghal Hidage*, which dates from Alfred's reign, names the burhs that existed in the 880s and also lists the number of *hides* (a common unit of measurement) they contained. These measurements were necessary to calculate how many men would be required to man the walls and defend the burh, emphasizing their military and defensive purpose. Settlement by the ordinary folk of Wessex, or the families of the men who guarded the walls, may have been a gradual process that happened over time, unless burhs were developed on the sites of existing settlements.

It is not clear where Alfred got the idea for his system of fortifications; some have suggested that he may have drawn inspiration from the fortified encampments made by the Vikings. Among these was the winter camp they had constructed at Repton during their Mercian campaign in 873. Alfred could certainly have seen these fortifications, such as the one constructed at Thanet, or any defences that might have been constructed around Chippenham or Exeter, and any of the other towns from which he tried to pull Guthrum. Alternatively, he may also have drawn his inspiration from Mercian and even Continental models. The great Mercian king Offa had constructed earthworks and other fortifications, most notably Offa's Dyke along the border of Wales. There is also wider evidence of many major Mercian cities having been fortified in the eighth and early ninth centuries. His wife was Mercian, and, as has already been stated, Alfred had strong connections with Mercia. He had stayed there for some time, so he cannot have been ignorant of the history or the military infrastructure of the kingdom.

Perhaps it is no coincidence that Alfred's building programme began in the very same decade when Mercia technically recognised his overlordship and Æthelred, a prominent Mercian lord and experienced warrior, became his most powerful ally. It has been remarked that during the 880s and 890s Alfred's court was 'positively crawling' with Mercians, including members of Ealswith's family and various clerics, as well as the new Lord of the Mercians himself. It was most likely during the first half of the 880s that Alfred first met his daughter's future husband, perhaps even during one of the campaigns against the Danes that decade, which will be described later in this chapter.

Learned Barbarians

By the time that Alfred began to lay down plans for his great building programme, Æthelflæd would probably have been approaching her tenth birthday. Her youngest surviving sibling and second brother, Æthelweard, was born about 880, but her other brother, Edward, was closest to her in age. With renewed peace and a measure of stability in the early part of the decade, the children could continue their education and preparation for adult life in earnest. This may have started a few years before, but the tumultuous events of Christmas and spring of 878 would have interrupted any such preparations.

It has often been said that Alfred did not learn to read until he was well into his forties. This is not, in fact, correct. The Latin word *illiterati*, from which we derive the term illiterate, did not necessarily mean the same thing as it did today. A person might be considered such because they did not know how to read and write in Latin, the language of education, the church and government. Yet a person ignorant of Latin could be literate in their own mother tongue of French, German, English, Welsh or anything else. Alfred seems to have mastered reading in his mother tongue of Old English or Anglo-Saxon by the time he was twelve years old. It was Latin that he did not learn until his later life.[4]

We know from other evidence that Alfred had a great love for the Old English literature and writings. His oldest children would probably have been given their earliest education in the household by their tutors (some encouragement and input from their parents and relatives might not have been impossible). It is known that his youngest son, Æthelweard, had the most extensive education, probably because he was destined for the Church at an early age. By the time he reached the requisite age in around 887–890, Alfred's reforms had reached the educational system and he had established a school at his court. Early medieval European monarchs have hardly left behind any traces of literary achievements or pursuits, but Alfred was one of the rare exceptions as he translated in whole or part a number of important literary, historical and philosophical works during his later years. Yet this did not happen until he learned Latin in the second half of the 880s, when his educational reforms began. In the first half of the decade, this movement was still in the future and his efforts were being channelled into strengthening the defences of his kingdom.

In his childhood Alfred certainly had a tutor, and this tutor would probably have taught his other siblings as well. What exactly would they have been taught? Certainly, some form of basic literacy seems to have been involved. Writing was quite a specialist skill that was more often than not the preserve of clerics, but reading seems to have been more common. This reading may well have included the various 'works of the English tongue' alluded to in Asser and other sources, which Alfred enjoyed so much. Short and simple texts could have been used as a basis for helping children learn their letters and master the basic structure of words and grammar.

Alongside reading, another important skill was memorisation. An anecdote in Asser recounted one of Alfred's earliest literary experiences, in which his mother showed her children a beautifully illuminated book of poetry and told them she would give it to the first of them who learned it. The young Alfred is said to have been so attracted by the book that he immediately took it to his tutor, who read it to him until the child Alfred had committed it to memory and was able to recite it back to his mother.[5] There is some doubt over the credibility of this story, but there may be some grain of truth in it. The memorisation of large amounts of texts for the purposes of oral recitation is a skill that has been largely lost in the modern age. Yet in the Anglo-Saxon age it was considered an important aspect of secular education for aristocratic children. Although early Saxon noble saints are said to have heard poetry recited in the lordly mead hall (or even learned it themselves), poetry was more than just a form of entertainment. It could be instructive. In our surviving corpus of Anglo-Saxon literature there exists a sub-genre of what could be called 'wisdom literature'. Some of this consists of short verses providing advice and metaphorical examples of ideal values and attributes. Such as,

> These fitly belong: gold on a man's sword as an exotic ornament and jewellery on a woman;
>
> A good poet to the people, to menfolk armed strife, and defend the civic security against war.
>
> A shield necessarily goes with a soldier, an arrow with a poacher, a ring necessarily goes with a bride, books with the student, the Eucharist with the holy man, and with the heathen sins.[6]

Other poems were devoted to mythology. Although this could be a highly fictionalised and sometimes fantastical representation of the world and of past events, it could represent an important form of folk memory for the tribe, kingdom or people. In a culture that had a strong oral tradition, it was considered important for the young generation to learn about the popular 'history' and heroic mythology of their forbears in the form of mythopoetic literature. Would Alfred have heard famous epic poems like the famous *Beowulf*? It is quite likely, although the royal line of kings who feature in that poem were claimed as ancestors of the ancient East Anglian royal line. We can learn from sources such as Asser that Alfred knew of the legendary ancestry of his own family line, which claimed descent from the fifth-century warlord Cerdic (who may have been a Romano-Briton) and was aware of his more distant, legendary ancestors, who were said to have included the ancient Germanic-Scandinavian gods like Odin.

Youngsters would also have been instructed in the manners and behaviour that was considered suitable for nobles of the time. We don't have any surviving books of etiquette for the Anglo-Saxon age like the ones which survive from the thirteenth century and after, but we can look at contemporary writings from places like the Carolingian Empire. Asser mentions how Alfred gave noble children 'instruction in all virtuous behaviour'. Three quarters of a century earlier, the Frankish noblewoman Dhouda had penned her *Liber Manualis*, an instructive manual for her absent son in which she advised him, among other things, to

> be Humble and Chaste in Body, be ready to give proper service, show yourself constantly kind to all people, both to the great and the not so great.... Frequently give assistance to widows and

> orphans, give food and drink to pilgrims, offer hospitality, stretch out your hands with apparel for the naked. Be a strong and fair judge in legal disputes; never take a bribe; never oppress anyone for the great Giver will repay you.[7]

In this we see some reflection of the some of the ideal values and behaviours that nobles were supposed to espouse even into the later Middle Ages like loyalty, charity, and upholding law and justice. Another passage also refers to honouring clerics and the sacraments, which would cover another noble value: piety.

There does not seem to have been any intrinsic bias against allowing girls to have education in the later ninth century, although most examples of literary pursuits that we know of come from the hagiographical works related to male saints, and in Alfred's biography we do find the occasional reference to women in the literary sphere. It is known that in later centuries mothers were often expected to oversee the very earliest aspects of their children's education, sometimes both male and female children. They might teach them the rudiments of reading in the domestic setting before they had their first tutor, and the story from Asser related above does hint at a conscientious mother taking an interest in the educational development of her offspring.

Traditionally, girls destined for the Church may have been educated in a nunnery, or spent some years there as a child before leaving to marry. Two of Alfred's ultimately went into the Church: the aforementioned son Æthelweard, but also the second of his three daughters, named Æthelgifu. Young people who entered religious institutions could expect the highest level of education available at the time, although the ravages of the Viking raids must have had some impact. It is known that in the eleventh century the German nun Hildegard of Bingen not only corresponded with male clerics in more than one language but also wrote works on religion and medicine. Five centuries before, the Saxon royal woman St Hilda became Abbess of Whitby and her institution became famous throughout the land for the clerics and churchmen who were educated there.[8]

There are allusions to all of Alfred's five children, including his two daughters who did not go into the Church, having enjoyed an education. His youngest children seem to have benefited from his educational reforms, but there is no reason to assume that Æthelflæd would not have had a tutor like her brother Edward before these reforms started. They may even have had the same tutor. Did she hear (and perhaps even read) the works of literature and poetry that her father had been so enthralled by in his own youth? It seems very likely, and there is evidence from her later life to suggest that she fostered a literary culture in the court she would later head in Mercia.[9]

Priests, monks and clerics employed as tutors would probably have taught their students religious as well as secular texts. In fact, Saxon literature included many religious motifs and themes from the very earliest period. Wisdom literature such as *The Maxims* (quoted above) draw heavily upon Biblical wisdom literature such as the Book of Proverbs. The Psalms also seem to have been an ever-popular choice for recitation and study with their poetic beauty and sympathetic portrayals of the challenges and struggles of the human condition. It is known that in the later Middle Ages psalters (small books containing the Psalms) were often used by tutors as a primer to help children learn and practise their Latin. The simple layout, with short sentences or verses, makes it clear why these were considered a good starting point for youngsters, or indeed older students mastering the language for the first time. Alfred was particularly keen on the Psalms, not just for their educational value but also for their spiritual merits. In the spirit of the original authors, he drew on them for wisdom, inspiration and encouragement in his darkest times. Perhaps it is no wonder that he chose to include a number of them in his great translation project in the last decade of his life.[10]

There were also saint's lives and theological works, although aristocratic children might not have been exposed to these in the schoolroom. Anglo-Saxon clerics did not always limit their writings and study to religious themes and subjects. The eighth-century monk Bede composed his famous *Ecclesiastical History of the English People*, a work which has caused him to be dubbed the Father of English History. Bede wrote mostly in Latin, but his works were widely distributed and translated. In the centuries after his death, his works were found in monastic libraries in Europe and even beyond.[11]

Alfred certainly knew about Bede, who had died only 120 years before his birth. His works were probably only as far removed as the works of Austen and Dickens are in our own time. The West Saxon king also held the monastic author in very high regard, choosing parts of his *Ecclesiastical History* to include in his later programme of translation. What is intriguing about Bede and other clerical authors of the eighth and ninth centuries is certain passages in their work that can challenge modern preconceptions about the age. It has often been stated that people in the later Middle Ages (from about the thirteenth century onwards) did not believe the earth was flat. This was indeed the case, but this knowledge was certainly widespread in Europe from a far earlier date. Bede had written about the earth as 'round like a ball' and even alluded to the moon affecting the tides. He was not the first to have done so. The late Roman author Boethius had made a passing reference to this as common knowledge two centuries before Bede.

Closer to Alfred's lifetime there was the aforementioned Alcuin of York. As his name suggests he was originally based at an abbey in York, and wrote a remarkable poem about it that suggests that the abbey possessed an extensive library of manuscripts including a number of works by classical writers, possibly including Pliny's (that is Pliny the Elder AD 23–79), *Natural History* and perhaps even some love poetry by the Roman poet Ovid. This heritage of learning and scholarship cannot help but cause us to admire the men (and in a few cases women) behind it – even its it is grudging. Danish and Norse culture may have been sophisticated in many ways, producing great artwork and craftsmanship. Undoubtedly, they were also excellent sailors and navigators with their own mythopoetic tradition. However, contrary to what some recent authors have suggested, they seem to have been rather backwards when it came to technical scientific and astronomical knowledge in comparison to their literate Christian European contemporaries with their prized ancient books on poetry and the natural world.[12]

A Woman's Place

Alongside her literary education, Æthelflæd must have spent the first decade of the 880s undergoing training and instruction in the traditional roles and duties of a young noblewoman. In literature, the ideal attributes of a young noblewoman were often spelled out quite clearly in passages like this one from *The Maxims*:

> ... the woman must excel as one cherished among her people,
> and be buoyant of mood, keep confidences,

> be open-heartedly generous with horses and treasure,
> in deliberation over the mead, in the presence of the troop of companions,
> she must always and everywhere greet first the chief of those princes and instantly offer the chalice to her lord's hand,
> and she must know what is prudent for them both as rulers of the hall.[13]

It was a sentiment echoed in other poetic works such as *The Husband's Message* and *Beowulf*, in which royal spouses acted jointly as givers of gold, the queen greeted victorious warriors, and was expected to be adorned in such precious finery as well as giving it out. Her husband had to have gold to maintain his 'fine estate' and his wife also had to maintain the royal dignity and the ostentatious display of wealth. So her 'jewel-spangled' body and clothing was as important as being a good and generous hostess. Even in these works, although women held a lofty and exalted position, the husband was still referred as her lord or *hlaford*.[14] It may simply have been a noble courtesy, but also reflected a position of technical subordination, which married women were supposed to adopt. These roles were all in the none-too-distant future for the girl Æthelflæd as she approached her early teens.

Many of the terms and phrases applied to Anglo-Saxon women throughout the social scale also give us some clue to the roles young women and girls were expected to play. Property or goods that were passed down the female line were said to have gone to the 'spindle side' as opposed to the male line, which was the 'spear side'. It has even been suggested that the Old English term *wifman* (the origin of the term 'woman', but translated as 'wife-man' as it was also the origin of 'wife') may be related to weaving.[15]

The production of cloth and the processes involved became inextricably linked with female identity; there are even examples from the pre-Christian era of women buried with spindles or spindle whorls. These items are typically found with burials of older children from about the age of twelve, when they began to take part in 'adult' tasks.[16] The production of cloth was not simply a useful skill – it was a vitally important occupation at the heart of society. Of course all people had to be clothed, but clothing could be a mark of social status. Regardless of its fineness and expense, it was usually women who made it, alongside soft furnishings such as tapestries or bed coverings. In the pre-Christian religion of some European societies, including those of ancient Germany, Holland and Scandinavia, the act of weaving even took on a supernatural significance. The course of fate was described in terms of weaving, and today it is thought that in some cultures there was a belief in the so-called 'fate-weavers' – immortal women of possibly divine status who determined the fates of all humanity on a never ending tapestry. The Danish warlord Ubba Ragnarsson's raven banner had been woven by his three sisters, and was said have been imbued with magical powers and had an almost totemic quality because of its associations with the old Norse religion.[17]

In aristocratic circles the name 'peace-weaver' came to be applied to another ideal attribute of women in matters of diplomacy and the moderating influence they could have on their menfolk. Early medieval women were supposed to be weavers of Christian peace alongside the cloth they made for the everyday needs of their family. We are used to images from film and television of medieval women gathered together with their ladies and engaged in activities such as sewing and embroidery. This is probably quite an accurate picture of the day-to-day activities the young Æthelflæd would have taken part in alongside her sisters, mother, servants and the ladies of the court. In the royal court, there would probably have been many slaves and servants involved in the working of cloth, but even upper-class women must have had the ability to do some of the work themselves. At their level of society, the items they produced must have been fine and intricate – fit, as the proverb says, for a king.[18]

When she was not so occupied, an intelligent girl like Æthelflæd cannot have failed to notice the military activities and preparations that her father and the other prominent men of the kingdom were involved in. Even if Alfred did not personally oversee and visit all of the burhs he planned to construct, his daughter and family may well have seen some of them during their circuits of the kingdom. It is easy to imagine Alfred's curious children asking him or his officials about the fortifications that were cropping up all over the kingdom and the preparations being made to defend them. These defences were soon to be tested once more – the Danes were returning.

Return of the Danes

After 880, the *Life of Alfred* and other sources kept an almost obsessive record of the movement of the Vikings on the Continent, especially in France. Their raiding activities in Britain did not come to an end with Guthrum's defeat in 878. Guthrum was but one leader of one force (albeit a large one) of Danish warriors. There were countless other war bands that were not bound by any agreements he had made. The sources are largely quiet about Alfred's actions against the 'heathens' in the 880s, perhaps for reasons of political expediency. There is a passing reference to a campaign in Epsom, Surrey, in 882, which comes from a charter and is not mentioned in any of the chronicle sources. They only record an engagement at sea against 'four crews of Danish men' that same year.[19]

Three years later, a Danish army that had been active in France attacked Rochester in Kent. Asser mentions that they built some kind of fortification around the town or, as the Chronicle suggests, around their camp. Both sources agree that the battle was won by the efforts of the townspeople to resist the invaders and defend themselves until, apparently, the king arrived with his soldiers and the Danes retreated to their boats and subsequently to France – or at least some of them did. The entries for the following year are somewhat confused but suggest a prolonged effort to dislodge and resist Danish forces; there is the very real possibility that they were considering or attempting an invasion of the south-western regions of Wessex. The Danes who did not leave for France after Rochester apparently chose to come to terms with Alfred – an agreement which echoes former arrangements with the exchange of hostages and oaths. This was no more successful than any previous arrangement, as the Danes continued raiding 'the Southern banks of the Thames'. Soon, a group of Danes who had been living in East Anglia went to join their fellows and formed a camp in Benfleet in Essex. Thankfully for Alfred, this came to nothing. The forces camped at Benfleet degenerated into factions who fell to quarrelling and a 'ghastly commotion'. Ultimately, the East Anglians returned home and the rest went back to France to re-join their fellows.[20]

Alfred and Wessex may have had a narrow escape, but it was a close-run thing. Alfred's next action suggests the events of 885 had unsettled him enough for him to strike back at those he considered to have broken their oaths: he sent a fleet to raid East Anglia. Was Alfred once again trying to play the Vikings at their own game by going 'a-Viking' on them? At first his attempt was successful – the men aboard Alfred's ships routed a force of 'pirates' and reportedly captured sixteen of the ships and killed their crews. Their minor victory was to be reversed when, on their way 'homeward with their booty', the Alfredian fleet was intercepted by a large Viking fleet and defeated.[21]

The following year, Alfred managed to 'take possession' of London and 'restore' the freedom of the city. London at that time was technically part of the kingdom of Mercia, although it had changed hands several times in the 870s. A Danish army had wintered there in 871/2, and another had established a toehold in 879. Considering their activities in Essex and Kent the year before, it is possible that Alfred considered the city a potential target for Danish armies and raiding parties. It is interesting that Asser stated that Alfred took the city 'after the burning of cities and the massacre of peoples'.[22] Had he only taken the great Roman city after a prolonged military campaign? Could the city or its surrounding regions even have been under Danish control?

Alfred's restoration of London followed a pattern that was to become usual, with the building of a burh and the desire to resettle the population into it, moving them out of their old settlement of Lundenwic and into a newly rebuilt one situated within the span of the walls of the old Roman city, much of which had fallen into ruin. He now took the opportunity to assert his authority. The restoration of the city was followed by a political act which became fairly typical of Alfred's reign: the king now styled himself not just as king of Wessex, but as king of the Anglo-Saxons. The *Anglo-Saxon Chronicle*, with its typical brevity, simply says that the whole of the 'English nation' that was not under Danish control 'turned to him' in his capacity as their self-appointed overlord. After his triumphal entry and the city's submission Alfred handed control over London to Lord Æthelred of Mercia. It had, after all, been a Mercian city in the past and the inhabitants may have still identified themselves with Mercia.[23]

It has been suggested that the handover of London may have had another dimension. It may have been a wedding gift from Alfred to his new son-in-law. We do not know exactly when Lord Æthelred of Mercia was married to Æthelflæd, but 886 is a reasonable and commonly accepted date.[24] At sixteen, Æthelflæd would have been of a suitable and usual age for marriage. We do not know where the marriage took place, but medieval royal marriages were well-planned affairs, and they had probably been betrothed for some time.[25] If the marriage did happen a year or two later, it is possible that London might have been a betrothal gift. Notwithstanding the finer details, we know that within a decade of the attack on Chippenham a West Saxon princess followed the example of her aunt some thirty years before and embarked on a journey to Mercia to commence her married life.

6

WILD BOAR OF MERCIA

The wild boar belongs in the woods, secure in the strength
of his tusks,
A good man belongs in his native land, forging his reputation
The javelin belongs in the hand.... the sword belongs in the lap,
a lordly iron weapon

The Maxims

Despite how little we know about Æthelflæd, even less is known for certain about the origins and early years of her husband, Æthelred of Mercia. It is estimated, from the date of his death and from the time at which we know he came to the attention of Alfred, that he was somewhat older than her. He was already an adult when he took control of Mercia around 880, which would make him at least ten years her senior. Such disparity in age between marriage partners was not at all uncommon throughout the Middle Ages and beyond. If we are to take ten years as the minimum gap between the ages of the two then this would place

Æthelred's birth around 860 or the late 850s, firmly in the reign of King Burgred.

Some have identified Æthelred with a nobleman named in a charter during the reign of King Ceolwulf. It is possible that he was the same person, although as the glossary of this book itself shows the name was rather common and it could just as easily have been another person who was entirely unrelated.[1] He would have been rather a young man during Ceolwulf's reign if we are to assume the 860 date for his birth. It was not impossible for younger men to play a role in politics if their fathers or royal forbears had died. King Alfred himself would not have been much more than fifteen when the third of his four brother died in 865.

More intriguingly, it has been argued that he may have been a relation of Alfred's own father-in-law, the aforementioned ealdorman of the Gaini, Æthelred 'mucel'. If this was indeed the case, then the Lord of the Mercians was a distant cousin of his wife.[2] Again, marriages to relatives were not uncommon. In later years, marriages between close relatives were technically banned by the Church, but even these could be overcome with a papal dispensation. Even if he was not directly related, there was one man in Mercia who had a connection with Alfred of Wessex before his marriage. This man was one Æthelwulf, the brother of Ealswith (whether older or younger we do not know) and so the maternal uncle of his wife. This Æthelwulf probably succeeded his father as ealdorman of the people of the Gaini.[3] Other suggestions are that he may have been related to one ealdorman Æthelwulf of Berkshire, or to the ancient ealdormen of the Hwicce including Æthelmund, who died around 800. The Hwicce was a tribal region of ancient provenance (it had once been a kingdom) that encompassed most of Gloucestershire and Worcestershire.

Interestingly, when Æthelred first appears in the historical record it is in a charter from 883, 'granting privileges' to Berkeley Abbey (also known as Berkeley Minster).[4] Joan Wolfe, a biographer of Æthelflæd, identified the abbey as being in Wessex, but this appears to be incorrect, as it was actually located in Gloucestershire until its dissolution in the twelfth century.[5] Much of the modern county of Gloucestershire was part of English Mercia instead of Wessex, although borders could be fluid at that time, and the county is flanked to the west by Berkshire and Wantage, King Alfred's own birthplace. The charter granted the privileges in return for land to be given to man named Cynewulf (his title is not given) at a place called 'Stoke Bishop'. The precise location of this area is hard to identify. There is a suburb of Bristol of that name today (the city was established later) and the area of the modern city seems to have been in West Saxon hands at this time. There is also the village of Bishopstoke in modern-day Hampshire, but the former seems to be more consistent, considering its associations with landholders in Gloucestershire and Warwickshire. Throughout his career, Æthelred seems to have had a strong affinity and associations with Gloucestershire, Worcestershire and the surrounding regions. After he married the daughter of Alfred, the couple established themselves in Gloucester, and they were later buried there. They were also patrons of St Peter's in Worcester and their friend the bishop of Worcester throughout their lives. All these connections suggest that Æthelred may have been a Gloucestershire or Worcestershire man born and bred.

We also don't know entirely *how* he came to power. It was mentioned in chapter four that there are some suspicions over the demise of King Ceolwulf. Æthelred appeared on the scene a few years later. One theory that has been posited for this lost period of Mercian history claims that after his defeat at the hands of Alfred, Guthrum went back to Mercia 'to complete the partition' or to demand more land from the king of Mercia. This proved to be too much for the nobles of Mercia, clinging on to what remained of their kingdom, and they deposed Ceolwulf (or perhaps even had him killed) and then regrouped to choose somebody to lead them who was more prepared to serve Mercian interests. This man was Æthelred, perhaps a military man and almost certainly a man experienced in rulership if he was indeed from an ancient noble line.

Soon afterwards, it is argued, the Mercian polity chose to throw in their lot with the king of Wessex, who had so recently defeated the Danes. At the same time, they launched a campaign against their neighbours in Gwyneth – not an expansionist war, but a war intended to prevent the Welsh from making a dangerous alliance with their Viking allies against them. It did not work; the Vikings were able to make camps in the border regions between Wales and Mercia. Of course, the latter scenario contradicts the author's above posited one, which holds that the Battle of Conwy may have taken place earlier than the traditional date of 881, and claimed the life of Ceolwulf. Either may be correct, but perhaps the above is more likely. The purpose of speculation here is simply to present the reader with an explanation of what *may* have happened, how and roughly when, because the sources are not always precise about this. Others may make stronger arguments, or new evidence may come to light in the future; until then, the reader can make up their own mind.[6]

The earliest charters show that Lord Æthelred had accepted Alfred as his overlord by at least 883. One from the following year refers to him as the ealdorman who 'by gift and divine grace supported in the rule of the Mercian people'.[7] Overlordship in Anglo-Saxon England could be a rather complicated matter involving ties of loyalty and obedience of various kinds such as military obligation, tribute or deference to the superior royal in political matters. In Æthelred's case this did not mean he could not act independently, as there are other charters showing him granting lands on his own without any reference to Alfred as his overlord. In fact, in Mercian charters he is often given more grandiose titles such as 'Dux', a Latin term meaning ruler, commander or general (which is the origin of the modern title of duke), 'procurator' or protector and 'subregulus', or sub-king. These were titles 'aspiring to divine grace' and several charters other than the one mentioned above speak of Lord Æthelred holding his position in these terms. The words the Mercians used to refer to their lord were 'verging on the royal'. If they were not allowed to officially call him king, they could call him everything short of it, especially when he acted independently of his West Saxon overlord.[8]

Æthelred was certainly a renowned warrior and warlord in his own right. It is hard to imagine that he would have been chosen as ruler of Mercia had he not been. Early Medieval kings were supposed to be war leaders. Of course, they had to have other attributes as well, but being able to subdue their rivals or other neighbouring kingdoms was always a useful skill. It not only gave the ruler glory and renown, but could allow him to reward his followers. It has been suggested that he may have played a role in the mysterious London campaign of 883 referred to in the last chapter, perhaps even a leading role left unmentioned in any West Saxon sources.[9] He also proved his mettle in campaigns against the Welsh. Alfred's biographer, Asser, whom the king met a little while before the probable year of his daughter's marriage, 886, referred to two Welsh rulers, the kings of Glwysing and Gwent, having submitted to Alfred to escape the 'tyranny' of the Lord of the Mercians in 885. This is a rather daring criticism of the closest ally and kinsman of the king of Wessex, but of course Asser was himself Welsh and had a certain affinity with his countrymen and it is possible that his book was not originally intended for a West Saxon or Mercian readership.[10] Glwysing and Gwent in Wales spanned the Severn estuary and would have been close enough to English Mercia to allow for the English to make raids and excursions into their territory. Were the beleaguered Welsh of these regions, already hard pressed by the heirs of Rhodri the Great of Gwyneth, forced to resort to submitting to an English king to prevent attacks from Æthelred of Mercia as well, effectively complaining to his father-in-law, who could bring him into line?

Naturally his marriage was one of political convenience, as most royal and aristocratic marriages tended to be. It is probably for this reason that Lord Æthelred has earned a rather unfairly negative reputation in fictional literature regarding Æthelflæd. He is usually cast as the unpleasant, unwanted and much older husband to the young and naïve West Saxon princess who falls hopelessly in love with somebody else. At best he is unloving and distant, at worst abusive, and some novelists have gone so far as to write of the spunkier and older version of Æthelflæd leaving him. This picture probably owes more to modern, Western views of romantic love (and a certain aversion to arranged marriage) than it does to reality. Women in the Anglo-Saxon age are believed to have had certain rights, including the right to own their own property and goods instead of these automatically coming under the control of their husbands when they married. The evidence for this comes from certain law codes, which distinguish between the goods of the husband and those of the wife. It has also been suggested that women had the right to choose to leave their husbands, and even to take their children with them. There was also the traditional *morgengifu* or 'morning gift'. This is defined as 'the gift made by the husband to the wife on the morning after the consummation of the marriage'. It remained the property of the wife, essentially to do with as she pleased.[11] It has been suggested that the cities of London and Oxford may have been part of a *morgengifu* from Æthelred to Alfred's daughter. It is an interesting theory, and it is known that London was ceded back to West Saxon control on the death of the former, perhaps at the behest of Lady Æthelflæd.

They were married for twenty-five years. What little evidence we do have for their relationship reveals mutual co-operation and trust, resulting mostly from political and military necessity. Æthelflæd's name appears alongside that of her husband in many charters from the mid-880s onwards. Most of this evidence comes from the early years of the tenth century until the death of Lord Æthelred in 911, especially from the last five years of the marriage. It is entirely possible that the events of the first two decades of the marriage went unrecorded simply because it was unremarkable. Æthelflæd's mother Ealswith also gets hardly any mention in the sources, barely even appearing in charters. This does not mean she was not involved in the life of her husband and family, it's just that most of her actions were not in the category of what was usually recorded (land transactions, wars, political intrigue, etc.). Her daughter is a little more visible in administrative records such as charters, perhaps because there was no prohibition on Mercian royal ladies holding the title of queen. She certainly seems to have been more active in the day-to-day business of rulership during her husband's tenure of Mercia than her mother had been. It must have been eminently useful for Æthelred, who was always cast as the faithful vassal of Alfred, to have the daughter of Alfred by his side affirming and supporting him as a capable consort.

After the death of King Alfred around 899, the lord of the Mercia's submission to Wessex seems to have come to an end. He still co-operated with Alfred's heir – his brother-in-law Edward, known to history as Edward the Elder – and sometimes even fought alongside him, but the nature of their political relationship does seem to have changed at the very end of the ninth century.

7

MOST NEEDFUL TO KNOW 886–992

In 886, a teenage West Saxon princess left the land of her birth to begin her married life in Mercia. In recent years, a tradition has developed around this event. It is said that Æthelflæd's wedding party was attacked by a group of Danes with the intention of interrupting or threatening the alliance between the two kingdoms. The story recounts how the resourceful young Æthelflæd used a ditch as a defensive structure so that she and her retainers could shore themselves up within it, and then repelled their attackers from their advantageous position.[1] Another version says that her dowry was looted and she and her attendants had to take refuge in a 'castle' or church until they were able to regroup and kill all their assailants. According to this version the whole engagement was rather less successful, as although the enemy was routed only three people survived: Æthelflæd, one of her maidservants and a bodyguard.[2] There is sadly no evidence for this fascinating story in any of the contemporary sources, so it is probably a later medieval or even a modern invention. Perhaps it was intended to illustrate the intelligence of Alfred's daughter, who learned to use the land to her advantage, and was prepared to do her utmost to protect her interests. These characteristics would certainly come to the fore in her later life.

Although only a teenager, Æthelflæd was not a scared child leaving all she knew to marry a stranger in a strange land. Lord Æthelred had been known to her father for at least four years, and had been present at the West Saxon court on a number of occasions. She would have met him there, perhaps when the family attended church or were feasting and socialising in the hall. Her position as the firstborn child of the king of Wessex, and the scion of an ancient Mercian noble dynasty, would have meant that she was raised and prepared for a certain lifestyle from birth. Rulers did not normally put firstborn children into the Church; that role was normally reserved for the younger children in larger families. Since she had come through the more perilous years of infancy when so many children died, she was expected to marry some man of wealth, power or influence. That's what older royal princesses had done since time immemorial, and there was no reason why she should have questioned or sought to go against such an ancient custom. It is always unwise to put modern attitudes into the minds of historical people, so we must not assume that Æthelflæd entered into married life full of hopes about enjoying the bliss of romantic love or, conversely, railing against the unfairness of her lot. At least her husband was of almost equal rank and status to her father, even if men did not call him king. At least, not in her father's presence. Nevertheless, she would be the co-ruler of a region comparable in size to her native Wessex with a proud and ancient history.

It is entirely possible, that, unlike in the story related above, Æthelflæd travelled to Mercia in the company of her new husband and his retainers, especially if the marriage took place sometime during or shortly before the handover of London. Lord Æthelred would hardly have wanted to offend his West Saxon overlord and new father-in-law by allowing his daughter to make such a dangerous journey through territory crawling with Danes – or risk the safety of his new wife, for that matter. She was just too valuable an asset. When she arrived there, she was fortunate enough to have established family ties to the Mercian nobility in the form of her mother's brother Æthelwulf, the ealdorman mentioned in the previous chapter. He too had been to her father's court, and she may also have met him in the years before her marriage. He held land in Gloucestershire, and did not die until 901; they moved in the same circles for fifteen years.[3]

We can be sure that Æthelflæd's new life in Mercia did not require her to sever all ties to Wessex. Her husband was one of the most important allies of her father and would have already accompanied him on campaign. In the years after their marriage, such warfare could remain a frequent occurrence. Like Alfred, the rulers of Mercia would have traversed their kingdom, residing at various estates and great buildings. They seem to have chosen to eventually settle in Gloucester, however. This was the former Roman city where Guthrum and his army had spent part of the winter of 877 before launching the famous attack on Alfred at Chippenham. It was less than 50 miles away from Wessex, an ideal distance for keeping up to speed with the news and developments at the West Saxon court, and also only a day or two's journey away from some of Alfred's favourite estates. They may have resided in the royal palace at Kingsholm, the original location of which is still not certainly known, although some clues may have been turned up by recent archaeological excavations.[4]

Over time Lord Æthelred chose to establish the city as his 'principal centre of power'. So it is quite possible that the royal couple would have chosen to stay there as often as they could. Less than two decades later they would be involved in a daring project that would establish the city as the spiritual centre in their kingdom, where they would both eventually choose to be buried.[5]

Though the Mercians were a proud people, whose kings had once been overlords of most of England, the authority and power of the kingdom had waned under the Danish onslaught. Really it had been waning since the early ninth century, but the Viking wars had only made the situation worse. Lord Æthelred has been credited with having helped to restore the fortunes of his homeland, as well as successfully holding it against the Danes.[6] In the years immediately following their marriage, he and his wife began following a similar course to Alfred in Wessex by establishing or restoring fortified settlements in strategic locations throughout their kingdom. Æthelflæd is well known for employing this strategy in the second decade of the tenth century, and that was certainly her most prolific period of fortress building, but she had started to get involved in cooperation with her husband. The first city they turned their attention to seems to have been Worcester. A charter that dates from between 889 and 899 mentions that the royal couple had 'ordered the borough at Worcester to be built for the protection of all the people, and also to exalt the praise of God therein'. It is estimated that the burh had been established around 890. Once again they had chosen a city of ancient Roman provenance. The city had boasted its own bishop for centuries. By 890 that office had been held for nearly twenty years by the erstwhile Wærferth, a man who was described in the charter as the 'friend' of rulers of Mercia.[7] A charter from the close of the 880s asked for the monks of the abbey to sing Psalms and Masses for the souls of Æthelflæd and her husband. Such was the reciprocal relationship between the Church and its founders or patrons. They established it, and it provided for the spiritual good of its founders in life and after death.

Their next foundation may have been Shrewsbury, the county capital of Shropshire. There is evidence that a settlement existed from an earlier period and that it may have once been the capital of the Welsh kingdom of Powys. It has been suggested that an Anglo-Saxon fortified burh existed there as early as 800, but it does not show up in surviving Mercian charters before 900. Stansbury suggests it was established by Æthelred and Æthelflæd before they met there with their council or witan in 901. There is also a local tradition that the church of St Alkmund was established by Æthelflæd. Alkmund or Ealhmund was a relatively obscure saint, said to have been a son of the king of Northumbria who was murdered at the behest of a rival king in the late eighth century.[8]

Yet Anglo-Saxon royals were not just supposed to be generous to the Church; they were also meant to be good lords (or ladies) to their nobles and their people. In the earliest part of the Saxon period, the seventh and eighth centuries, kings were described in terms of 'ring-givers', 'gold-givers' or 'gold friends'. In the simplest and most pragmatic terms, this meant that the king rewarded service in battle with a share of the loot, not unlike the Danes so despised by the chroniclers of a later age. By the golden age of Anglo-Saxon England, this had taken the more concrete form of gifts of land, or items that symbolised a loyal bond between lord and subject. Æthelflæd's aunt Æthelswith made a grant of fifteen hides to one Cuthwulf in a charter dated 868.

What is intriguing about this particular text is the reference to Cuthwulf in the original Latin as *fideli meo ministro*, 'my faithful minster', not just 'minster'. Clearly the queen of Mercia believed in rewarding loyal service, though not without the consent of her husband and lord.

One such reward may have been the Æthelswith ring. Æthelswith, Æthelflæd's immediate predecessor as queen of Mercia, seems to have taken her responsibility as treasure-giver quite literally, as the gold ring inscribed with her name (now an exhibit in the British Museum) appears to demonstrate. Measuring 26 mm on its inside diameter, it appears to have been too large to wear on an average finger, and may have been intended to wear over a glove, or perhaps on a necklace. It is inscribed with the queen's royal title, Æthelswith Regna, though the inscription is positioned on the inside, and not easily visible. There exist two interpretations of this piece: the first is that it may have belonged the queen herself, and the second is that it was a gift to a retainer. The latter is favoured by the author. The *Agnus Dei* design appears appropriate for a gift from a Christian queen, perhaps to an equally pious servant. We do not know of any such surviving personal gift from the Lord and Lady of the Mercians to their retainers, but the way they chose to refer to certain people in their charters suggests that they too believed in rewarding loyalty and good service.

Revival in Wessex

In Wessex, at the time of his daughter's marriage and shortly before, Alfred began one of the projects that would define his reign and his legacy. It was to be a programme of literary and cultural reform on an almost unprecedented scale. Asser related how the king 'suffered great distress inwardly and outwardly' because of his lack of learning and his knowledge of the 'divine learning and liberal arts'.[9] In the period known as the High Middle Ages, which began in the later eleventh century, the liberal arts consisted of seven distinct disciplines. There was the trivium of grammar (basically mastery of Latin), logic and rhetoric (which related to public speaking, persuasion and debate), and the quadrivium of geometry, arithmetic, music and astronomy. These were the subjects that were supposed to be taught and studied at major educational institutions such as court and cathedral schools, the forerunners of the great universities. They were supposed to be the fundamental basis of the secular education system from the ancient period and into the early modern age.

Apparently, it was an affliction that troubled the entire kingdom. To right the wrong Alfred sought out men of learning from throughout Britain and even the Continent to institute a system of educational reform (which the king hoped would result in moral reform as well) in his kingdom. This would ultimately include the translation of various classical, biblical and early medieval works, in whole or in part, and the establishment of a court school in the West Saxon court modelled on ancient Carolingian lines. Alfred's plans were indeed ambitious – he intended to make all his notable men or their sons learn their letters and familiarise themselves with works most needful to know (most of which were part of his translation programme), and he wanted to revive monasticism. Both learning and monastic devotion, we are told, had lapsed in Wessex, because of the Danish incursions as well as the laxity of the nobility and the clergy. It probably is not true that there was no educational system or that learning had completely died out as Alfred himself had learned to read in his own tongue before he was a teenager, but something does seem to have happened. The final passages of the *Life of Alfred* recount how the king went as far as to threaten his 'ealdormen and reeves and thegns' with the forfeiture of their positions if they did not enthusiastically apply themselves 'much more attentively to the pursuit of wisdom'. So passionate was the king that the project would occupy much of his energy and attention in the last decade of his life.[10]

The works Alfred and his scholarly fellows chose included Bede's *Ecclesiastical History* as well as a collection of stories about saints and martyrs. Other works that were not of English origin included *The Consolation of Philosophy* by the sixth-century Roman nobleman Anicius Manlius Severinus Boethius, *Pastoral Care* by Gregory the Great (the Pope who had originally sent Augustine on his mission to convert the English), the *Dialogues* of the other St Augustine (Augustine of Hippo, best known for his *Confessions*) and *The Histories Against the Pagans* by Paulus Orosius, another late Roman author from what is today western Spain. They also included the first fifty Psalms out of the total of 150 contained the Bible.

Although Alfred has sometimes been credited with translating and editing these works himself, he did not. He had help from various clerics drawn from across the British Isles and eventually (allegedly because not enough could be found on his home soil) from the Continent. Two of the clerics who came to the assistance of the king were Mercians. One was Wærferth, bishop of Worcester, a man who looms prominently in the contemporary sources and returned to the Mercian court when his services were no longer required in Wessex. He undoubtedly became known to Alfred's daughter there. The other was Plegmund, 'an estimable man richly endowed with learning' who was appointed Archbishop of Canterbury in 890.[11] There was also the Welshman Asser, along with two men from the Continent. One was called John and was known as the 'Old Saxon' because he originally came from the area of Germany whence the Anglo-Saxons traced their own origins, and the other was Grimbald, who was of French origin. Grimbald would go on to become the co-founder of the New Minster in Winchester, the institution that would be known to history as Hyde Abbey, where Alfred himself was initially buried. John, on the other hand, was not so well received. Alfred established him as the abbot of the abbey he founded at Athelney but disaffected clerics ended up trying to assassinate him in his own church.

What motivated Alfred's zealous, almost obsessive desire for reform? In part this was spelled out in his own writings, most notably in the preface he wrote to Gregory's *Pastoral Care*. Alfred believed that the time before the coming of the Danes had been a golden age in Britain, when wise and godly rule had bought manifold blessings. These had been, in the opinion of the king,

> happy times throughout England ... how the kings who ruled over the people were obedient to God and to his messengers, and how they both upheld peace and authority at home, and how they extended their territory abroad, and how they prospered in warfare and in wisdom.[12]

It would be easy to dismiss Alfred's attitude as rose-tinted nostalgia for the 'good old days', and perhaps he was being something of an idealist. Yet there may have been some grain of truth in what he believed. In the late eighth century, the great Frankish king and Holy Roman Emperor Charlemagne had looked across the Channel for scholars to institute a similar programme of reform in his own realm. He had found what he sought with men such as Alcuin of York, the British cleric who is often lauded as a leading figure in the Carolingian Renaissance. Sixty years later, the number and quality of manuscripts produced in England had significantly declined, and some complained that few clerics could be found who had a good command of Latin.

However, Alfred was not simply yearning for the glories of a bygone age. He saw in the past a very practical model for rulership and government. Had not heaven blessed Charlemagne, and his contemporary Offa of Mercia, not only with stability in their own kingdoms, but victory in war and expanded their authority far and wide? Offa had held sway over much of England, and his Frankish compatriot had carved out a huge empire. If the sins of Alfred's people had brought upon them the scourge of the Northmen, who had taken one kingdom after another, then a return to obedience, wisdom and diligent rule could restore the fortunes of the people becoming known as the English. It is even possible that Mercian influence may have rubbed off on Alfred, helping him formulate his idea of a unified kingdom of the Anglo-Saxons. In 890, at the height of the reform programme, the *Anglo-Saxon Chronicle* was started. Alfred wanted not only to emulate the glories of the past, but also to preserve the history of his time for future generations. In common with a lot of medieval chronicles, the *Anglo-Saxon Chronicle*'s account does not actually begin in 890 but many centuries before, at the birth of Christ. Some accounts went back even further, starting at the creation of the world. Much of the early material for the history of Britain was copied or borrowed from earlier writers, such as Gildas and Bede.

The *Chronicle* is often accused of pro-West Saxon bias, ignoring events outside the kingdom and those involved in them. It is true that the creation of the *Chronicle* was part of an exercise in image management for Alfred, who naturally wanted to make himself look good and cast himself as the heroic saviour of his people. Yet it still serves as an invaluable source for scholars of the period. Over time scribes created different manuscripts or versions of the *Chronicle* in different places, and sometimes recorded different events with their own slant. It is believed to have been in a Mercian version of the *Chronicle* that the so-called *Mercian Register* appeared, which is our main source for the activities of Æthelflæd in the tenth century.[13]

It was always a good idea for medieval kings and nobles to establish and support churches, monasteries and abbeys. The Anglo-Saxons had been doing it since the seventh century, and Alfred was no exception – nor would his daughter and son-in-law stray from this practice, as will be shown later. He established an abbey on the site of his former refuge at Athelney, and one at Shaftesbury. This made sense. Churches and religious foundations could be established anywhere, but there was particular merit in establishing them on notable sites, such as the locations of great military victories, or places that were devoted to particular saints. For instance, Æthelflæd and Æthelred established their capital at Gloucester and built a great church dedicated to St Oswald, a seventh-century king not of Mercia but of Northumbria.

Curiously, despite the fact that Church reform came to be an important feature of Alfred's reign, the king himself did not have much role in it. He left the actual business of reform, such as establishing new dioceses, to churchmen like Grimbald. Alfred's piety had a very practical turn; he was quite prepared to give to the Church when he was able, but also siphon off Church lands and revenues when he needed them for the defence of the kingdom. Clerics may have complained about lands that were promised to them being given to others, but the king would have seen the necessity of defending his lands (and by extension its Church) to the last days of his reign. His religious pragmatism is also demonstrated in his association with the cult of St Edmund, king of East Anglia, who had died when he was nineteen years old. Alfred 'pumped investment' into the town of Bury St Edmund's, which became the centre of the cult and a useful source of revenue, as well as a Christian enclave on the borders of the area known to history as the Danelaw.[14]

Despite his cultural activity, time was advancing on Alfred. He was in his late thirties when he began his programme of reform in earnest – not a great age by modern standards, but many of his family members had died in their thirties or forties. His father had made it past fifty, but that was before the Danes came to ravage Wessex. Besides, many of the old order were passing away, men who had known or crossed swords with him as a youth. Archbishop Æthelred, a man who had opposed Alfred the in the coup of 878, was dead a decade later. He had been one of the only men involved in the events of 878 to retain his position afterwards. Kings could, in theory, oppose and depose archbishops, but such actions very rarely went down well. Alfred seems to have been content to leave the prelate in place after he won back his kingdom, and perhaps the archbishop himself believed that God had demonstrated his approval of Alfred in his victories. Then, in 890, Guthrum – the man who Alfred had installed as king of East Anglia under the baptismal name of Æthelstan – passed away. For the last four years of his life, Guthrum had been the neighbour of the new rulers of Mercia. After the events of the 880s, establishing the Danelaw with Alfred, Guthrum seems to have been quite content to observe the terms of the treaty and settle down to rule in East Anglia. The same could not be said of other raiders and adventurers. Barely two years after the death of the man who had briefly occupied Wessex and driven Alfred out, another great Viking army landed.

8

THE HEATHENS RAGE 892–899

Why do the heathen rage, and the people imagine a vain thing?
The Kings of the Earth set themselves, and the rulers take counsel together, against the Lord and his anointed.

Psalm 2

Æthelflæd was twenty-two and had been the co-ruler of Mercia for about six years when the Danes returned. In truth they did not even return to Mercia, but according the *Chronicle* an army came from France and landed with 250 ships at Appledore in Kent. There was apparently some kind of fortification on the site which was 'half-made' and occupied only by 'a few peasant men'.[1] True to form, the Danes established their own camp on the site. Then another eighty ships landed at Milton in the same county under the leadership of a man who would replace Guthrum as a notorious opponent of Alfred and his allies for the next few years: Hæsten. Hæsten was a Viking adventurer who had previously raided in North Africa and Spain before trying to sack Rome, although he never actually reached the sacred city.

The two armies seem to have been targeting an area of Wessex left unprotected by the new fortifications. Alfred responded to the situation quickly, bringing an army with him. The *Anglo-Saxon Chronicle* then proceeds to give a detailed account of campaigning that spanned the next year and more. In a way, it resembled some of the earlier campaigns of Alfred's reign, except that he now made better use of his resources and his newly reformed defence system.

> Then King Alfred gathered his army and went so that he camped between the two raiding armies ... then afterwards they went through the forest [the Wealden Forest, which stretches over several counties] in gangs and mounted groups ... The King separated his army in two, so that there was always half at home and half out, except for those who held the fortresses.[2]

Alfred's intention was apparently to prevent the Danes from roaming freely around the countryside or breaking out of their fortresses. He also sent out men to 'harass Viking raiding parties' and prevent communication with then.[3] Although smaller, he seems to have considered Hæsten's force to be the more dangerous, probably because of their location between Rochester and Canterbury, and because near the camp an ancient trackway ran across the North Downs, all the way to Winchester. Curiously, after a few months Alfred resorted to the age-old method of dealing with Danish raiders: negotiation. Alfred bought Lord Æthelred with him to meet the Danish warlord. The *Anglo-Saxon Chronicle* recorded (sometime after the event) how the subsequent agreement involved the traditional exchange of hostages, including two sons of Hæsten, who were baptised with Alfred and Æthelred acting as their godparents. It also mentioned the king giving 'a great deal of money' to the Danish warlord. Money to make him disband his army? Was Alfred again resorting the tactics of the 870s, naively believing that Hæsten had peaceful intent?[4]

In any case, as ever, it did not do him much good. Hæsten's army moved on, but did not go far. They resettled at Benfleet in Essex, the neighbouring county to the north. There follows in the sources another account covering almost two years of fighting against one or both armies that landed in 892. These events were chaotic, messy and confusing and the contemporary accounts reflect this. In the words of Edoardo Albert, it is not easy for the historian to impose order on what occurred, especially as so much was often happening at once.[5]

The Appledore army broke out of the camp they had occupied for a year in the Easter of 893 and sailed up the Thames estuary to land and pillage in Essex, disappearing for a while only to re-emerge in Hampshire, Surrey and Berkshire to go 'a-Viking'. They were eventually intercepted near Farnham in Surrey by part of the Wessex fyrd under the command of the atheling Edward, the elder of Æthelflæd's two brothers. There were about two to four years between them, so he would have been eighteen at the youngest but more likely on the cusp of his twenties. His father had commanded forces at his age, and he would have been trained at arms from childhood, but he did not have the direct battlefield experience of his forbears. Nevertheless, he was about to be tested. The battle appears to have started before the atheling arrived, with most of the fighting being done by local men; then he came, 'clashing in dense array with the foemen at Farnham. There was no delay, the young men leaped against the prepared defences ... they duly exulted, being set free by the prince's arrival, like sheep bought to the pastures under the usual onslaught of predators'.[6] Edward's role is hardly mentioned in the usual sources; he gets this dramatic appraisal in Æthelweard's *Chronicle*. Needless to say, the battle was a victory for the English. With the unnamed Danish commander wounded, the 'foes' abandoned their booty and fled to Thorney Island with the English in hot pursuit. Elated by victory, Edward fell afoul of the logistics of war. He could not besiege the beleaguered Danes at Thorney forever, for his men had used up their provisions and their agreed terms of service were coming to an end. They would have simply gone home, or back to garrison duty in one of the boroughs – fortunately this did not happen, as Lord Æthelred saved the day.

In *The Warrior Chronicles*, as in many other works of fiction, Lord Æthelred gets a very bad rap. In the fifth instalment of Bernard Cornwell's series *The Burning Land*, it is the ever-resourceful Uhtred of Bebbanburg who saves the day at Farnham. In the style of a good storyteller, the hero of the tale takes all the credit and none are left to bask in the limelight. In reality, there is no record of any Uhtred. Æthelred arrived with his forces from London, and the Danes shored up at Thorney decided to negotiate with him and Edward. The agreement was a straightforward exchange of hostages with the usual admonition to leave the area, but it was far from the end.

The war continued on and off for a further two years, and in some respects resembled the campaigns earlier in his reign with Alfred and his allies. The account of what happened after Farnham is somewhat garbled. The Appledore Vikings may have retreated to East Anglia, but they next seemed to appear with

Hæsten at Benfleet, and now there was a greater challenge: a third Viking army to contend with. This was a force that comprised men from East Anglia and Northumbria, so they were not foreign adventurers as previous forces had been, but men who had settled in England, but still chose to come to the aid of their fellows. They landed at Exeter in the weeks after Easter 893. Alfred was now 'assailed in the West (by the new Viking army) and raided in the East (by Hæsten)'.[7] He chose to deal with the threat in the west, leaving the Londoners to deal with their bad neighbour in Benfleet. London, as has already been shown, had been handed over to the control of Æthelred. The Lord of the Mercians played a major role in much of the campaigning in or near Mercian territory throughout the years 892 to 896. In London, as at Farnham, he seems to have proved a capable commander, and it is entirely possible that Mercian forces under him helped to lead the Londoners in their next bold move. They launched an attack on Hæsten in his own fortress, taking the defenders by surprise, 'killing those found in the open and storming the fortification after a short, fierce fight'.[8] They were rewarded with the plunder from the Viking warlord's raiding, plus some of his boats and many of the women and children who had been left behind. Those of high status would have been kept for ransom, and the others were probably sold into slavery. The Anglo-Saxons saw nothing wrong with the practice; in fact, slaves were common long before the Vikings came.

Their main quarry, and leader of the force at Benfleet, Hæsten had escaped with most of his men, which seems to have been a remarkable talent of his. He soon reappeared, like a spectre emerging from the mists and fens. Benfleet was gone, but he established a new camp at nearby Shoebury. Then, using the boats that some of the East Anglians who had joined him brought with them (his own having been captured or destroyed), he made a remarkable 185-mile dash across England to the Welsh borders, where they built another fortified camp at Buttington (in the modern county of Powys), snugly surrounded by the Welsh hills and in the shadow of Offa's Dyke. The Danish army had made a remarkable trek through hostile territory, apparently undetected by the garrisons of the Mercian and West Saxon burhs, which testifies to the remarkable mobility and resourcefulness of the Viking forces. In the early months of 894 Hæsten's forces began raiding in Powys, and they were now perilously close to the Danish army in the West Country that Alfred was still dealing with, but again the tables turned quickly. Right when Hæsten was recouping his losses by pillaging in Wales, his fellows of the Northumbrian/East Anglian army withdrew from Devonshire and decided to return home. Pinned down by Alfred's army, it is likely they simply decided that staying was pointless and unprofitable. They sailed back to their home territory, skirting the south coast. There is a story recounted in the *Anglo-Saxon Chronicle* that they stopped along the way to raid Sussex and attempted to attack the city of Chichester, only to be repelled by the inhabitants, who killed 'many hundreds' of their number. By the autumn of that year, Alfred was back in London.[9]

But the war was not over, especially not for Lord Æthelred, who still had Hæsten's army on his doorstep. Late the previous year, Æthelred had been pursuing Hæsten from the south. Two other nobles, the erstwhile ealdormen Æthelnoth of Somerset and Æthelhelm of Wiltshire, came up from the south having also been tracking their foes for some time. Now they knew where Hæsten was based, and the combined forces made ready to strike. The ensuing siege, which was focused on the Viking camp near to the modern village of Buttington, deserves to be better known as an important example of Welsh–English military co-operation. The *Chronicle* reports how the forces of the three ealdormen combined, along with thegns from the West Country and the Welsh borders 'west of the Severn' who had been 'employed at home on the works' (presumably the construction of the burhs). Their numbers were bolstered by 'some part of the Welsh people'.[10] This 'part' may have been quite a considerable number, as the Welsh Merfynion dynasty of the time ruled much of Wales, including the kingdoms of Dyfed, Gwynedd and Powys, and had considerable resources to draw upon. Ironically, the dynasty had been an ancient enemy of the Mercians, their king Rhodri Mawr and his son having been killed in battle against them. It seems that by 893 the hatred or fear of the Danes had resulted in a pragmatic alliance between the former enemies.[11]

The size of the Anglo-Welsh army, of which Lord Æthelred seems to have been one of the main leaders, must have been considerable. Sadly no numbers are given in the sources, but it seems to have been sufficiently large to lay successful siege the Danish forces for some weeks, forcing them to such desperate straits as eating their horses because they were unable to send out any foraging parties; reportedly, some also starved to death. In desperation, Hæsten decided to break out and attempt to cross the River Severn. We do not know where the ensuing battle was fought; the *Anglo-Saxon Chronicle* only records that the Christians were victorious but suffered many losses. The only name recorded was that of a thegn called Ordheah. The Danes reportedly lost many more soldiers. Whilst this engagement was celebrated as a great victory, it was far from decisive as Hæsten and many of his troops escaped. According the sources, they made it back to their camps in East Anglia and regrouped with the remnants of the army from Devon, getting more ships. Leaving their womenfolk in East Anglia, they set out again.[12]

However, something had changed by the time the Danish forces had set out again in late 894: they were no longer led by Hæsten. He disappears from the records sometime after the return to Essex following the mauling at Buttington. It is known that before they set out again from East Anglia, sometime in late 893, Alfred had returned Hæsten's wife and children to him after they had been in his care for nearly a year. It is doubtful that Hæsten was so struck by Alfred's act of mercy that he simply withdrew; he was a seasoned warrior and leader, after all. It is more likely that he simply retired and went home because his age was catching up with him. Sources suggest that Hæsten had been raiding for nearly forty years, which would mean he was in his late forties or, more likely, his early fifties. He would have been a wealthy man, considering his activities earlier in his career in France and the Mediterranean, and probably just saw no further reason to stay in England. He left the remnants of the army, comprised of the two original armies from Appledore and Benfleet, alongside the other which had settled in England. Two years on from the new Viking army's arrival in 892, Alfred and his allies were still unable to extricate them.

What was Æthelflæd doing in these years? Her charters are few for the whole decade of the 890s; most of them are for the decade before, or the two afterwards. It was probably sometime in the last decade of the tenth century that Æthelflæd's only surviving child was born. She was a daughter named Ælfwyn. As with her mother, we are not certain of the date of Ælfwyn's birth, but it was probably early in Æthelflæd's marriage. The first charters which refer to her come from 903 onwards, at which time she must have been old enough to act as a witness, which probably meant she was at least in her teens by that date.[13] We do not know why Æthelflæd and Lord Æthelred did not have any more children. In the twelfth century, the famous chronicler and author William of Malmesbury said that the birth of Ælfwyn almost killed her mother, and that soon afterwards she took a sort of informal vow to abstain from sexual relations with her husband.[14]

William may have had access to sources lost to us today, and we should not entirely discount the testimony of medieval writers. It is possible that Æthelflæd may have had an especially difficult birth and, fearing for her life, did not want to have another child. However, there could have been other reasons. Kathleen Herbert suggested that it may have been a pragmatic political act, that Æthelflæd was using her body to prevent the conception of a male Mercian heir who could threaten the alliance between Mercia and Wessex.[15] Yet it is also possible that there was some biological or gynaecological reason. Perhaps Æthelflæd simply did not conceive again. We know that something similar happened to the mother of Henry Tudor in the fifteenth century, as she never had any more children after giving birth to him at fourteen. Another possibility is that Æthelflæd did have other pregnancies which ended in miscarriage or stillbirth. These tragic situations were all too common at the time, and tend to go unrecorded.

We do know of another important child who was born in the middle of the 890s, most likely 895; a child who would become the son that Æthelflæd never had, and ultimately the first officially recognized king of all the English. This was Æthelstan, the son of Edward. His mother's name is unknown, and it is widely believed that he was illegitimate (although it is possible there may have been an informal marriage between his mother and Edward). Perhaps his father and mother met when he was home from the wars, or even on campaign. Edward was well into his teens or early twenties, quite the normal age for a young man to have been fathering children at the time. When Æthelstan reached the appropriate age, he was sent to Mercia for his education, and was later raised by his aunt and uncle in the Mercian court. He will emerge again later.

In short, we do not know much of what Æthelflæd was doing in the four years of campaigning between 892 and 896, or much of the decade. The problem is that it is actions like grants and exchange of land which tend to leave behind physical traces in the form charters. Is it possible that Alfred's daughter might have accompanied her husband on campaign? Certainly it's possible that she did when the Danish army were in Mercia, or dangerously close to Mercia. She had been married for the sake of the alliance with Mercia, and would not have wanted to let her people or her family down. Perhaps her mere presence would have been enough to encourage those in the armies of Wessex and Mercia with a show of solidarity, especially at the campaign near Buttington where her father was not present.

Of course, she could have done her duty just as well by staying at home to run the household or oversee the court. Most noblewomen played similar roles throughout the Middle Ages, and it was in no way considered demeaning or belittling. Contrary to media depictions, medieval noblewomen were not supposed to be wallflowers, or just breeding mares. Managing households was not just about ordering servants around; noblewomen would have to have some knowledge of financial and economic affairs, and some grasp of the law might have helped to be able to resolve disputes between tenants. Asser referred to Alfred in his later years doing something similar:

> King Alfred used to sit at judicial hearings for the benefit both of his nobles and the common people, since they frequently disagreed violently among themselves at assemblies of ealdormen or reeves, to the point where virtually none of them could agree that any judgement reached by the ealdormen or reeves in question was just. Under pressure of intransigent and obdurate disagreement, the separate parties would undertake to submit to the king's judgement, a procedure which both parties hastened to implement.

Sometimes, Asser said, these judgements would be questioned and the king would take the trouble to examine not only the matter but the soundness of the judgement as well as those who made it. Of course, Asser wanted to idealise his patron, and present him as a paragon of justice and virtue, but undoubtedly there was some truth in what he says. The Anglo-Saxons had reeves, who were local officials in charge of matters pertaining to order (some were shire-reeves, which is the origin of the term sheriff), but the ultimate source of law, justice, and order was supposed to be the king. We know that Alfred took a very active interest in the law; in fact he invented his own legal codes, becoming very interested in their implementation. Throughout the centuries kings were expected to provide justice for the good of their subjects, and female rulers were expected to adopt a similar role when it was required. In the later Middle Ages, queens were expected to act as mediators, interceding with their husbands on behalf of others. There are a few cautionary tales of royal women in the early

Middle Ages. We have already heard of the wicked Eadburh, the daughter of Offa whose murderous jealously supposedly cleared the way for Alfred's grandfather to claim the throne of Wessex. There was another such wicked woman in literature, one Queen Tryrth, who appeared in the famous epic poem *Beowulf*. She was described as 'proud and perverse, pernicious to her people. No hero but her husband, however bold, dared by day so much as turn his head in her direction – this was far too dangerous.' Dangerous because such a man was likely to end up dead. The reason for her being branded as perverse and pernicious was explained in no uncertain terms a few lines later: 'It is not right for a queen … to behave like this, for a peace-weaver to deprive a dear man of his life because she fancies she has been insulted.'

In short, a woman had to be smart and resourceful to be able to rule successfully. Another useful attribute would have been the ability to work with others, and to take advice from councillors, advisers or peers. Donald Stansbury has speculated that, for these reasons, Æthelflæd might not have succeeded by having an extremely forceful or domineering personality. It truth, it was never advisable for medieval noblewomen to display too much strength. If they did, they ran the risk of being judged and condemned by their male compatriots as unnatural or unfeminine and stepping far outside the acceptable mores of the time.[16] Eadburh and Thryth were condemned because they had failed quite spectacularly in their role of peace-weaver. Murdering rivals was obviously a shocking action, but perhaps it was meant to be so, conceived as the very worst extreme to which a queen might go to protect her interests and assuage her pride. Another explanation is that, despite being 'up to her neck' in politics, Æthelflæd did not do the things which these women had, namely 'behaving like a tyrant' to borrow from Asser's account. The 'bad' women were those who wore the proverbial trousers in their relationship, manipulating spouses who did not keep them in check and eliminating anyone who got in their way. The ideal was perhaps a sort of happy medium of mutual co-operation in which women could rule their household, reward their followers, patronise the Church, work alongside their husbands for the good of their kingdom and, just as in poetry, bring honour and glory to their people. The reality was often different, but in some ways Æthelflæd was fortunate that the kingdoms of her birth and her marriage were united against a common enemy and faced no serious threats from within.

Back the Barricades

As always, the armies of Mercia and Wessex were not able to rest easy for long after the departure of Hæsten in mid-994. Even with the grizzled warlord gone, there was still a sizeable army abroad in East Anglia, licking their wounds from the mauling in Wales but still largely intact. Late in that same year, they established a new fortification twenty miles north of London on the River Lea, probably near to Hertford. The fort was well situated, in wetland fed by three rivers, and the Danes could easily guide their boats into Mercian territory or London for raids. By the summer of 995 the men of London had attacked the fortress, but they were beaten back with heavy losses. It was time for the king to act. After a year or more of not directly taking part in the action, King Alfred and his army marched on London. Afraid that the Vikings would try to steal the harvest supplies coming into the city, Alfred sought to find a place where he could block their ships. He moved his camp to a suitable place, and ordered his men to start constructing earthen ramparts on each bank of the river. He was building a 'double burh', an interesting practice that Alfred seems to have borrowed from the Continent.[17]

The Danes also seem to have been familiar with the tactic, perhaps from the experiences of some of Hæsten's former soldiers in western Francia, and guessed what Alfred intended. Rather than stay and be penned in or risk open battle against a superior force, they once again broke out, abandoning their ships and marching across the country. They sent the women and children home to East Anglia again, and travelled to the ever-popular Mercia, near the Welsh borders, settling at Bridgnorth in Shropshire. Once again the English fyrd were in hot pursuit, the people in London having seized the ships left behind. However, despite driving them away Alfred still had not fully vanquished his enemies. Unlike in the 870s, there had been no decisive pitched battles. They had escaped his grasp again, and re-established themselves elsewhere. It must have seemed that another chase and siege were imminent. This time, though, the political situation was what turned against the Danes. The previous year, Alfred's trusted friend and ally ealdorman Æthelnoth had made approaches to the Danish king of York, Gunfrith. Gunfrith seems to have responded well to their overtures for peace. Quite simply, the Danes at Bridgnorth could not expect much help from their fellows in Northumbria, and they were holed up in hostile Mercia, ruled by the son-in-law of Alfred. After three years, they did not have much plunder to show for their efforts. In the middle of 996, the army simply disbanded and left. The *Anglo-Saxon Chronicle* reports that many went back to Northumbria, and others managed to procure boats and went across the channel to France.[18]

Finally, four years after they had come, the last Great Heathen Army of Alfred's reign left his kingdom. The chroniclers were keen to emphasise the role of Alfred's military reforms in the victory but also credited the forces of nature, mentioning a famine and a possible cattle plague that stopped them from 'greatly afflicting' the English as they had done before. This same alleged plague had killed several English nobles and thegns. Alfred had not actually played a major role in the last major campaign of his reign – the action that had most involved him was the effort against the Danes in the West Country in 893–4. In truth, his son Edward and the ealdorman Æthelred and other nobles had done more through their forces. Alfred was on old man, at least by the standards of the time. He was in his forties, and seems to have suffered from ill health in the last years of reign. He was probably delegating as much responsibility to the younger generation as was necessary. Of course, his reforms did help. Whereas in his younger days Viking armies had could manoeuvre and operate freely all over Wessex and Mercia, by the last decade of the tenth century the new burhs meant that they could not so freely attack and capture towns and cities in the protected areas, and seem to have restricted most of their raiding to the countryside. Also, Alfred's more mobile forces were capable of setting out to pursue and intercept their enemies more often from their bases in the burhs. Alfred's reforms had worked to blunt the teeth of the Danes, even if they could not stop them coming altogether.[19]

Only one more engagement, which took place in 896, was at sea. Once again the main source for this event is the *Anglo-Saxon Chronicle*, which reported that several ships, from the same areas of the Danelaw as before, 'greatly harassed ... by piracies' the coasts of Wessex. Alfred's boats were reported to have been larger than those of the Vikings, with sixty oars or more, and were supposed to be higher so that the attackers could shoot arrows down at their opponents. This time the response of the king was to make use of some of his newly built ships. It was innovations like these that resulted in writers of the modern age hailing Alfred as the father of the English navy. This was probably not entirely correct; Alfred's navy was nothing like the permanent, dedicated maritime force of our own time, and he was not the first ruler to build ships. It was a useful idea, but with one major drawback that was soon to become apparent.[20]

Alfred's ships had their first outing in 896, when they were sent to intercept six Viking boats that were raiding the area around the Isle of Wight and Devon. They caught up with them at an estuary of unknown location, and decided to use it to block their exit to get back into the open waters of the sea. Several of the ships ended up stuck at low tide, and vicious hand-to-hand fighting ensued. The Viking ships, being smaller and lighter, were able to float first when the tide came in, and what was left of their crew could row them past 'the still stranded English ships' and away.[21] There was a minor victory for the English; though they had lost men the Vikings had also suffered badly, and two of the six Viking ships that had come for the raiding did not have sufficient crew left to get home. In the end these ships were taken, and their surviving crew bought before King Alfred. On this occasion, he decided to have them promptly hanged. He was no longer in a magnanimous mood when it came to obdurate pirates. Besides, in Alfred's view, these men were worse than pirates: they had broken their oaths to leave the kingdom and desist from raiding in it. If there was one kind of person Alfred despised, it was an oathbreaker.[22]

Death of Kings

Finally, peace had come. There is no record of any more armies setting foot on West Saxon soil for the remainder of the king's life. The *Anglo-Saxon Chronicle* is quiet on the closing years of the tenth century and on Alfred's activities during these years, most likely because he did not do a lot that was worthy of note. Many authors assume that he would have indulged in his lifelong passion for hunting, a pursuit that both men and women enjoyed. Illustrations from the 1200s onwards depict women hawking, and even stalking animals armed with bows and arrows. They are usually depicted alongside other women, so they may not have gone out in mixed groups with men – or at least not men they were not related or married to – but hunt they did.[23] Alfred might well have passed on his love for the pastime to his sons and daughters, at least those who did not do into the Church. The king also continued with his translation projects, focusing on the Psalms. It was also in his later years that he is credited with developing his famous candle clocks. These were sets of six 12-inch-long candles, marked with a notch at every inch to keep the hours of the day. When these kept going out, because of 'violence of the wind', they were fashioned into a type of lantern constructed of wood and horn. Apparently Alfred had certain relics that he liked to keep with him at all times, and it was for these that he commissioned the candle clocks, probably one for reach reliquary or altar.[24]

It is possible that Alfred's delegation of responsibilities in his later years caused him to appoint his son Edward as a sub-king of part of his territory, possibly Kent. His father had done the same thing, as did others in other countries. It was a good way to confirm that Alfred favoured his son for the kingship. He had proved his mettle on the battlefield in the campaigning against Hæsten and his army. However, Edward was not the undisputed heir. Alfred's brother's sons were grown men, approaching their thirties by that time. They had been passed over in favour of their uncle when they were children because he had seemed like the best person for the job, and he had eventually proved himself at Edington.

Alfred's will, possibly drawn up in the late 880s, was mostly concerned with the disposal of his lands and property. In the king's version of events detailed in the document, he had asked his brother Æthelred on his ascension to the throne to divide their landed inheritance and give him his share (possibly in a similar arrangement to that their father had made, bequeathing certain regions to his sons). Unable to do this, King Æthelred is supposed to have said that he would happily allow Alfred to inherit all the land they held jointly, and anything else they would acquire at his death. Later, the two brothers agreed 'in the witness of all the councillors of the West Saxons that whichever of us lived longer should succeed to both the lands and the treasures and to all the other's possessions except the part which each of us had bequeathed to his children'. After Æthelred's death, it is mentioned that there was some dispute over property. This does not seem to have involved the crown, but rather the property that had been held jointly by Alfred and his brother. Conveniently, the king was able to produce his brother's will to justify his claim in this case. These nephews had not forgotten their claim to the throne, or to their inheritance, and may have felt themselves hard done by with the terms of the will. Yet for the time being, they could only wait to see how things could pan out. They may not have known the exact terms of the will. Either way, they did not have long to wait.[25]

There was one other event of remark in Alfred's closing years, one which, on the face of it, does not appear very important. In about 898, a meeting or conference was convened in London to make decisions about the layout of a street grid 'that would stretch from Thames Street to Cheapside'. The aging King Alfred attended, of course, but so did a number of other important delegates including Wærferth, bishop of Worcester; Plegmund, archbishop of Canterbury; Edward, Alfred's son; and Æthelflæd and her husband. It was at this gathering that Æthelflæd may well have learned the rudiments of town planning (notwithstanding what she had gleaned from her father when he was establishing the burhs of Wessex the previous decade), which she would put to use in her later career in Mercia. It has been suggested that the design of the city was also based on Roman models, and this conscious mimicking of all things Roman was a very deliberate part of Alfred's policy for the restoration of his kingdom. As with much that Alfred did, this also rubbed off on his children, and especially his eldest daughter. This will be explored in more detail in chapter eleven. We can see that in the years after her marriage Æthelflæd would have had cause not just to maintain contact with Wessex but probably also to visit his court with her husband or other dignitaries from Wessex.

On 26 October 899, King Alfred died at the age of fifty or fifty-one. He had ruled Wessex for twenty-seven years. The *Anglo-Saxon Chronicle* records only the date, the duration of his reign and that 'he was king over all the English nation, except that part which was under the power of the Danes'. We cannot know with certainty when his daughter last saw him alive; it may well have been during the campaigns of the 890s, or during the period of peace afterwards. We know that her husband had a lot to do with Alfred throughout the last two decades of his reign, and they were close allies so they may well have continued to visit one another. The news of Alfred's death would have reached Æthelflæd quickly. It was probably not unexpected considering that fifty was a ripe old age by the standards of the time, but this does not mean Æthelflæd did not grieve. By 899 she would have been twenty-nine. She had been two years old (or even less) at the time of his ascension and would not have remembered a time when he was not the king, except for that fateful six months in the wilds of Somerset. Her life, and the lives of those she loved the most, had been shaped by the war with the Danes, and in the last decade and a half Alfred had brought it to an end. He had also helped to establish a sacred and mystical concept of kingship 'as a task he had been given by God and as a King he felt he was accountable to God'. In truth, Alfred had been something of a micro-manager, insisting on getting involved in disputes and resolving them, managing administration and finance and 'fixing' the problems of his state.[26]

His will may have been read out soon after his death. It was not unusual, dividing lands and possessions between family members. He left one estate to Æthelflæd, corresponding to the village of Wellow in modern Hampshire. We don't know why he left it to her, but she may have requested it. Perhaps the village held some special attraction or sentimental value for her. The only problem was that Alfred also left the same estate – or an estate of the same name – to his youngest daughter, Ælfthryth. Perhaps he intended for them to share the land. To Æthelred he bequeathed a sword worth 100 mancuses. A mancus was originally a gold coin from the Byzantine Empire, but it could also be a unit of measurement in silver coins. Either way, a mancus was a lot of money, and a sword worth 100 mancuses would have been a valuable and special gift. It may have been ornately decorated with gold and jewels, reminiscent of some of the stunningly beautiful and elaborate weapon fittings uncovered with the Staffordshire Hoard.

Naturally, Alfred's eldest son and heir, Edward, received most in his will. In the event, the witan also elected him as Alfred's successor on the throne of Wessex. While the chroniclers had tried to present Alfred as the model of Christian kingship, the way that his nephews had basically been cut out of the succession, the questions over what happened with Ceolwulf many years before and certain arrangements with Guthrum all reveal a darker side to Alfred. He could be ruthlessly pragmatic, sometimes even sly and deceitful when it served his ends. He probably thought he had to be ruthless in order to survive. Did he use his guile (or other, more obvious means) to influence the West Saxon council to choose his son for the throne? It is possible, and in any case it seemed to have been a successful transition. Yet in the years following Alfred's death, Edward and his siblings would face the greatest of challenges from an adversary uncomfortably close to home.

9

THE KING OF THE PAGANS
OCTOBER 899–902

In the first chapter, the sons of Alfred's brother Æthelred were mentioned. Their names were Æthelhelm and Æthelwold, and they had been no more than small children when their father died. By the time of Alfred's death they would have been approaching their thirties, and at least one of them felt hard done by regarding the terms of Alfred's will. Within weeks of Alfred's death, Æthelwold rebelled. His intention was almost certainly to claim the throne of Wessex. He may have been harbouring resentment for years, and now he and his brother had been sidelined not only by his uncle's will but by the witan's choice of his cousin as king. Alfred's will was in some ways one of the most controversial aspects of his reign. In it, he bequeathed a total of eleven estates to his nephews: eight to the older Æthelhelm, and three to young Æthelwold. Was he deliberately denying his nephews the endowments that they might have needed to establish themselves as serious contenders to the throne? Did he ensure that they did not have the support of the nobility?[1]

Either way, the *Anglo-Saxon Chronicle* reports the rebellion thus:

> Then Æthelwold … rode and seized the manor at Wimborne and at Tywnham against the will of the king and his counsellors. Then the king [Edward] rode with an army until he camped at Badbury near Wimborne, and Æthelwold stayed inside that manor with the men who had given him their allegiance, and had barricaded all the gates against him, and they said they would either live or die there.[2]

Justin Pollard suggests that this may not have been a simple act of rebellion, but a demand from the atheling Æthelwold for the witan to accept him as king. He had seized an ancestrally significant region where his own father had been buried, rejecting the lands in Sussex and Surrey which his uncle had given to him. It also appears he had found a woman he favoured as his wife – according to the sources she was a nun whom he had 'abducted', though it is possible she was a royal woman who had left a nunnery willingly or had just been sent there for an education and had not taken any vows. Whatever his intention may have been, this coup attempt failed. The next sentence reports that the atheling escaped the siege by night. He ended up in Northumbria, where in a remarkable turn of events a 'raiding army' accepted him as their king. Æthelwold's coup in Wessex may have failed for a time, but now he had his kingdom – just not the kingdom anyone would have expected. At large in Northumbria, and with an army of his own, the son of King Æthelred would be a thorn in the flesh of the new king of Wessex. Edward's newest and greatest enemy was not a pagan Dane, but his own cousin.

Æthelwold's career after the flight from Wessex is worthy of remark. He came to be styled as 'King of the Pagans' and he ruled in Northumbria for up to three years. He is even known to have minted his own coins. Why were the pagan Vikings of York prepared to accept on ostensibly Christian Saxon, a relative of the despised Alfred, as their ruler? First, not all of them were necessarily pagans. There may have been a significant Christian population in York and Northumbria. It is certainly known that there was still an archbishop of York operating in his ancient seat in the city, and the pagan Danes do not seem to have caused him any trouble. Perhaps the chance to have a Christian on the throne of Northumbria for the first time in nearly a century was simply too good an opportunity for the Christians of the region to ignore.[3]

Of course, having a West Saxon atheling with a grievance was politically useful to those who wanted to undermine Alfred's dynasty and their ambitions. Alfred had taken to referring to himself as king of all the Saxons before his death, and he had determinedly established his lordship over Mercia. He had made Guthrum his godson, and established him as the king of East Anglia. It is possible that even at this stage the Vikings of the north feared that Alfred's descendants might try to establish hegemony over the rest of what had formerly been the Anglo-Saxon lands. It may have simply been a case of political pragmatism trumping the bonds of nationality, family and religion.[4] It has even been suggested that Æthelwold denounced Christianity to be accepted in Northumbria, but this does not appear very likely. The chroniclers were already critical enough of Æthelwold, so it's hardly likely they would have pulled any punches for an apostate who had abandoned the God of his fathers. Æthelwold's rebellion emphasised the disunity at the heart of the West Saxon regime, but at the turn of the tenth century it may have appeared to Alfred's children that the threat had been negated for a time. In the summer of 900, only months after Æthelwold's rebellion, Edward was crowned.

We do not know how Æthelflæd felt about her cousin's rebellion and setting himself up as the king of Northumbria. Some novelists have chosen to depict them as close friends and even unofficial allies, with Æthelflæd sympathising with Æthelwold if not quietly condoning his actions. It does seem doubtful that she would have dared to openly align herself with a man who had aligned himself as the enemy of her brother.

Back in Wessex, two significant events took place, one of which would be a determining factor in the future of both Wessex and Mercia. The first concerned Æthelstan, the firstborn child of Edward, who had been born around 895. There was a story that, shortly before his death, Alfred had singled out this grandson for a special privilege: he had girded him with a sword belt, thus demonstrating that he favoured the boy for future kingship and high office. It was a sign that the king of Wessex not only favoured his son as his successor, but his son's dynasty and heirs. By the time of Edward's coronation Æthelstan would have been at least five years old, and when the time came for him to be sent for fosterage his father decided to send him to the Mercian court to be raised by Æthelflæd and her husband. If he was sent there at the usual age of about seven, this would probably have taken place sometime around 902.

The same year, Æthelstan's grandmother Ealswith died. It has been said that after her husband's death she had retired to a nunnery. This was not an unusual course of action for a widowed consort, especially if she was beyond childbearing age and no longer sought after as a bride. Although she is hardly visible in the records, it is intriguing that in his will Alfred left to his wife estates that were located at or near the sites of his greatest victories – Edington and Ashdown – and at his birthplace, Wantage. It is also quite possible that in her last years she became involved in the establishment of the convent of St Mary in Winchester, which later became known as the Nunnaminster; although the building was not completed until around 908, it is credited as her foundation.[5] While she may have spent her last three years at the nunnery, or somewhere nearby, she chose to be buried next to her husband in the newly consecrated New Minster located nearby in the city of Winchester. Over twenty years later, their son would also be buried there. The bones were moved several times in the subsequent centuries, first of all to Hyde Abbey. After the Dissolution of the Monasteries and rebuilding in the modern age, the site of Alfred and his family's remains are lost to us today.

What would the woman described in a later source as the 'Great and dear Lady of the English' have made of the events of the first years of the tenth century? In the last years of her husband's life, peace had once again been secured. She had seen two of her daughters well married, one to the Lord of the Mercians and the other, young Ælfthryth, to the Count of Flanders around 893. She had also lived to see at least two of her grandchildren, Æthelflæd's daughter Ælfwyn and Edward's son Æthelstan, and possibly a daughter of Edward's also. Ælfthryth had children but went to live with her husband on the Continent, and although her parents may have heard of their births they probably did not see her children in person very often. Her middle daughter became a nun at her father's foundation at Shaftesbury, and her second son Æthelweard also went into the Church. Far gone were the days when she had married the second son of the king of Wessex and all had almost been lost to the armies of Guthrum. Yet by the opening years of the tenth century, there was cause for concern again through the nephew whom she had known and who had been raised at her husband's court alongside her own children.

In 902 Æthelwold made his presence felt in Wessex, letting his cousins know that he had not forgotten his claim to the throne. He landed with a Viking fleet in Essex, then part of the kingdom of Wessex. Surprisingly, we are told that the people of the region very quickly submitted to Æthelwold. But was this so surprising? Essex had been part of the 'expanded Wessex from the early ninth century' but it had been lost during the treaty between Alfred and Guthrum. Hæsten had been able to establish his main base there at Benfleet.[6] We know that the Danes of Northumbria had already accepted Æthelwold as their king, so the submission of Essex may have been largely due to its Danish population. What happened next seems to bear this out. Æthelwold went into East Anglia to 'draw the communities of East Anglia into his plans'. The *Anglo-Saxon Chronicle* puts it across more strongly, saying that he persuaded or even 'seduced' them to break their peace treaties with Mercia and Wessex. In the records, his actions are depicted as little more than an annoyance and inconvenience, but in fact Æthelwold may have been the most powerful man in England for a short time, able to draw support from almost every kingdom and posing a major threat to the status quo established by his uncle and inherited by his cousins. He may indeed be one of the forgotten kings of this period.

With his army from Essex and East Anglia, the West Saxon prince spent much of the autumn of 902 passing through Mercia and Wessex, eventually reaching Cricklade in Berkshire 'where they seized all that they could grab' before turning back to East Anglia.[7] Clearly this was not an army intended for full-scale conquest, at least not yet. For the most part they seem to have simply ravaged royal estates, an action designed to deny their enemies revenues and support. It was also a good way of undermining the trust that the general populace had in their rightful lords, making the rulers appear unable to protect their people.

The events of 902 are an interesting and revealing example of Anglo-Danish collaboration, showing that, contrary to what certain chroniclers and sources suggest, the two groups were not always irreconcilable. When there was some practical reason, or when it served the purposes of both, they were happy to fight together. Such is human nature; examples of this kind of cross-cultural collaboration can be found amongst supposedly implacable enemies throughout history. Æthelwold could offer the Danes of East Anglia and the surrounding regions centralised leadership and 'dramatic opportunities' for plunder.[8] It is also possible that they considered joining with him as an opportunity to strike back at the Mercians and West Saxons, against whom they may have still held a grudge after the events of the previous decades. Æthelwold may have been avoiding a pitched battle with the rulers of the two kingdoms (perhaps he did yet consider his position strong enough), but his activities that year did give him the opportunity to wreak havoc in the lands of his foes and undermine the authority of the king of Wessex. Had Æthelwold been intending to take over the kingdom it is more likely that he would have gone after Edward himself.

The king of Wessex responded to this invasion by raising his own forces and to giving chase to his cousin as his forces headed back to where they had come from – a rather tardy response considering that they had already been active for some time, but the specific circumstances are not reported. Perhaps the attack came as such a surprise to Edward that he did not have the time to prepare. When he did give chase in late 902 the king of Wessex showed that he was not averse to using the same tactics as his adversaries. It is reported that he 'raided all their lands between the dykes and the [Ouse], all as far North as the Fens' (presumably the fenlands around modern-day Norfolk or the region of Ely in Cambridgeshire).[9] It is argued that Edward did not distinguish between English and Anglo-Danish in his harrying of these regions. They had submitted to Æthelwold, and so as far as he was concerned they deserved everything they got. Edward and Æthelwold's armies finally met in an engagement in Cambridgeshire in December 902 that was arguably as decisive as Alfred's victories. For the account, we must once again turn to the *Anglo-Saxon Chronicle*:

> Then when they wanted to go back out from there [Cambridgeshire], he [King Edward] ordered it to be announced to all his army that they should go out together, then the Kentish remained there against his command, and he had sent seven messengers to them. Then they were surrounded there by the raiding army and they fought there. And there they killed ealdorman Sigewulf and ealdorman Sigehelm and Eadwold the King's

> thegn, and Abbot Cenwulf and Sigebert son of Sigewulf ... .and many others.[10]

The other side seems to have lost less prominent men, but those who did die were of the utmost importance. They included a king called Eohric, probably a Danish king of East Anglia, and a mysterious figure named Beorhsige who was reported to have been the son of an atheling. Last of all, the combat saw the end of Æthelwold himself. In a strange twist of fate, the battle actually seems to have been a victory for the Danes, who soundly defeated the men of Kent, but the death of Æthelwold removed Edward's greatest rival.

The legacy of the Battle of the Holme, as it has come to be known, has been much discussed by historians. It has been suggested that, in becoming king of Northumbria and securing the submission of Essex, it was in fact Æthelwold who was the first relative of Alfred to come closest to uniting England. 'Had Æthelwold won the battle ... England could, we may fairly guess, have been united in a different matter, involving much less warfare than ultimately proved to be the case.'

There is one other intriguing counter-factual possibility that emerges from the deaths at the Battle of Holme. The Beorhsige mentioned above is said to have been the son of an atheling named Beornoth. Who was this atheling? He appears to have been of Anglo-Saxon origin, judging from the name and the title. Dorothy Whitelock, the great twentieth-century historian and scholar, suggested that these men were members of the Mercian 'B' dynasty (so called because its members all had names beginning with B), of whom King Alfred's brother-in-law Burgred had been the last king. Were these men claimants to the throne of

Mercia from an ancient dynasty that had been pushed aside by Æthelred when he took power? Had they not died, could they have been known to history for having gone all the way and claimed the kingdom in the place of the ageing Lord Æthelred and his wife?[11]

Æthelwold had died, and with him a possible claim to the throne of Mercia. The battle in which they died had occurred on Danish territory that bordered English Mercia, and yet no Mercian troops are known to have taken part in the battle, which in some ways seems unusual. Were the Mercian royal couple happy to allow Edward to deal with Æthelwold by himself? Or could there have been help from Mercia that went unrecorded? The presence of Beorhsige could well have come to their notice. Quite possibly, they would have been relieved at the outcome of the battle, and the non-attendance of their armies may not have been due to indifference or tacit support of Æthelwold. It seems to have been in 902 that Lord Æthelred of Mercia first showed signs of an unidentified illness that would leave him debilitated for long periods, and his wife Æthelflæd in charge. Her apprenticeship for power could not have started any more dramatically, with a war between her brother and cousin and the settlement of a group of Danes in part of her kingdom (the Wirral peninsula near Chester). The significance of this settlement only became apparent a few years later, but they seem to have been led by a man named Ingimund, who originally hailed from the Viking settlements in Ireland around Dublin.

The account of the events on the westernmost border of Mercia in 902 comes from Irish annals instead of Saxon sources, but they are important because they provide the first recorded account of Æthelflæd acting in an independent capacity, at the age of thirty-two, nine years before she became the officially recognised ruler of Mercia. Ingimund and some of his fellows had been driven out of Ireland the year before and had travelled to Wales, but they had found a hostile reception there and so sailed further along the coast towards Chester. The sources imply that the rulers of Mercia were already there, and so they may well have been suspicious of the Viking leader who had entered their territory. They had good reason to be nervous. The strategic value of the Wirral peninsula cannot have been lost on the Mercians or the Vikings. It was an estuary where the rivers Dee and Mersey met, and provided a safe harbour for ships, and easy access along the rivers to Northumbria and into Mercia, with all the opportunities for plunder that this afforded. Rather than tolerating a potentially dangerous Viking army on their doorstep, Æthelred and Æthelflæd opted for direct action and diplomacy. In the event, Ingimund was willing to accommodate diplomatic negotiations; in fact, the sources suggest he may have initiated them. We are told that he went to Æthelflæd – and she is specifically named as queen – when her husband was incapacitated and 'asked her for land where he could settle and build stalls and houses because he was weary of war'.[12]

Like her father before her, Æthelflæd chose the diplomatic option instead of engaging in a battle she might not win when approached by a Viking leader who seemed to be amiable. He did not want to fight, he said; he just wanted to settle. If the sources can be believed, Æthelflæd had done something which her Welsh neighbours had been unwilling or unable to do – she had been prepared to talk with a potentially dangerous enemy, and she had come to a peaceful settlement with him.

Were these the actions of an intelligent and accommodating leader in embryo, or a somewhat foolhardy and naive optimist? Perhaps they display a combination of both, but there is little evidence that Æthelflæd was weak, reckless or out of touch with the realities of her age. As a woman, according to the ancient customs of her people, she was supposed to act as a peace-weaver and try to avert hostilities between warring parties. As a leader, she was about to take centre stage.

10

SCOURGE OF THE HEATHENS 902–911

She greeted the chief of Geats, and being of wise understanding,
Gave thanks to God because her desire – That she might put her
trust in some noble warrior for help against violent outrages –
was realized.

Beowulf

We know nothing of the nature of Lord Æthelred's illness, but if the sources are to be believed it took a similar form to that which afflicted Æthelflæd's father, with intermittent bouts of debilitating poor health. In healthy spells he may well have enjoyed a normal life, able to fulfil all of his duties as ruler of Mercia. When Æthelflæd had her first rapprochement with Ingimund as detailed above her husband may well have been in his early forties. By the standards of the time he was approaching his twilight years, but despite his period of illness he was still a formidable warrior. The first decade of the tenth century was also the time when he and his wife seem to have been most active politically and economically. Many of their charters date from this time, dealing with grants of land. However, the Mercian royal couple were also performing the roles expected of them as Christian rulers. This included granting land to churches, including their favoured foundation of St Peter's in Worcester (mentioned in the previous chapters) and another foundation at Much Wenlock in Shropshire. The latter foundation may be interesting, as the small town is not far from Shrewsbury, which some have argued was established in the earliest part of the tenth century by Æthelflæd and her husband. A charter of 901 records a grant of land to this mysterious church, and intriguingly a gift of a chalice worth thirty mancuses in honour of one St Mildburg.[1] The chalice was most likely intended for religious services such as the Mass. Perhaps the royal couple had visited the church, or chosen it for its strategic location near to their new town. The dedication is also interesting. Mildburg was an eighth-century Mercian abbess, later canonised. She was also said to have been the daughter of a Mercian sub-king who, according to one story, had run away from the prince who wanted to marry her and subsequently entered a Benedictine Abbey in or near Wenlock. Her tomb, located in the original and unidentified abbey in which she had chosen to serve, became a cult centre. The website devoted to the abbey built there later by the Normans claims that this original abbey was destroyed by the Danes, but the saint and her cult seem to have been known to the rulers of Mercia, and their patronisation of an ecclesiastical foundation in or near Much Wenlock in 901 suggests that they were once again choosing to honour local saints at or near a site where they had established a fortified settlement. It appears the rulers of Mercia were hedging their bets, and trying to ensure that they had divine support for their foundations and their actions.[2]

While his sister and brother-in-law were making their bequests of land and their expensive gifts to retainers and clerics, the king of Wessex was not necessarily having so much luck. This is not to say that Edward was impious, but even after his foremost rival Æthelwold had died in battle Edward still had to deal with the army that he had raised. He did so in the way that many of his forbears had done before him: he paid them off. The *Anglo-Saxon Chronicle* merely records that the king 'concluded a peace' with his enemies, but there is evidence of some financial exaction. It cannot have been anything less than embarrassing to the son of the man who had beaten the Danes back twice without having to pay them, ensuring the continued independence of his kingdom.[3]

The embarrassment was only temporary for a young king in his first few years on the throne. The remainder of his rule would prove altogether more successful, but he did not succeed alone. As Æthelred of Mercia had been an erstwhile ally of his father, so Edward also had an important ally in his sister, Æthelflæd. Perhaps surprisingly, he did not follow the example of his ancestors by forging a marriage alliance with Mercia. There was only one marriageable female on his sister's side of the family, and that was her daughter Ælfwyn, who may have been in her early teens by the early years of the tenth century. Edward had sons, the oldest of whom was Æthelstan. After his marriage (or his relationship) with the boy's mother ended, he married twice more. His second wife was Ælfflæd, the daughter of none other than his cousin and Æthelwold's older brother, Æthelhelm. She bore him two known sons, and no fewer than six daughters. As the eldest of Edward's offspring was probably no more than seven, a marriage to Ælfwyn was out of the question for the time being; instead, Edward sent his son to his aunt and uncle in Mercia for fosterage. Young Æthelstan may have spent much of his early life in the kingdom being educated, possibly at Worcester under the tutelage of the Bishop Wærferth and his fellows. Æthelred and Æthelflæd may have established a court school there like the ones established in Wessex on the ancient Carolingian model, which focused on a similar curriculum and subjects. Although Æthelflæd may have missed out on the full impact of her father's educational reforms in Wessex, it did not mean that her successors had to. Bishop Wærferth, her 'faithful friend', had been one of the leading figures in this flourishing education system after all. There has been some suggestion that Æthelstan may have been educated alongside his cousin Ælfwyn. Whilst it is interesting to think of the two youngsters being educated by the same tutor in the same room, Ælfwyn was, as stated above, quite a bit older than her cousin, perhaps as much as eight or nine years his senior, so when she was ending her education he may have just been starting his. Michael Wood suggests that when not involved in academic study Æthelstan would have enjoyed hunting in the Forest of Dean with the thegns of Mercia, and perhaps with his aunt and uncle too. This was of course a pleasure activity, but it was also a way of fostering a relationship with the powerful families of the kingdom whom he would one day fight alongside and whose council and support he would need.

After the rebellion of Æthelwold the kingdoms of Wessex and Mercia enjoyed another period of relative peace, but it was not to last. The next challenge for Æthelflæd and her husband was to come from Ingimund, the Viking warlord whom she had given permission to settle in the Wirral peninsula. Sometime in 906, the *Annals of Ireland* give us an account of an insurrection launched by Ingimund and his forces in which they tried to seize the town of Chester. The account is detailed, and rather interesting in the sense that it shows a somewhat unexpected side to Æthelflæd: the ruthless pragmatist, prepared to resort to any means necessary to achieve her ends. It must be noted that the Irish annals are treated with some suspicion by historians, and are believed to have been written about a century after the events they record, but the Irish connections of those involved in the siege of Chester and the long and detailed account that is given suggest there may well be some truth to it.[4]

It begins by relating the settlement of Ingimund, then elaborates:

> What resulted was that when he saw the wealthy city [Chester] … he yearned to possess them. Ingimund came then to the chieftains of the Norwegians and Danes … and said that they were not well off unless they had good lands, and that they all ought to go and seize Chester and possess it with its wealth and lands … What he said was, 'Let us entreat and implore them ourselves first, and if we do not get them *good lands* willingly like that, let us fight for them by force.' All the chieftains of the Norwegians and Danes consented to that.
>
> Ingimund returned home after that, having arranged for a hosting to follow him. Although they held that council secretly, the queen learned of it. The queen then gathered a large army about her from the adjoining regions, and filled the city of Chester with her troops.[5]

How did Æthelflæd learn of Ingimund's plans? Did the Mercians have a network of spies? It is an intriguing possibility, but the Irish annals' account continues below:

> The armies of the Danes and the Norwegians mustered to attack Chester ... They came to attack the city- and there was a great army with many freemen in the city to meet them. When the troops who were in the city saw, from the city wall, the many hosts of the Danes and Norwegians coming to attack them, they sent messengers to the King of the Saxons, who was sick ... to ask his advice and the advice of the Queen. He advised that they do battle outside, near the city, with the gate ... open, and that they choose a troop of horsemen to be concealed on the inside; and those of the people of the city who would be strongest in battle should flee back into the city as if defeated, and when most of the army of the Norwegians had come in through the gate ... the troop that was in hiding beyond should close the gate after that horde, and without pretending any more they should attack the throng that had come into the city and kill them all.
>
> Everything was done accordingly, and the Danes and Norwegians were frightfully slaughtered in that way. Great as that massacre was, however, the Norwegians did not abandon the city, for they were hard and savage; but they all said that they would make many hurdles, and place props under them, and that they would make a hole in the wall underneath them.[6]

Having failed to dislodge their Viking foes with this strategic feint, the rulers of Mercia decided to resort to the tried and tested tactic of dividing their enemies. It is in this part of the account that the Irish connection becomes apparent. It is alleged that there were a number of Irish soldiers among the Viking forces, mostly fosterlings (perhaps young men from Irish noble families), to whom Æthelred and Æthelflæd sent messengers, appealing to the common ties that their shared Christian religion had forged between them, and encouraging the Irish to side with them, their fellow Christians, against their pagan Viking overlords. The plan seems to have worked, for the two parties devised a strategy to overcome the Viking foe using trickery. The Irish were supposed to 'ask the Danes what gifts in lands and property they would give to the people who would betray the city to them. If they will make terms for that, bring them to swear an oath in a place where it would be convenient to kill them, and when they are taking the oath on their swords and their shields, as is their custom, they will put aside all their weapons.'[7]

The plan worked, and when the Danes had put down their weapons they were slaughtered by the army and the townspeople. Yet the occupation of Chester was not over. The annals account at this point states that there remained in the city many Norwegian Vikings – Ingimund's army had apparently comprised both Danes and Norwegians. The Irish had hated the Danes and, we are told, had been happy to co-operate with the English against them. They do not seem to have felt the same way about the Norwegians. To rid their city of them, the people of Chester and the remainder of the defenders resorted to pelting the Norwegians beneath their makeshift defences with anything that was to hand. Eventually, in the culmination of the siege which has become a famous historical anecdote they threw beehives and ale at them 'so that they could not move', forcing the beleaguered Vikings to finally abandon the city.[8]

The story of the siege is a dramatic tale of the plucky English and Irish co-operating against the pagan foe, and it also shows us that Æthelflæd was aware of political necessity and military strategy. She emerges as an intelligent and resourceful woman, trusted by her people, who was nevertheless prepared to resort to underhand tactics and deceit – the same sort of tactics for which the Vikings were despised. Yet it also suggests that even though she had been forewarned of an attempt to take Chester, and despite preparing the army, the Mercians had not been able to repel their enemies entirely. The Vikings had occupied the city, or parts of the city, and had held onto it for a time. Perhaps their own tactics in the early part of the campaign of 906 had turned on them, and they had closed the gates at an inopportune time. It would appear that the lesson had been learned, for the *Anglo-Saxon Chronicle* recounts that the following year 907 the city of Chester was re-fortified. Its silence on the attack on the city the year before, and Æthelflæd's role in the events, is something that we cannot understand with absolute certainly. Perhaps there was a level of embellishment or exaggeration in the Irish version of events; the men across the Irish sea certainly knew about Æthelflæd, and they seem to have been rather impressed with her. She received more attention in the *Annals of Ireland* than her husband or her father, although some of the attention may have been altruistic. She had, after all, adopted a pro-Irish policy at Chester and had appealed to the common religion of her people and theirs but had also pointed out the way that Irish clerics had reportedly been treated with as much honour as Englishmen.[9] The battle for Chester is perhaps reported precisely because it is exceptional. Did other Vikings settle in English Mercia? If so, how many settled peacefully? There must have been many who were happy to simply establish themselves and to farm, trade, marry and live their lives as ordinary citizens without craving more land, and this simply went unreported in the sources because it did not stand out. These people might well have set up their own local hierarchy, with reeves or similar officials, but ultimately accepted the authority of Æthelred and Æthelflæd. In the course of time, many of the settlers may even have converted to Christianity and moved into nearby cities like Chester, even worshipping in the churches there.

The account of the battle for Chester certainly suggests that the power and influence of Æthelflæd was growing considering her husband's illness. She is hailed in no uncertain terms as the undisputed queen of Mercia, not by the lesser title of lady, which was later given to her in English sources. Of course, it may be that the Irish annalists were simply unaware of the political relations between Wessex and Mercia in the early tenth century, which meant that the former had never regarded Æthelred of Mercia as the king. Whatever their reasons, Æthelflæd's position of power and trust carried with it certain roles and expectations. There had been strong and powerful queens before who had granted land and performed other actions in their own right, but there was a fine line between independence of action and will, and tyranny. Of course, the difference was that Æthelflæd was not a queen (not technically anyway), and she was trying to maintain peace in her kingdom and defeat those who turned out to be their mutual enemies – and that was acceptable, even in a woman.

Interestingly, the re-fortification of Chester may have been followed, according to a 'later tradition', by the foundation of yet another church dedicated or re-dedicated to another Old English saint. Æthelflæd was following her usual pattern, giving thanks to God and hoping to ensure the support of God and the saints by establishing a basis for the Christian community and worship in the city she and her husband had successfully wrested back from Viking control. This time she chose Werburgh, another seventh-century royal woman and, very appropriately, the daughter of a Mercian king, who chose to become a nun and by turn established other nunneries, eventually rising through the ranks to become an abbess. A church dedicated to St Werburgh still stands in Chester today, on or near the original site of the minster that was very probably established by the Lady of the Mercians in the city in which she achieved her first victory. There is another twist to the story of the church, and one which presaged a later and far more famous event. It rededication in Chester seems to have resulted from the moving of the relics of St Werburgh from their original resting place in Hambury in Staffordshire, which was still under Danish occupation in the first decade of the tenth century. By means fair or foul, the Mercians had rescued one of their ancient saints from the pagans. They were about to do so again.[10]

The recovery of the bones of St Oswald in the year 909 would go down in history, and enter the realms of legend as a daring sortie into Danish-occupied territory by plucky Saxons in a daring operation masterminded by their beloved ruler Æthelflæd. There are some interesting parallels with legends that grew up surrounding the stealing of the remains of St Mark from Egypt by the Venetians in the ninth century. Nothing was written until much later, but the chroniclers produced an embellished version full of adventure, with the saint supernaturally protecting his saviours and the two Venetian merchants responsible covering their cargo with pork to prevent searches by Muslim guards. In truth, we are not entirely certain of what role Æthelflæd played in this event. It is possible that it was planned by her, and possible that others were involved. The *Anglo-Saxon Chronicle* only records that some of the bones of the saint were translated from Bardney, in Danish-occupied Lincolnshire, to Gloucester (only some because his relics were divided between several sites). It mentions nothing about who did it, why, or who was involved. But then, it does not mention the siege of Gloucester and other events either. Clearly the translation itself was considered significant, so some elaboration is required. Oswald, like many of the other saints that Æthelflæd and Æthelred were attracted to, lived in the seventh century, arguably part of the golden age of Saxon Christianity, which stretched into the eighth century with writers like Bede, Aldhelm and Alcuin.

Oswald was not just a royal saint, however. He was something particularly special: a canonized king, the most potent of all the royal saints from the time. Oswald of the dynasty of the Idings had ruled the kingdom of Northumbria from 634 to 642, a brief but famous reign in which he founded the monastery of Lindisfarne with the help of the Irish monk Aidan and helped to permanently establish Christianity in his kingdom. Oswald had, according to his main biographer Bede, spent much of his youth in Ireland as an exile after the death of his father in battle against his uncle, King Edwin. The irony of Oswald's life is that he himself was killed in turn by the last great pagan king of Mercia,

Penda, at or near Oswestry in Shropshire. We have already seen that the Mercian royal couple seem to have been very attracted to the cults of ancient royal saints (and Æthelflæd would continue to be). Most were obscure, their cults often relegated to the locality associated with them. Oswald was the crowning glory of royal saints: several institutions laid claim to his relics, and there were many stories of miracles attributed to him. He is still regarded as a saint today and is venerated in many countries and by the Eastern Orthodox Church.

Gloucester had no historical connection with Oswald at all, but the priory there, initially dedicated to St Peter, was rededicated to the saint when the Lord and Lady of the Mercians had rescued him from a ruined shell destroyed by the pagans and brought him to a grand new church in their capital, where he would be reinterred in splendour. St Oswald's following was never large, but during this time enjoyed a golden age of fame and recognition, and the building itself had 'sumptuous adornments of sculpture and liturgical ornaments'. Surely the efforts of the Lord and Lady of the Mercians to rescue the saint and build a grand church for him would, in their minds, have met with his and his God's approval? It may seem reckless to us today for a small party to have been sent into hostile territory to retrieve a few bones, but the significance of saints and their cults to medieval European Christian belief and practice would have made such an operation seem to be of the utmost importance. Besides which, the Mercian royal couple may have felt that they were in particular need of this saint's intercession and help. According to his hagiographers, his devotion to Christ had allowed him to achieve victory in battle, and to reclaim his father's throne. The Vikings had first landed in his kingdom and had ravaged Lindisfarne. Their coming had been a punishment from God upon the Saxons for their impiety and immorality, but now the rulers of Mercia were attempting to undo the damage, not only by restoring and refortifying cities and sponsoring men of learning but also by making sure that the holy men and women of their people were honoured amongst the populace. More than this, by translating their relics the Lord and Lady of the Mercians may well have believed they were tapping into the sacred power of the saint, giving their new towns and cities extra protection.

Soon, the efforts of Wessex and Mercia would move beyond simply defending the borders of their kingdom and shoring up fortresses, which had been their main policy for so long. They were about to take the fight to the enemy. The attack on Chester, as well as other events such as a treaty Edward, king of Wessex had made some years before, suggest that there was increasing tension on the borders and frontier territory of the Anglo-Saxon kingdoms with the arrival of Vikings from Ireland, and their rulers considered themselves increasingly vulnerable. King Edward of Wessex was prepared to use negotiation when it was necessary, or when he was pushed to it by his inferior position, but he was not a peace-weaver like women were supposed to be, and as the first decade of the tenth century came to an end he decided to invade Northumbria. The *Anglo-Saxon Chronicle* reports that Mercia and Wessex combined their armies. In five weeks they ravaged the land, killed many men and seized much plunder. That the army consisted of men from both the main Saxon kingdoms suggests that Lord Æthelred was present, possibly leading the Mercian forces in actions which would prove detrimental to Mercian interests. Now probably in his fifties, the

Lord of the Mercians was still prepared to ride out at the head of his army alongside his West Saxon allies against the pagans – except that not all the Danes were pagans anymore. Many former raiders had now settled, and some were starting to convert to Christianity or at least were happy to allow Christianity to thrive. They had become 'as vulnerable to attack as their victims had once been'. It has been suggested that the operation into the Danelaw was when St Oswald's remains were retrieved, but this is reported before the campaign in the *Anglo-Saxon Chronicle*, and there is no reason to assume that the saint had not already been translated to Gloucester.[11]

On the occasion of the campaign of 909, it is possible to feel some sympathy for Danes. Edward's attack seems to have been largely unprovoked, although he feared the influence of the Hiberno-Norse Vikings who were coming over from Ireland on the increasingly fragmented northern part of the Danelaw. These Dublin Vikings had already attacked his sister and brother-in-law in Chester, but that had been nearly three years before. Wessex and Mercia may well have feared the potential for further attacks under new leaders who did not honour arrangements and treaties that had been made between the Saxons and the Danes. The Danes responded to aggression with aggression. In August 910, the Danes took the opportunity afforded by Edward's absence from Mercia (he had gone home and was in Kent) to attack the kingdom in what cannot have been anything other than a reprisal for what had happened the year before. Using ships, they took their army directly into Mercia via the River Severn where they ravaged the land, just as Edward and his allies had done months before; according to Æthelweard's *Chronicle* they got as far as the River Avon near the border with Wessex.[12] True to form, they collected much plunder, and sought to return to their homes in the north having taught the Mercians a lesson that they hoped they would not soon forget. However, the Mercians had not been idle. In a reversal of the campaign of the previous year, the Mercians reinforced their army with men from Wessex. At Tettenhall, or Wednesfield, near to the modern city of Wolverhampton, a Mercian army intercepted their foes in what may well have been a deliberate trap. The source above tells us that the Vikings were so weighed down with plunder and elated by their victory that they were taken completely by surprise when crossing a bridge. Perhaps this was so, but perhaps the Saxons were also prepared to ambush them, and attacked when their adversaries were penned in and unable to retreat. Other battles were won in a similar way. Nearly 500 years later, the Scottish hero William Wallace won the Battle of Stirling Bridge by attacking when the English army was still in the process of crossing said bridge and forming up on the other side. The *Anglo-Saxon Chronicle* reports that Edward attacked the Vikings from behind, and reports the death of a number of Viking nobles and important officials in the battle, as well as the loss of the two kings. It does not mention the presence of Mercian forces under the leadership of Æthelred or his wife.[13]

Needless to say, Tettenhall was a great victory for the Saxons, in which two Viking 'kings', named Halfdan and Eowils, were killed alongside many thousands of ordinary men. Æthelweard recounted the victory with great relish, and in one of his most famous lines remarked that a great number of the enemy 'hastened to the hall of hell'.[14] The Saxons had won another great victory, although arguably the battle had been a direct consequence of their own actions against the Northumbrians. Either way, the battle had another long-term effect. The cull of the northern Viking elite served to weaken and destabilise the region. This weakness was about to be used to the advantage of the Saxons in a daring campaign of re-conquest launched in eight years after Tettenhall. In the immediate aftermath, they had every reason to simply revel in their victory. Its significance cannot have been lost on them – the battle had been fought and won on 5 August 910, the feast day of St Oswald.

Heaven had just granted the English the greatest victory against their 'heathen' enemies in years, on the very day that commemorated the martyrdom of the great king St Oswald. How could the men and women of Mercia and Wessex not see it as a sign of divine favour? Yet victories, even divinely ordained, meant little if they were not followed up by action. Shortly after the battle, Æthelflæd emerges in the historical record as an independent agent for the first time. A sentence in the Mercian Register (the Mercian addition to *the Anglo-Saxon Chronicle*) records that she built a fortress at a site which is now identified as Bridgnorth in Shropshire. It might not seem like much, but as we have already seen this had been a key aspect of her father's strategy in Wessex in the previous century, and it had been carried over into Mercia by Æthelflæd and her husband. Ever the pragmatist, she set about shoring up the defences of her kingdom by overseeing the building of her first recorded burh at the unidentified site of Bremesburh. There are several possible locations for this, including the town of Bromsgrove in Warwickshire, and perhaps even the aforementioned Bridgnorth, which is only 13 miles away from Tettenhall, although she was later recorded as building a burh in that very place. Nothing more is mentioned in the chronicles until the following year, 911, when at the age of forty-one, close on the heels of their great victory, she and her people were dealt the bitterest of blows. Æthelred, Lord of the Mercians, was dead.

11

LADY OF THE MERCIANS 911–916

As with many other of events of this time, we do not know exactly when Lord Æthelred of Mercia died, where he died or how old he was. This lack of detail is frustrating for the biographer, and is why we must read between the lines from the available sources. His death is recorded very shortly after the battle of Tettenhall in most versions of the *Anglo-Saxon Chronicle* so we may assume that it happened relatively early in the year 911. The Irish sources suggest that he had been ill for some years before his death, but his demise so soon after the battle raises the possibility that one may have been related to the other. Was he mortally wounded in the melee, as another Æthelred had been over thirty years before? It is possible, but at nearly fifty he may simply have died of natural causes at what was then a good old age.[1]

His death was another event which altered the course of events significantly. When their husbands died, royal women would often retreat from public life to make way for the heir. This seems to have been what Ealswith had done, but her eldest daughter did not follow her example. After the burial of her husband at the newly consecrated St Oswald's Minster in Gloucester, Æthelflæd faced the most difficult choice of her life. Should she hand over power to one of her nobles or family members and retire to some nunnery, or go on pilgrimage like her aunt had? For the last twenty-five years she had played an active role in the economic, diplomatic and political activities of her kingdom, but it was not uncommon for nobles and ruling women to enter religious houses in their older years as a form of penance, or just because they wanted to spend the rest of their life in peace. Her mother had done so, and she could have done without suffering any reproach.

In a sense, Æthelred could not have died at a worse time. After the campaign of 909–10, the Saxons and Danes were on a war footing once again, and Edward was continuing his efforts to regain ancient English territory by conquest, beginning with the policy of building burhs. Mercia was vulnerable to reprisals and to the ravages of roving armies, and the victory of the combined armies of Mercia and Wessex would prove to be a double-edged sword, removing all those in a position to oppose the bands of Hiberno-Norse Vikings that came over to Britain from Dublin in the first decades of the tenth century.[2] The Mercians needed a strong, capable leader, not a succession crisis. Realistically, there do not seem to have been any Mercian athelings who rushed to claim the throne after the death of the Lord of the Mercians, though with some effort one could perhaps have been found from the bloodline of a long-dead king. There was Æthelstan, the ward and nephew of the deceased ruler whose relationship to his Mercian Aunt and Uncle may have been so close that they considered him their adoptive son. At fifteen or sixteen he may have been old enough to rule in theory, though perhaps not in fact. He could have gained experience on the battlefield during the campaign in Northumbria, but he was far off the seasoned leader that Æthelred had been when he had taken the reins of power from Ceolwulf so many years before. Of course, there was always his father, Edward, king of Wessex, who would probably have been only too happy to take the throne of his nearest neighbour as well. The kingdom had been technically subject to the rule of the kings of Wessex since Alfred's day, but in reality Mercia had kept up a tradition of self-rule, with its leaders more than capable of acting independently even if Wessex did not recognise them as kings. They may have been prepared to accept the West Saxons as their overlords, but few in Mercia would have wanted their kingdom to be effectively annexed by their southern neighbour.

Thus, there was only one viable heir who remained. A person who was half Mercian by blood, and whose family claimed descent from the proud and ancient warrior kings of Wessex and overlords of the other Saxon kingdoms like Offa and Penda. It was Æthelflæd. The sources suggest that she had been an active and capable consort to her husband, and women had acted in that capacity before. One such notable woman had been Cynethryth, the wife of the redoubtable Offa, whose 'control had extended over the monasteries of the kingdom' and who had held power during the minority of her son. It was quite possible for women to hold power in the capacity of regent for underage heirs, and many other women had done so on the Continent, especially in France. Furthermore, Mercian queens had more status than their West Saxon counterparts, who were not even allowed to carry the title. If there was anywhere an Anglo-Saxon royal lady could hold power in the opening years of the tenth century, it was in Mercia.[3]

For all this, a woman had never been elected to rule any Anglo-Saxon kingdom in her own right. In the event, it was a combination of the challenging circumstances of the time, the traditions of the kingdom she ruled and her own undoubted personal qualities which made this unprecedented step acceptable to the powerbrokers of Mercia. She could offer Mercia stability, continuity and strong rule at a time of uncertainty. What was more, to have chosen her the Mercian witan must have known that she could be trusted with power. The siege of Chester, and her involvement in the rebuilding of Gloucester, as well as the way her father allowed her to attend the meeting in London, must have proved their confidence was well placed.

We do not know of any formal declaration or meeting of the witan in which Æthelflæd was appointed as the first Englishwoman to rule a kingdom in her own right. There may have been something like this, or there may not have been. Certainly, she could not have become ruler without the support and consent of her nobles. In her role as leader she would sit at the head of the witan and bear ultimate responsibility for dispensing justice in the kingdom among the nobles as well as those lower down the social scale. These nobles, in ages past, had been known to turn on unwanted and unpopular rulers. Even men had to tread carefully. Alfred had nearly been deposed, and so his daughter had to be even more certain that she did not do anything that would have made her controversial or unpopular. This is one reason why it is highly unlikely that she engaged in the various love affairs that many novelists have accorded to her. Her people had chosen her because they trusted her and because something of her leadership ability had shown though; it would have been absurd for her to have jeopardised everything by sleeping with the enemy. As to her spiritual wellbeing, she had arranged for the monks of Worcester to say masses and prayers for the souls of herself and her family, and she had established or endowed many other churches. She did not have to retire to a nunnery to gain expiation for her sins.

So it was that from the time that she was accepted by her people in early 911 Æthelflæd came to be referred to by the title that has been used throughout this book, 'Lady of the Mercians' or *mrycna hlæfdige*. It is the first time, to the best of our knowledge, that the term 'lady' had been used in any kind of political sense, to denote the position or office of the person who held it. It developed as the female version of her husband's title, Lord of the Mercians (*mrycna hlaford*), and in Latin charters and sources from outside Wessex and Mercia she was granted equivalent royal titles including the Latin 'gubernator' and in Irish and Welsh sources 'queen'. Æthelflæd was now holding a position and title equivalent if not equal to that which her husband had held. Perhaps surprisingly, this situation was satisfactory even to her brother Edward of Wessex, who had been cultivating the relationship with his sister and brother-in-law for many years.[4]

That did not, however, stop him from seizing London and Oxford shortly after the death of the Lord of the Mercians. If his sister raised any objection there is no record of it, although the Mercians who held and administered those regions may well have had cause for complaint. As we have seen, the re-capture of London in 885 had been a joint effort, in which her father and husband had played a role before King Alfred had ceremoniously handed the city back to the Mercians. Perhaps Edward of Wessex believed that the death of the Lord of the Mercians bought to and end any arrangements his father had made over control of the city. Perhaps there had been some unwritten agreement between the parties that Edward was acting upon, although this would have been unlikely if London had indeed been part of Æthelflæd's *morgengifu*, which she was supposedly entitled to keep. Whatever happened, the new Lady of the Mercians again displayed her political sense, and may well have decided that the alliance between Wessex and Mercia was too important to jeopardise in a dispute over a border city, and a city which required a considerable amount of manpower and resources to defend. She decided to let the matter pass, as it was the least of her concerns. In the long run, it probably proved beneficial.[5]

The Mercians and their rulers had begun to flex their muscles in the years before Æthelred's death (as has been shown in the previous chapters) by invading Viking territory, raiding Northumbria and rescuing the bones of St Oswald. Overcoming the trauma of losing her husband, Æthelflæd began to emulate her brother, launching an aggressive campaign against the enemy concentrated in the northern and westernmost parts of her kingdom. Edward had presaged this campaign by encouraging his nobles to buy up land in the Danelaw. It is possible that his sister was doing the same thing, as there is an interesting charter dated from 914 in which a man named Ealhhelm, who was called a 'friend' of the Lady of the Mercians, was granted two hides of land near Derbyshire in return for '60 swine and 300 solidi'. Stanton is near to Burton upon Trent in Derbyshire, and was over (or dangerously close to) the border with the Danelaw. The Anglo-Saxons were, it appears, engaging in a form of colonisation by stealth, designed to lull their enemies into a false sense of security or undermine their hold on their territory from within.[6]

Edward and his sister also began following their father's example by building fortresses in strategic areas, sometimes from scratch and sometimes using existing defences. They occasionally brought armies with them to clear their paths of any Vikings. Æthelflæd was especially prolific, building or restoring nine fortresses in the space of five years (not counting the two or three before Lord Æthelred's death). The *Anglo-Saxon Chronicle* provides an account of this building programme, but much of what Æthelflæd was doing is best understood in the wider context of the military actions of her family at that time. The battle of Tettenhall had toppled the leaders of Northumbria, leaving it open to opportunists from Ireland, so the English response was twofold: to press home their advantage, and at the same time secure their kingdoms against the new wave of Viking settlers from Ireland. Their methods were more assertive and aggressive than before. Instead of just shoring up their defences in case the Vikings came and attacked them, they had begun a concerted effort to strike at the enemy by open warfare or subtler means, like encroaching on their territory to build their new towns. The siblings hoped to crush the surrounded Danelaw and its kings, or at least force them to capitulate. This may have seemed harsh, and even a breach of their father's treaty with Guthrum, but as far as the siblings were concerned this was the best way of protecting Wessex in the long term.

To this effect, in 912 Edward built Hereford while his sister began to set her eye to various sites around Mercia. She had, according to the twentieth-century historian Frank Stenton, a good eye for detail and the lie of the land, rather like her father. The locations of her burhs may sound impressive on the page simply for their number, but seeing them plotted on a map allows

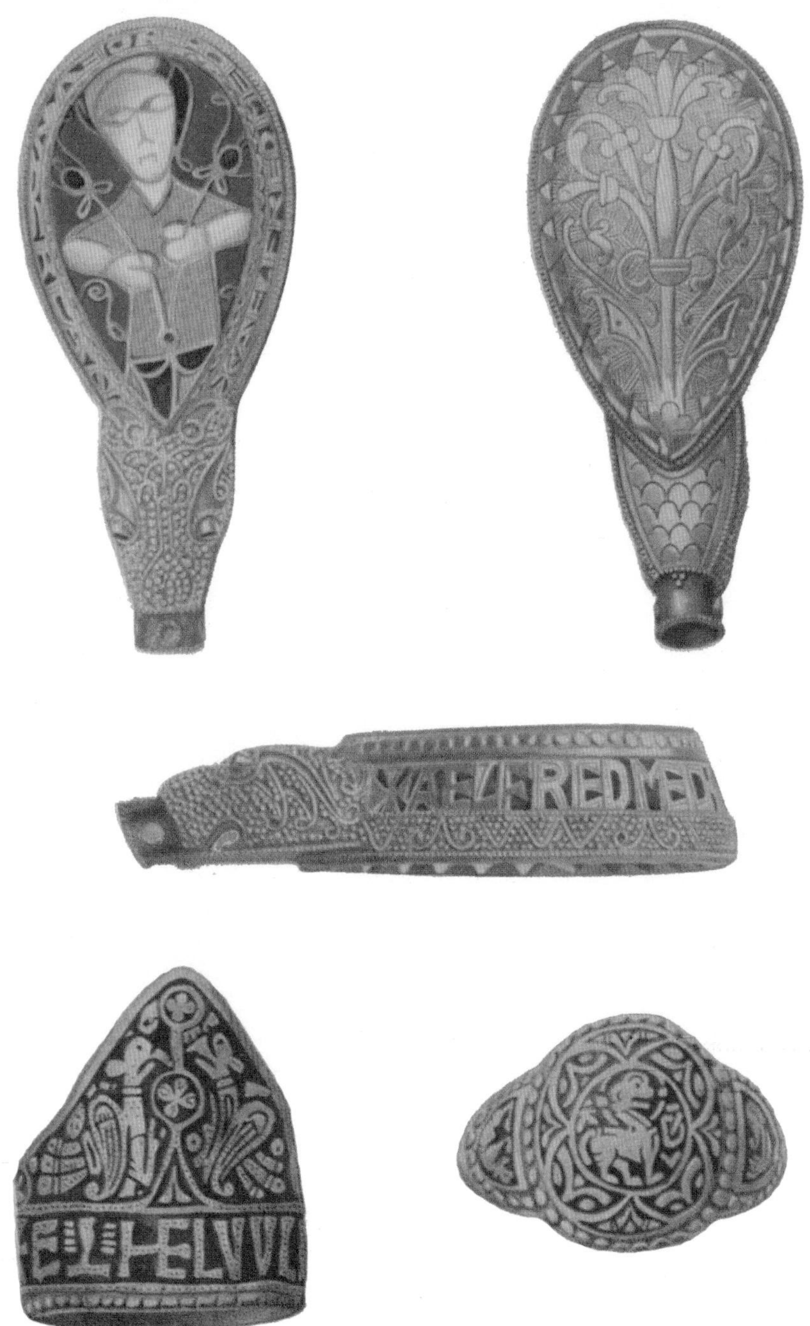

Top: The Alfred Jewel, found near Athelney in 1963. The text on the side, rendered in modern English, reads, 'Alfred ordered me to be made.' (Courtesy of Jonathan Reeve)

Above left: The ring of Æthelflæd's grandfather, Æthelwulf. (Courtesy of Jonathan Reeve)

Above right: The ring of Æthelflæd's aunt, Æthelswith. (Courtesy of Jonathan Reeve)

The statue of King Alfred in Wantage. (Courtesy of James Platt)

Map of England at the turn of the tenth century. Cropped down by the author from the map 'The Political Development of England' from the website *Kemble Anglo-Saxon Charters: Maps of Anglo-Saxon England*. (Used with permission of Simon Keynes)

Map of Southern England in the ninth century from *Kemble Anglo-Saxon Charters: Maps of Anglo-Saxon England*, 'Southern England in the Ninth Century'. (Used with permission of Simon Keynes)

G. F. Watts' *Alfred Inciting the Saxons to Resist the Landing of the Danes*. (Courtesy of Jonathan Reeve)

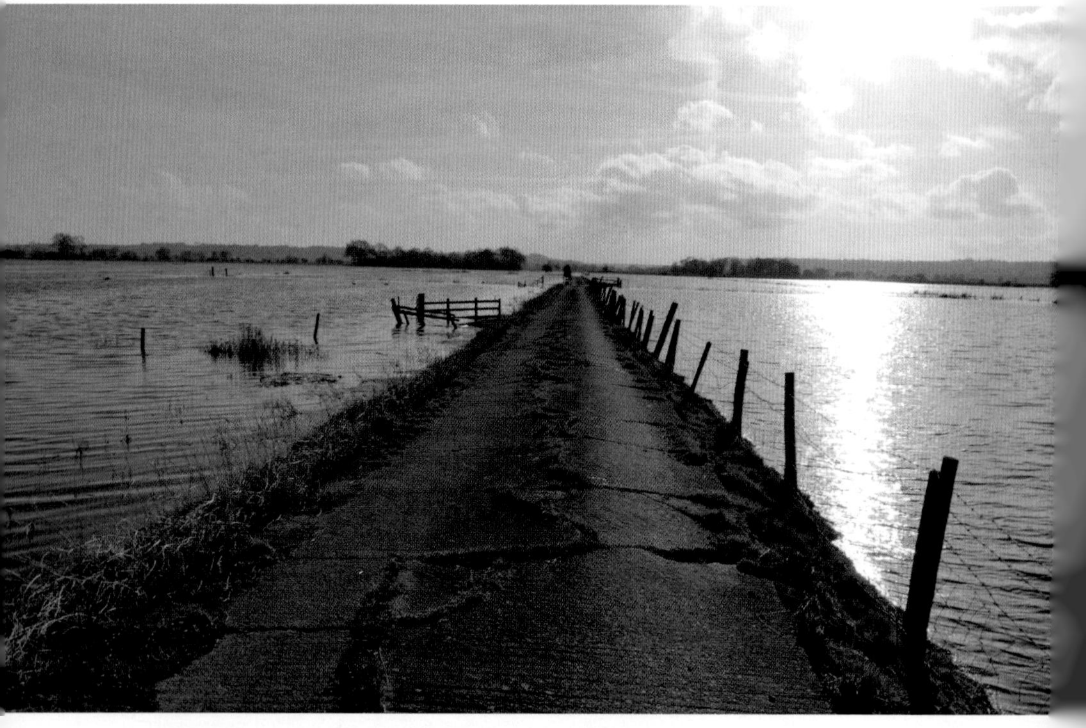

The impenetrable Somerset levels. Alfred hid from the Danes here, in Athelney. (Courtesy of Nick Sarebi under Creative Commons)

Above: Athelney in Somerset, where Alfred hid out with his family. (Courtesy of Jonathan Reeve)

Right: A manuscript page from the *Anglo-Saxon Chronicle*, which Alfred is thought to have commissioned. (Courtesy of the British Library)

Above: The Coronation Stone in Kingston upon Thames. Athelstan, Æthelflæd's adopted son, is thought to have been the first Anglo-Saxon king crowned here. (Courtesy of Jonathan Reeve)

Below: The ruins of St Oswald's Priory, Gloucester. Although it was very much a spiritual centre of Æthelflæd's Mercia, it declined in importance and wealth during the following century, and by the time it was destroyed during the English Civil War it was nothing more than a parish church dedicated to St Mary. (Courtesy of Rebecca Sillence)

Manuscript image of King Athelstan, the nephew of Æthelfæd and grandson of Alfred the Great, presenting a book to St Cuthbert. It is the most famous image of the first king of all England, and illustrates his piety and literacy – characteristics he shared with his aunt. Illuminated manuscript from Bede's Life of St Cuthbert.

A carved stone slab discovered in excavations at St Oswald's. It is believed to have been the base of a cross. It probably dates from the late ninth century, when the church was first established by the Lord and Lady of the Mercians, but before it was rededicated to St Oswald following the interment of his relics *c*. 909. (Courtesy of Fæ under Creative Commons)

Statue of Æthelflæd outside Tamworth Castle. The statue was raised in 1918 on the millennial anniversary of her death. Although the statue is a highly romanticized Edwardian version, it does represent the two aspects of her character. There is the maternal and nurturing side in how she has her arm around her young nephew and surrogate son Athelstan, and in her other hand she holds a sword, indicating her preparedness to fight for her cause and her people. (Courtesy of Humphrey Bolton under Creative Commons)

the viewer a deeper understanding of the strategy she was putting into effect, as close as we might be able to get to understanding the motivations and intentions of the great lady today. In the year after her husband's death she built two burhs: one the unidentified Scargeat, and the other at Bridgnorth. The Shropshire town of was of significance, as the Danish armies had encamped there during Alfred and Æthelred's last campaign of 992–6. It was also close to the site of the battle of Tettenhall, fought only two years before. According to Æthelweard, the Danes had been intercepted when they were approaching the bridge there. That Æthelflæd chose to fortify the site suggests that she saw it as a potential weak spot, a chink in the armour of her kingdom that needed to be protected.[7]

The geographical location is also interesting. Starting with Chester (where the Danes had also once briefly made an encampment) and then Shrewsbury and Bridgnorth, and finally the former Roman towns of Worcester and Gloucester, which Æthelred and Æthelflæd had worked on in the earliest part of their reign, Mercia now had a complete chain of five fortified towns. These stretched from the northernmost to the southernmost reaches of the kingdom's western border with Wales, the region from which the Dublin Vikings had sought to enter the kingdom in the first decade of the century.

Edward I would later be credited with a ring of castles including Harlech, Beaumaris and Caernarfon designed to subdue north Wales after his conquest in the late thirteenth century, as well as establishing new towns which he aimed to fill with English settlers. There is an intriguing foreshadowing in the work Æthelflæd completed with the building of her burhs nearly four centuries before by securing one of the most porous and vulnerable borders of her kingdom. Yet while Edward's castles were intended to consolidate his conquest of Wales and enforce his authority, Æthelflæd seems to have been asserting her lordship by ensuring her kingdom was well defended. Her new burhs were more than just defensive structures, however; they were also planned towns. Inside the walls of many burhs the streets were laid out neatly according to the old Roman pattern, with four main streets intersected north to south and east to west, and smaller side streets veering off them. People were encouraged to settle, and the men who served in the garrison may have been given 'burgage' plots within the town where they could live with their families. They had all the facilities they required, with new churches or restored old ones, and some of the towns had their own mints for producing coins which would serve the economy of the kingdom.

There is a silver penny in the British Museum attributed to Edward the Elder, which appears to depict a fortress of some description, and it is believed that it may actually have come from a Mercian mint set up by his sister. Perhaps she approved of the design. It was certainly relevant to what she was doing at the time, and it sent an unequivocal message to any raiders and invaders who might want to take their chances on the western border. In the same year, Edward also built two burhs in northern Wessex, one at Hertford and the other at Witham in Essex. Brother and sister were using the same policy, strengthening their defences and pushing the boundaries of their territory. The message was clear: decades after the Danish Conquest, the English were regaining their strength under the offspring of Alfred. They were a force to be reckoned with again.[8]

In the following year, during the summer of 913, Æthelflæd took the daring step of building two more fortresses in far more precarious locations at Stafford and Tamworth. Both lie in the modern county of Staffordshire, and were on the very borders of the Danelaw. Tamworth today is a quiet and pleasant market town nestled between the bustling cities of Stafford, Derby and Birmingham, its name taken from the local river, the Tame. Today its significance in the Anglo-Saxon age is largely forgotten, only occasionally celebrated in local tradition and historical events. In the tenth century, the town had a certain resonance for the people of Mercia. It had in the been the capital of Mercia during its golden age under Offa, and even before, but had been decimated by the invading Danes in 874 and had become a 'backwater' in disputed territory between English Mercia and the Danelaw. Æthelflæd and her husband had made their capital far to the south-west at Gloucester, but now she turned her attention back to the ancient city, once a potent symbol of the glory and pride of her kingdom. The *Anglo-Saxon Chronicle* tells us that she came to Tamworth, a town that may have been reduced to little more than ruins clustered with a few hovels, with the ordinary folk of Mercia. Reportedly the church of St Editha was little more than 'a heap of blackened ruins'.[9]

There is a local tradition that Æthelflæd's burh was situated on the site of the present Tamworth Castle, and she is sometimes even credited with originally building the castle. As Don Stansbury says, the Lady of the Mercians did not build castles, nor did any of her Anglo-Saxon predecessors, or at least not castles as we would know them. That said, the present castle is situated well within the walls of the town proposed by a short report on local history in the Tamworth library. These, we are told, encompassed the area from 'the river Tame West of the Lady Bridge, down Marmion Street on to Mill Lane, then across

Bolebridge Street and the river Anker', an area some 16,000 yards long, the lines of which the later medieval walls followed. It is suggested that the fortifications constructed at Tamworth were not just simple walls, and that behind the main palisade there was a 'walkway 8 feet wide' and behind that another walkway on a lower level, and the ramparts were equipped with gatehouses large enough to accommodate guardrooms. In other words, these ramparts may have been reminiscent of the elaborate ramparts of later medieval towns, cities and castles.

The royal and ecclesiastical centre of the town would have consisted of a royal palace or other residence, and a church, possibly as small as a royal chapel or as large as a parish church, sometimes even a minster or abbey. Whilst the possibility that the royal residence was situated on the site of the modern castle cannot entirely be ruled out, there is some support in the archaeological evidence for another location near to the present-day St Editha's church. It is known that a royal palace existed on or near this site in Offa's day. There is speculation that it was his own palace, and it is known that at least one of his charters was issued from Tamworth, most likely from his royal palace there, and it is widely believed that St Editha's dates back to the early ninth century. It would make sense for Æthelflæd to have constructed some kind of royal residence on the site as the royal centre of the newly rebuilt town. What better way to establish her authority as the heiress of Offa and the ancient Mercian royal dynasty? Also, what better way to prove that she was a good lord?[10]

The rebuilding of Tamworth may have been more than a symbolic act designed to boost the morale of the Mercians. In the account of the rebuilding in the *Anglo-Saxon Chronicle* there is the interesting statement that Æthelflæd enacted the rebuilding of the town 'with the help of God'. Was there some conflict in the retaking of the town? Although none is reported, it was right on the edge of the Danish territory and it has been deducted from place-name evidence that were Danish settlements and farmsteads built 'right up to Tamworth', separated only by several miles of forest. The natural resources of the region would have been useful to the soldiers and commoners of Mercia as building material for the walls of their town. Certainly Æthelflæd is credited with having pushed back a Danish advance in order to rebuild the town, so there may well have been border raids and skirmishes right up until the construction, which could account for the remark in the chronicle. Was the rebuilding of the town intended as a deliberate challenge to the local Danish rulers and settlers, a very palpable statement of her authority in disputed and dangerous territory?[11]

Shortly after she had finished her business in Tamworth in mid-913, Æthelflæd moved onto her next project, building the fortified town that would become known as Stafford. Like Tamworth, Stafford was also close to the border of the Danelaw. Again, the precise location of Æthelflæd's burh there is not known with any certainty. Some think it was near to the castle constructed after the Norman Conquest, which is located a few miles west of the present town centre. Stansbury believed that it was located on the meander of the River Sow, encompassing Greengate Street and Bridge Street – in other words, the area corresponding to the later medieval town. Archaeological excavations and local knowledge suggest an alternative site forming a rectangle 'on the west side of Greengate Street ... Earl Street on the west, Stafford and Broad Streets to the North, and

Mill Street to the South' with St Mary's church in the centre, spanning roughly 400 by 200 metres, 1200 metres in total and equivalent in Anglo-Saxon times to the measurement of 960 hides. If Æthelflæd used the same calculations as those in the *Burghal Hidage* then every hide would have been expected to support one man for the garrison of the city, which would have totalled 960 men. This suggests something about the amount of planning and administration that would have been required to maintain the defences of such a settlement. It seems that Stafford was divided into two, with a fortress on one side and an industrial area on the other, the latter containing a royal or ecclesiastical centre. Interestingly, there has been found what is thought to have been part of a book clasp in the area near the modern-day St Bertelin's church. Æthelflæd, like her father, was literate and keen to promote literacy. Could the book the clasp belonged to have come from one of the original settlers just after 913, perhaps a cleric attached to one of the churches there? Or a nobleman who took the admonitions of Alfred and his children about the pursuit of learning seriously? It is interesting to speculate that the book had some personal connection to the Lady of the Mercians, perhaps being a gift from her to somebody, but unless more concrete evidence is found we cannot know anything for certain.[12]

Next, in 914, while her brother built a double burh at Buckingham, Æthelflæd built Eddisbury in Cheshire along with Warwick, the county town of Warwickshire. The *Annals of Ireland* also tell us that in the same year Æthelflæd stepped into the shoes of a peace-weaver once again when she made an alliance with the people of the British kingdoms surrounding Mercia, described as 'the men of Alba and the Britons'. These were the kingdoms of Strathclyde, an ancient British kingdom which covered south-western Scotland and parts of what is now north-western England including Cumbria, and Alba, the kingdom which would ultimately become Scotland. The act was done, supposedly 'by her own cleverness'. In other words, the alliance was not made at the behest of her brother, or even the British rulers, but was sought by Æthelflæd of her own volition. Under its terms, they were supposed to come to her aid if Vikings attacked her, and vice versa. There is no independent verification of this account, but the location of the burhs Æthelflæd built after 913 do suggest that she was increasingly concerned about threats from the north of her kingdom, so an alliance with kingdoms in these regions would have made sound strategic sense, and, as we have already seen, Æthelflæd had plenty of that. She was also gaining a reputation for being as much a formidable enemy as an erstwhile ally. The Irish annals remark that after 916 'her fame spread everywhere'. It had certainly spread across the Irish Sea, as this was the second anecdote that the annalist had chosen to record involving her. Indeed, the stories that became attached to her in these sources suggest she must have had a rather charismatic personality. Later sources tell us her nephew was an affable and personable man, so it's possible his aunt shared the same characteristics. It was unusual for a woman to do what she was doing and to be successful, and her actions were not only remarkable but were also remarked upon favourably. Those who wrote about her seemed to have genuinely *liked* and admired her as a person, whether from personal acquaintance or second-hand knowledge. The Lady of the Mercians was already doing more than building towns – she was making her mark on history.[13]

Moving back to the discussion of her building projects, the northern burhs were the unidentified *Weardbyring* (possibly Whitchurch in Shropshire), Chirbury (in the same county) and Runcorn (Cheshire). Her other unknown burh, at a place called *Scargeat* in the *Anglo-Saxon Chronicle*, may also have been close to the northern border of her kingdom. The name may mean something like 'border gap', and there were gaps in the line of defences along the northern border. She was trusting her brother to secure the regions to the south and the east. He had been doing just that with his own burhs at Waldon in Essex and Towcester in Northamptonshire, as well as the one at Bedford, which had been recaptured from the Danes. No notable military campaigns or engagements are recorded in this first half of the second decade of the tenth century, when the brother-and-sister team were building their fortifications. It has been suggested, however, that the record of the building of Mercia's fortifications may be incorrect, and that they may in fact have been part of a concerted campaign moving from west to north, then east to south, encircling the land and reclaiming or securing it as the Mercians went along. It is true that some of the burhs seem to be out of order, and the date of their building does not entirely make sense considering the careful and methodical nature of so much of what Alfred and his children did. In fact, the pattern of all the fortifications that they built suggests that they were involved in some kind of collaborative strategy resembling a type of pincer movement. Æthelflæd was moving in and enclosing the Danelaw.[14]

It is interesting to consider here the overall purpose of some of Æthelflæd's burhs. There are some which are unidentified, in some cases because they did not survive or develop into modern towns. All that might be left of them today is a few ditches, or raised promontories. Were they intended to be military camps and bases for garrisons (as may have been the case with Stafford for time), or were they royal centres with some domestic occupation? The latter designation would go some way towards explaining why some have not survived today when so many of her father's foundations did. It has already been mentioned how many of the burhs were laid out according to a simple plan of Roman origin, with two straight streets intersecting north to east, south to west, with smaller side streets coming off them. At the earliest stage, in King Alfred's day, the purpose of these fortified settlements was the protection and defence of the population and the area. However, the permanent residents of these burhs were also responsible for providing for their defence by paying some kind of tribute, or raising and equipping soldiers from the community.

The layout of Æthelflæd's burhs and the re-use of Roman sites has given rise to suggestions that Alfred and his progeny were consciously mimicking Roman and Continental designs in their programmes of building and cultural renewal. At Stafford there is also evidence for the production of pottery based on Roman designs and styles. Earlier Anglo-Saxon monarchs had been obsessed with all things Roman, even from the earliest times: the seventh-century Edwin of Northumbria is said to have had a special banner made in the Roman style to be carried before him. In the case of Alfred's family, the restoration of Roman towns may have simply proved convenient, but on a cultural level it was also a good way of demonstrating their ability with all things Roman, and by extension Christian. Alfred had of course visited Rome as a child, and looked at the Carolingian and Christian Roman past for inspiration. It is also possible that the

English had one more reason: they wanted to demonstrate to the Church that the Saxon kingdoms were not lapsed in their devotion and tolerant of paganism. Instead, they were doing their best to restore the golden age of learning and piety, reclaiming their territory and bringing it back under faithful Christian rule.[15]

One other intriguing artefact from this time is a coin. At first it does not seem to be anything special, just a simple silver penny that was traditionally attributed to Edward the Elder. Yet recent investigation on the name of the moneyer suggests that it was minted in Mercia and under Æthelflæd, not her brother. Unlike her forbear, Cynethryth, Æthelflæd did not go as far as to have herself depicted on a coin (at least no such coin has been found), but she was certainly minting them. The coin is believed to depict a tower erected as part of a burh, or possibly a church tower. The Lady of the Mercians' building projects were clearly close to her heart; she even chose to make them part of the public image that defined her reign. It was more than just an attractive image to use on a coin showing that the she was following in her father's footsteps as a master builder. The coin represented the success of the system of 'urban regeneration' which had begun nearly a decade before but which Æthelflæd ahd continued in earnest. She was trying to strengthen the economy as well as bringing peace and stability within the borders of her kingdom.[16]

There was one other advantage to Æthelflæd in what must have been a near-constant round of building between 912 and 916: it kept the able-bodied men of Mercia occupied. Since Roman times commanders had seen the advantage in keeping soldiers out of trouble by involving them in building projects, and the Lady of the Mercians may well have realised this too. She must have had a significant force of soldiers roving around the kingdom with her, and she would have needed the assistance of sheriffs, reeves, administrators and officials to deal with the day-to-day needs of her retinue. After they were built, the fortresses must have been garrisoned as those built by her father had been for their defence and the defence of those who would in time, it was hoped, settle there. They were also useful bases for future excursions into the surrounding territory. Æthelflæd was showing that she was every inch her father's daughter once again, managing and overseeing her operations carefully and with a view to the future. This must have occupied much of her time as well, as there are few surviving charters from the second decade of the tenth century. One, as mentioned above, was the daring grant to Ealhhelm in Derbyshire, and another confirmed some lands in Warwickshire, which had been destroyed by fire. She and her brother were making inexorable progress towards their goal of securing their kingdom and clawing back land. By the summer of 916 it must have seemed as though they were invincible, and anyone who doubted this would be convinced by the events of the next two years.

12

DAUGHTER OF GOD

Æthelflæd was, like her father, pious and highly educated. It is even possible that she was more educated than him, as he did not learn to read Latin or undertake more complicated studies of classical subjects until his later years. Her religious devotion is shown in her bequests to churches: the jewelled chalice in honour of St Milburg's church, the provision to St Peter's in Worcester for psalms, prayers and masses to be said for the good of herself and her family as well as their souls after death. Such were typical for a medieval Catholic of noble birth, and can be seen in wills and documents even into the early modern age.

Yet Æthelflæd was a lady of more than conventional piety. She had a sense of divine destiny, fostered by and quite probably inherited from her father during her upbringing in Wessex. So much of her later career in Mercia mirrored what her father had done before her: the building of the burhs, the almost obsessive planning that went into her rebuilding projects, the devotion to all things old and Anglo-Saxon including saints and literature. Although Æthelflæd never set foot outside the British

Isles, unlike her father (and her younger sister, who married the Count of Flanders), the evidence also shows that she was acutely aware of the legacy of Roman rule, especially in the form of the Roman Church.

Unlike her father, Æthelflæd had no definitive biography – only the Mercian Register, which records her building projects and an attack on Wales in 916. She had no Asser, although it is not hard to believe that, had he lived longer, her 'faithful friend' Bishop Wærferth could have served her in a similar capacity. As a result we have no record of any books that she was particularly keen on or that she commissioned and translated. Yet we know that she was literate, at least in English and quite possibly in other languages. After her marriage in her early teens, it is not impossible that she may have pursued some academic study in Mercia, perhaps under the tutelage of Wærferth, who had served her father and aided in his translations. So grateful was Alfred to the man that he even sent a copy of Gregory's *Pastoral Care* back to Mercia for him; like his daughter after, he addressed the bishop as 'dear' or 'beloved' to him.[1] As the book was sent to Mercia, it's entirely possible his daughter would have read it during the years of her married life in Mercia. In the introduction composed by her father she would have read his reminiscences on the actions of godly kings back in the golden age before the Viking invasions. She would also have read his musings on wisdom and the ideal attributes of a ruler, including admonitions to avoid pride 'lest through desire for renown in the world' a person should 'assume the leadership of the damned'. Eventually, her own daughter Ælfwyn and her nephew Æthelstan would be sent to Worcester to be educated, probably at or near to St Peter's Minster, where she may have established a school like those her father had set up in Wessex.[2]

We know that Alfred had his children given a basic education in English works, and Æthelflæd was no different. There were classics like Bede and Alcuin, as well as newly translated works such as those by St Gregory and Boethius, plus psalms, scripture, poetry and even some Latin. It is hard to discern exactly what her tastes in literature might have been, but we can make some guesses based on what was popular at the time. If the Worcester charter is anything to go by it seems that Æthelflæd knew her liturgy, for it specifies that the psalm *De Profundis* was to be sung for her and her family every day, and after their deaths the *Laudate Dominium*. The former is the name in the Latin liturgy for Psalm 130, which begins with the phrase 'Out of the Depths' (from which the Latin title is taken), and the latter is Psalm 113.[3]

We have already seen how the Anglo-Saxons had an impressive intellectual heritage, and how Æthelflæd's father had tried to revive it at his own court, blending it with Continental models such as that of the schools created at the Carolingian court. What, if anything could she have contributed to this literary culture? How could she have benefited from it? There is one interesting text which may provide the answer. It is a poem entitled *Judith*, with echoes of the epic tales of warriors and the high drama of saints' lives. But this poem is not about a heroic male warrior and nor does it contain monsters, unlike *Beowulf*, which is contained in the same manuscript. Its protagonist is a woman, at first glance quite an unremarkable one. Judith is the widow of a fairly substantial landowner, but it quickly becomes apparent that she is also something special. She is an armour-clad war leader, and she is also Jewish.

The ethnicity of the heroine may seem unusual, but the poem is in fact based on a book from the Apocrypha, the 'extra books' in the Old Testament that are included in the versions used by the Catholic and Eastern Orthodox churches. It is unfortunate that the original Book of Judith is not better known in Britain today. Whilst it is not a literary masterpiece (and the chronology of figures and events mentioned within is decidedly confused), it is an interesting read. Medieval people were more familiar with the story than modern audiences are as it was frequently depicted in medieval art, and Judith was a fairly popular first name given to girls. It was clearly popular enough in the later Saxon period for some unidentified author to write a poetic adaptation suiting the context of their own time. Indeed, it might also be said that the Saxons had a long tradition of converting Bible stories, and even theological concepts, into poetic form for the consumption of ordinary people who would never learn Latin, read the Bible or learn the psalter for themselves. Way back in the seventh century, a former cowherd turned monk called Cædmon made songs and poems out of many biblical accounts and shared them to disseminate biblical teaching among the common folk of Northumbria.

What does this have to do with Æthelflæd, other than that the story of Judith was popular during her lifetime? More, perhaps, than we might think. It is not known for certain when the poem based on the book was written, but it is widely believed that it dates from the early tenth century, and that Æthelflæd may have had something to do with its composition. Pauline Stafford suggests it was either written 'for or about' her, and the wider consensus is that the biblical heroine may have been used as a sort of allegorical representation of her and her career. When we examine the poem below, the reasons for this will become apparent.[4]

The poem, and the book it is based on, began with the people of ancient Israel in dire straits: their nation had been invaded by the pagan Assyrians and their allies, who had already conquered most of the surrounding states. The commander of the army, annoyed at how they had fled to their walled cities, threatened to the destroy them all. Events came to a head when Holofernes, the commander of the Persian army, brought his huge army to lay siege to a place called Bethulia (described as a mountain fortress, where most of the people were shored up). Terrified that they could not win with their lesser forces, the Israelites wanted to surrender until their own commander urged them to give it five days and to pray to God to save them, for the events could be a punishment from him.[5]

Sound familiar? A righteous nation set about on all sides by pagans intent on destruction and conquest? It is no wonder the book was turned into a poem, as the Anglo-Saxons must have (rightly or wrongly) identified themselves with the beleaguered Jewish people in the ancient setting. This is how the Apocryphal version begins, and so enters Judith. She comes across as a very ordinary person – in the original book a recently widowed woman of some property, in the poem a virgin. When she hears of the threats made, and her people's intention to surrender to the enemy, she is mortified and decides to take immediate and decisive action. She presents herself to the hosts of Israel, and tells them that she and her ladies will save their people before the five days are up. She then prays to God to guide her, and sheds her jewellery and finery before entering the enemy camp with her women.[6]

It is at this point that the Anglo-Saxon poem begins, after the beautiful Judith has entered the enemy camp, where the men have thrown a feast in honour of the lovely ladies.

Then Holofernes summoned the men to wine,
And splendidly prepared a mighty banquet,
To which he Prince of men commanded all his noble thanes …
This was the fourth day of which the elf-fair Lady Judith first,
Wise in her heart, had come to visit him[7]

It is interesting to note that the poem has been adapted to suit the needs of the tenth-century audience, with the followers of the king called 'thanes' and the reference to Judith being 'elf-fair'. Nowhere do elves appear in the original book, or anywhere in Hebraic mythology, but the Anglo-Saxons envisioned them as indescribably fair and beautiful creatures. It was the ultimate form of physical beauty for the people of Æthelflæd's day. Judith, however, was far more than just a pretty face; she was the ultimate *femme fatale*, as the rest of the poem demonstrates. When the men were soundly drunk, Holofernes, 'the enemy of the Saviour', retired to his bed and summoned Judith to be brought to him. Once more she was 'bedecked in jewels' and Holofernes 'intended to pollute the fair maid with sin'. The wise lady, instead of shying away from his sinful advances, played along.

On his bed the noble Lord fell down,
so drunk with wine that he knew no sense …
Then the maiden of the Lord, seized a sharp sword hardened with battle play,
And with her right hand drew it from its sheath,

> She then began to call upon the Lord of Heaven by his name ...
> and said these words
> 'To you God of Creation, joyous Spirit, and Son of the Almighty will I pray ...
> Grant me, heaven's Prince, a victory and true belief,
> that I may cut down with this sword the murderer ...
> Avenge now, mighty Lord, and glorious Giver of Fame
> That I have in my heart such bitterness, such heat within my breast' ...
> She took the heathen man fast by his hair,
> Pulled him towards her shamefully by hand,
> Skilfully placed the evil, hated wretch, in such a place as she could best control him.
> The fair-tressed one then struck her enemy with decorated sword
> So that she cut through half his neck ... then the gallant girl
> Severely smote the heathen hound again,
> So that his head rolled forth upon the floor ...
> Then in the fight had Judith won herself outstanding glory,
> As God granted her when Heaven's Prince gave her the victory[8]

Such violent imagery was not uncommon in the poetry of this period, which often celebrated battles and the heroic deeds of warriors. At first glance, however, the poem appears to be quite a shocking departure from the norm – this ostensibly righteous woman is playing the seductress, before beheading her victim with his own sword. Nor are her actions those of a frightened woman: on the contrary, they are premeditated and really quite calculating. This is hardly the typical image of a pious medieval lady. Yet there is not a hint of censure for Judith's actions. On the contrary, she is praised as a heroic handmaiden of God, vanquishing the heathen foe. Her killing Holofernes was an act of divine justice, and 'she is not a monster for her violent action, but rather a vanquisher of heathen forces'. She did not have an army, and was not a warrior; instead, she put her trust in God and he enabled her to succeed.[9]

There is certainly a parallel here with some of the comments made about Æthelflæd's career. Like the biblical heroine, she was engaged in a valiant struggle against a heathen foe to which most of the neighbouring kingdoms had already fallen. She took Derby, and went to Tamworth 'with the help of God'. Here, then, was a biblical precedent of a woman overcoming her enemies and the enemies of the Christian faith by placing herself in the hands of her God. The extract above also lauds Judith as the wisest of women – one might more accurately describe her as cunning and sly. Again, Æthelflæd was described in similar terms as acting 'by her own cleverness', and as one who had adopted her father's love of wisdom.[10]

Judith's fight was not done. The commander was dead, but there was still a war to fight, and there were still 200 lines to go in the poem. Having killed Holofernes, Judith was still in a dangerous situation, in the middle of the enemy camp. She made a quick escape back to the fortified city, passing Holofernes' severed head back to her women (who had conveniently smuggled in sacks among the food they had bought with them), and her next act was to encourage what was left of the beleaguered Israelite army to complete the fight and drive Holofernes' forces out of the land for good. The poem continues:

> The valiant heroines both departed thence at once,
> Till triumphing the brave maids came out of that host …

They hastened their way till glad in heart they reached the city wall.
There soldiers sat, and wakeful warriors in the fort kept watch
As Judith noble lady, prudent maid had ordered the sad people earlier when she set out
And then she spoke these words to the victorious people ...
"I tell you a most memorable thing
That you need mourn no longer in your hearts
The glorious Lord of Kings is good to you ...
Here you may clearly gaze, triumphant heroes ...
Upon the head of the most heathen general ...
Now I wish to pray to every man among the citizens
And warriors that you prepare yourselves quickly to fight ...
Bear forth linden shields before your breasts, and ring mailed corselets too ...
Cut down their officers with flashing swords ...
For your enemies are doomed to death and you shall have renown
Glory in Battle as Mighty God
Has shown you by this token in my hand[11]

Here we see Judith, like the noble ladies in chivalric romances of a later age, urging and encouraging her soldiers to acts of bravery. She does not act in a leadership role in the main battle, but she is undoubtedly the hero of the piece, and afterwards she is honoured by the victorious Israelite soldiers bringing her the armour of Holofernes as a trophy. Something very interesting is going on with female roles in this poem. Very often Judith is called a 'maiden', with all its implications of sexual purity. In the original book Judith is a widow, and the beginning of the poem is missing today so we don't know if virginity was mentioned in the adaptation. Nevertheless, she uses her feminine wiles and her knowledge of human nature to overcome her enemies. The distinction is important – Judith (and the Anglo-Saxon woman that would have heard about her) did not use her body for sinful actions, to lead men astray and into sin or to gain power and fame for herself, but in the service of God to save her people. Here, then, is another parallel with Æthelflæd, who according to a twelfth-century chronicle only had one child, and did so by her own personal choice.

Despite her more violent and cunning side, Judith stays well within the bounds of acceptable morality: she is the model pious lady in the context of the deadly conflict in which she is forced to act. Did Æthelflæd want to cast herself in the same mould? It seems very likely. She would certainly have identified with the biblical heroine and the struggle of her people against the pagans, gaining victory and eternal fame through her courage, endurance and piety. It is not hard to imagine that the story of Judith was a favourite of hers, and that she would have loved any poem developed from it.[12]

This is not to say that she conceived of her struggle against the Danes and Hiberno-Norse Vikings as a holy war in the sense that we would understand it or as later generations understood it, but perhaps she believed that, like Judith, she could have the support of God if she was faithful to Him. It is also possible that sponsoring a poem like this one, in which the protagonist was modelled on her, was an exercise in early medieval image management. Although literacy was on the increase thanks to Alfred's reforms, the way to get the poem and its message out would probably have been by oral dissemination, with it being read and recited in public, in the halls of royal and noble residences. By casting herself as God's holy maiden and a heroine in the mould of her forbears, all in the sight of her people, she could ensure that she had the support of her Christian neighbours and anybody who might have harboured doubts about the justness of her cause and her actions. As she did not have anybody to write a biography of her, she had to find another way to enhance her reputation. Thus, one of the most interesting and unusual poems in the Anglo-Saxon corpus may be seen as an attempt by the Lady of the Mercians and her supporters to create and promote her legend.

13

SHIELD MAIDEN
916–JUNE 918

Æthelflæd is best known, if she is even known at all, as a legendary warrior woman. The concept of such a woman has grown so popular in depictions of the Middle Ages that virtually every movie or TV series now has at least one weapon-wielding female. More specifically it is women of certain cultures, specifically 'Celtic' and Viking, who are most often cast as warriors because of the popularity of stories like that of the earlier Boudicca. The warrior woman, especially in the Middle Ages, has become a popular trope, but the figure is more problematic for historians.

Controversially, there is little direct evidence of warrior women in the earliest centuries of the Viking Age. There is evidence that Danish settlers may well have bought their womenfolk with them, or even taken in local women. These women would have worked as tradespeople with their husbands, although it should be said that this was not unique to Scandinavian women, as we know women of various nationalities worked in such professions in the later Middle Ages. Norse Mythology and religion does seem to provide many examples of powerful martial women, such as the Valkyries. However, many of the most important Norse Sagas were not written down until the twelfth and thirteenth centuries, and although they are fascinating they are retrospective and often highly fictionalised representations of the distant Viking past. Viking women may have had great opportunities for travel and exploration with their menfolk, and on occasion did take a leading role when circumstances required it of them, but the idea that they enjoyed more rights and freedom than other European women is open to question. It is possible that they may have taken part in warfare on occasion, but the notion that Viking women were fearsome armour-clad, sword-wielding warriors as a matter of routine seems to be more myth than fact. In reality they were probably no more likely to take up arms than any other medieval woman (as will be shown below, this was not necessarily uncommon in some situations), and were just as apt to adopt traditional roles as wives, mothers and keepers of the household.[1]

There is also one other misconception that ought to be addressed here: the idea that it was entirely unacceptable for Christian women in the Middle Ages to take any role in warfare. After all, Joan of Arc was not burned at the stake for wearing men's clothes and donning armour – she was burned for heresy, and the main charge against her was that she claimed to communicate directly with the saints. Throughout the Middle Ages, there were examples of women in Europe and beyond who assumed roles of leadership and, according to some chroniclers, even donned armour and fought. Between the eleventh and twelfth centuries there were several such women, like Matilda of Canossa or Matilda of Tuscany (1046–1115), Sichelgaita of Salerno (1040–90), Isabel of Conches (b. *c.* 1070) and reportedly several others. Of them, Matilda stands out as the only example of a woman who is actually said to have been trained to use weapons. Her career is also a truly fascinating example of what a medieval woman could do if she did not have the protection of a husband, brother or father. Born in 1046 in northern Italy to Boniface III, Marquis of Tuscany, and Beatrice of Lorraine, she was her parents' third child. Alongside her rumoured training at arms, she is reported to have enjoyed a high level of more conventional education, mastering three languages. Her father was assassinated when she was about six years old, and after the deaths of her mother and siblings she became the sole heiress to her parents' lands. Though she had married before her mother's death, her only known child, a daughter, died in infancy the year she was born, 1071, and her husband followed in 1076 when she was only thirty. The death of her husband also brought her a substantial land inheritance and the title Matilda of Canossa, which was based on the family name of her late husband. Matilda is most famous for her exploits in a conflict between the papacy and the monarchs of Europe that spanned the eleventh and twelfth centuries. She not only sided with Pope Gregory VII, but was by all accounts one of his most ardent supporters. Her involvement in the war resulted from the extensive and strategically important lands that she held. 'On her husband's death,' reported William of Malmesbury, 'she defended his dukedom against the Emperor, especially in Italy.' Her actions certainly pleased the Pope, who offered her remission of sins for her actions much in the way that his successor was to do for those who went on Crusade. William of Malmesbury wrote of the help she gave to the pontiff, and described her as a woman 'unmindful of her sex' who 'led into battle, woman as she was, the columns of men clad in mail'. Her biographer claimed that she went into battle clad in armour herself. Her role in the conflict famously culminated in a famous incident in which Emperor Henry IV himself submitted to the pontiff barefoot at Matilda's castle with the great lady in attendance. The submission had come about in no small part due to her efforts.[2]

Matilda shows us that it was not impossible for a woman to have been given martial training (provided what her biographer said about her was true). Indulgent or conscientious parents may have been willing to allow such a thing in certain circumstances. Of course, the story may have been invented to explain her later military exploits but it would hardly have been possible for a woman to use weapons without some training and practice. Three centuries after Matilda's death, another woman, Christine de Pisan, would write that it was fitting for lady to 'know how to use weapons and be familiar with everything that pertains to them, so that she might be ready to command her men if the need arises. She should know how to launch an attack or defend against one, if the situation calls for it.'[3]

Our second example is Sichelgaita of Salerno. A close contemporary of Matilda, she was the Lombard wife of Robert Guiscard, the Norman conqueror of Sicily. Her role in warfare was reported by one of the most famous female historians of the Middle Ages, Anna Komnene, daughter of the Byzantine Emperor Alexios I Komnenos. A story was told, reported Anna, that Sichelgaita had accompanied her husband on campaign, as she was wont to do, and in a battle against Byzantine forces was said to have seen the men running. When her admonition to 'halt and be men' failed, brave Sichelgaita is said to have 'grabbed a long spear' and charged at the runaways. The sight of the tall, muscular and possibly armour-clad woman unsurprisingly brought the men 'to their senses'. Anna seems to have grudgingly admired Sichelgaita, even though she was of a race Anna considered to be barbarian and was fighting against her people, the Byzantines.[4]

Moving beyond these two redoubtable Italian-born ladies, there is the third and final example. Isabel of Conches was a Norman woman who resided in England. She came to the attention of one of the main Anglo-Norman chroniclers of her age, Orderic Vitalis, who recounted how she would ride out 'armed as a knight amongst the knights, and she showed no less courage amongst the knights in hauberk then did the maid Camilla'. The fighting that she was involved in, however, came about because of a feud between Isabel's husband and the husband of another local noblewoman, Helewise, for whom Orderic did not have a good word. Incidentally, Isabel retired to a nunnery in her later life, an act which earned her further commendation from the chronicler.[5]

What these examples show is that, two centuries after Æthelflæd's life, it was more than possible for women to be involved in warfare, sometimes even alongside their husbands. This action was unusual enough to warrant comment from chroniclers, but common enough for there to have been three or four such women who were contemporaries or close contemporaries with one another. Whether or not their actions were approved of depended on the context and the sides which they chose to take. Matilda was a loyal servant of the Pope, and so writers who supported him spoke very well of her. Isabel of Conches was seen has having right on her side, rather than being the aggressor in the feud between her family and her neighbours. Sichelgaita proved more controversial, and was at one point accused of poisoning her husband. We only know about her military exploits because they came to the notice of an intelligent and curious Byzantine princess who wrote a book about the events of her time. There were others, too. Back in the tenth century, Gerberga, the wife of the Ottonian king Louis IV d'Outremer, 'led the defence of Laon' when her husband was in prison. Later, during her regency, she accompanied her son on campaign and 'helped direct the sieges of Dijon and other towns'. The rule seems to have been straightforward: if a woman had no choice but to fight to defend her home, her land and her people and to avenge the wrongs done to them, then her cause was deemed just and acceptable, all the more if she was forced into such a situation because she had no man to protect her. Such a woman was not unnatural or vicious, she was simply a good leader. She would do even better if she was seen to have been fighting a holy and righteous cause, for instance in a war for the Pope against his enemies, or defending Christian lands against the ravages of pagan Vikings.[6]

Before 916, Æthelflæd had only been involved in one major military engagement that we know of: the siege of Chester, nearly ten years before. There was also the possibly fictitious attack on her wedding party. She could only have learned about warfare from the men around her, from her father during childhood and then from her husband and brother in later life, as well as any advisers and deputies amongst her ealdormen and thegns, the military elite of her kingdom. We simply do not know if, like Matilda nearly two centuries later, she had any kind of formal training to use weapons or bear armour. Most historians have concluded that it is unlikely, and that the nature of her leadership probably did not involve personally fighting in the front line. Perhaps, like Joan of Arc over 500 years later, she donned armour for protection when she acted as a figurehead – it has been shown that Joan was often quite a passive figure when it came to the actual fighting and finer details of warfare, many important strategic decisions being made by her commanders. This does not seem to have been the case with Æthelflæd, as there is every indication, as we shall see, that Æthelflæd took the initiative, as well as a more active and decisive role in planning and command during her military engagements. Æthelflæd was known to 'command the army on horseback' as well as leading them into battle. She would certainly have been taught to ride, as this was a skill common to most of the social and military elite. At one time, riding a horse and bearing a spear had been the mark of a warrior. It has long been said that the Anglo-Saxons did not fight on horseback (although this hypothesis has been brought into question), but they certainly used them for transport and to ride to the site of battle.[7]

An interesting perspective on this matter comes from the suggestion that Æthelflæd was the inspiration for the character of Eowyn in J. R. R. Tolkien's *The Lord of the Rings*. Her character had learned the arts of war out of sheer necessity to assist in the defence of her people. It is not entirely outside the realms of possibility that the young Æthelflæd may have received rudimentary training to get used to a javelin-like short spear or sword (although these were almost exclusively high-status items), and perhaps even a shield because it was deemed necessary in the precarious situation her family was facing, perhaps even at her own request. Such weapons may have been useful to a mounted commander who presented something of a sitting target to enemy soldiers. So, it is likely that she donned some kind of armour for her own protection and rode out amongst her troops. Thus, it is also likely that she carried or wore a weapon of some description for symbolic reasons (to represent her nobility and rank).

However, learning to wield a spear or sword was a far cry from fighting on the front lines in a shield wall. There is no evidence that Æthelflæd ever did such a thing. It would have taken years of training and practice, and it might have been deemed that this final step was simply too dangerous. When she is described in military situations in the sources it is almost always in a leadership capacity as a sort of general, ordering or directing her army, but not actually among her thegns in the vicious struggle at the gates or walls of a town. More often than not, she seems to have succeeded by outthinking, outmanoeuvring, and sometimes outsmarting her enemies, even if this meant occasionally resorting to underhand tactics. Although it is something of a cliché, Æthelflæd made the best advantage of her sex by using her brains and not just relying on brawn to win her battles. When she needed military force, her army were there to provide it.

One of her most famous military actions, in the summer of 916, was one that none of the Mercians had planned for. The *Anglo-Saxon Chronicle* records that 'in this year … on the 16th of June Abbot Ecgberht who had done nothing to deserve it was slain along with his companions'. We know almost nothing about this Abbot Egbert (to use the modernised version of the name), where he came from or why he was killed. What becomes obvious from reading the rest of the passage in the chronicle is that he was in Wales. What he was doing there we also do not know, as his existence is not recorded anywhere except in this passage in the chronicle. He may have been on a diplomatic mission or personal errand at the behest of the Lady of the Mercians. It was not unknown for royals or great lords to send out prominent prelates on such business, especially if it related to their church or jurisdiction in some way, and of course abbots were often great men of high status themselves.[8]

There seems to be a lot that is left unsaid in the chronicle's account, however. Edward and Æthelflæd's fortress-building programme had not just encroached into Danish territory, but was also pushing at the borders of Welsh land with foundations at places like Shrewsbury and Hereford. There may well have been tension that we do not know about between Mercia and some of the Welsh kingdoms. We know that Rhodri Mawr, king of Gwynedd, and one of his sons were killed in battle against the 'Saxons' in the 870s. The *Anglo-Saxon Chronicle* shows that Æthelflæd's response was swift, decisive and ruthless. Within three days, we are told, she had raised an army and marched them into Wales to storm a place called Brecenanmere. The site is identified as being at Llangorse Lake itself, and the work of various historians can allow us to elaborate more on the individual ruler who was involved in the debacle surrounding Abbot Egbert's death. He was one Tewdr (the original Welsh version of the name we would render Tudor), king of Brycheiniog (modern-day Brecknockshire). There were two kings of this name that could have been alive at the right time. He may have been the one identified by Asser who had submitted to King Alfred years before, or his descendant Tewdyr ap Griffi ap Elise. When they reached their destination, Æthelflæd and her troops burned a crannog – a timber structure constructed on an artificial island typical to the Celtic nations of Britain – that belonging to King Tewdyr. Over thirty people were taken hostage, including the wife of the king himself, although Tewdyr was not present, perhaps having escaped. That was probably for the best, as the whole event was thoroughly humiliating.

It was a calculated act, but not one accompanied by unnecessary brutality. Æthelflæd could have inflicted more casualties or ravaged the land, but she chose not to. The point of the exercise had been to force a rapprochement and force the submission of Tewdyr. He did later submit, and presumably got his wife back when he did so.[9]

Obviously, the murder of an abbot was a shocking act which could not be ignored, but Æthelflæd's response may seem extreme. It is likely that the people behind the murder were men of the kingdom of Brycheiniog, and they may even have been known to King Tewdyr. They had killed an official and subject of the Lady of the Mercians who was supposed to have been under her protection (and may have been acting at her behest), and King Tewdyr had presumably done nothing about it. He had not rooted them out, delivered them up nor offered any kind of compensation (although we may question whether he had time to do so, only three days after the act). Æthelflæd, probably quite understandably, took the matter personally. It undermined her authority as a ruler, as well as depriving her and the men of her kingdom of their abbot. Did Tewdyr believe that the matter could be overlooked, and he could turn a blind eye simply because Mercia was ruled by a woman? Did he think her weak and feeble because of her sex? We do not know if the king had submitted to her as he had submitted to her father. In fact, many of the Welsh rulers seem to have shown more inclination towards her brother in Wessex, the man whom Asser had unashamedly labelled a tyrant to his Welsh people. She was nonetheless determined to uphold her reputation, and to show her adversaries that she was not a woman to be crossed. The incident at Llangorse those shows Æthelflæd at her most forceful. That she personally took control of the operation and marched at the head of her soldiers also reveals the nature of her leadership, which she also brought to the campaigns of the following two years.

The *Annals of Ireland* recount another incident recorded as having taken place in 914 which does not appear in the *Anglo-Saxon Chronicle*. We have already heard how the Irish source reports that the Lady of the Mercians made a mutually beneficial alliance with the Britons of Strathclyde and the Scots, her northern neighbours, that year. Before that, it records how an army of Danes and Hiberno-Norse Vikings 'came again to attack the Saxons', and the 'Saxons' responded accordingly:

> A hard and ferocious battle was fought between them, and there was great energy and heat and contention on both sides. Much noble blood was spilled in this battle; nevertheless, it was the Saxons who won victory and spoils after massacring the pagans. For the king of the pagans was taken ill, and he was carried out of the battle to a forest nearby, and he died there.[10]

The *Annals of Ireland* account goes on to say that the army was led by formidable a Saxon queen, presumably Æthelflæd, who, not content to allow her enemies to escape, ordered her soldiers to cut down the trees and go after their foes so 'the pagans were slaughtered by the queen … and her fame spread in all directions'. It is after this we get the first mention of the alliance between Æthelflæd and the Scots and Britons. There are various problems with the account in the Irish annals, one being that the date is almost certainly wrong. The forging of the alliance is usually dated to 917, not 914. The other problem is that the account is not corroborated by other sources, or rather this passage has been interpreted as referring to the Battle of Corbridge, which is mentioned in various sources as having been fought in 918, but they make absolutely no reference to the presence of Æthelflæd. This seems strange given that this military engagement was supposed to have made her famous to all the people in the surrounding regions. The jarl Ottir, a notorious raider and ally of Ragnar who came from Ireland, and who according to the account above died in 914, is mentioned later on in other accounts, which makes matters even more complicated.[11]

The Annals of the Four Masters, compiled from various early Irish annals, contains this entry for 916: 'Oitir and the foreigners went from Loch Dachaech to Alba; and Constantine, the son of Aedh, gave them battle, and Oitir was slain, with a slaughter of the foreigners along with him.'[12] The *Annals of Ulster* gives this more detailed account:

> The foreigners of Loch dá Chaech, i.e. Ragnall, king of the dark foreigners, and the two jarls, Oitir and Gragabai, forsook Ireland and proceeded afterwards against the men of Scotland. The men of Scotland, moreover, moved against them and they met on the bank of the Tyne in northern Saxonland. The heathens formed themselves into four battalions: a battalion with Gothfrith grandson of Ímar, a battalion with the two jarls, and a battalion with the young lords. There was also a battalion in ambush with Ragnall, which the men of Scotland did not see. The Scotsmen routed the three battalions which they saw, and made a very great slaughter of the heathens, including Oitir and Gragabai. Ragnall, however, then attacked in the rear of the Scotsmen, and made a

> slaughter of them, although none of their kings or earls was cut off. Nightfall caused the battle to be broken off.[13]

Here at least there is a reference to something happening near to English territory. It is believed that this passage refers also refers to the battle of Corbridge. We know about a battle of that name fought in 918 between the forces of King Constantine of Scotland and invaders led by Ragnall ua Ímair. The battle also involved a Northumbrian lord by the name of Ealdred. His father, Eadwulf, had been called 'king of the Saxons of the North' but Ealdred himself seems to have been the Lord of Bamburgh rather than an officially recognised king.

Ottir is only mentioned once in the *Anglo-Saxon Chronicle*, under the entry for the following year, 917 (or 918, as there is some confusion of dates here as well):

> Here in this year a great raiding ship-army came over here from the south from Brittany, and with them two jarls, Ohtor and Hroald, and went around west until they got into the mouth of the Severn, and raided in Wales everywhere by the sea, where it suited them, and took Cameleac, bishop in Archenfield, and led him with them to the ships; and then King Edward ransomed him back for 40 pounds. Then after that the whole raiding-army went up and wanted to go on a raid against Archenfield; then they were met by the men from Hereford and from Gloucester and from the nearest strongholds, and fought against them and put them to flight, and killed the jarl Hroald and the other Jarl Ohtor's brother and a great part of the raiding-army, and drove them into an enclosure and besieged them there until they gave them hostages, that they would leave King Edward's domain.[14]

This is the only account which suggests that Ottir actually strayed into English territory, or went anywhere near Mercia. We can see that the accounts in the various sources are somewhat confused and conflicting. It may be that the passage in the Irish annals actually reflects something that took place during this attack. We have already seen how chroniclers and annalists seem to have been enamoured of the Lady of the Mercians, and the writer of these annals seems to have been particularly keen on stories about the 'most famous Queen of the Saxons', and so he embellished his account to include the woman who had become a figure of myth across the Irish Sea.

It is interesting that the *Anglo-Saxon Chronicle* does not tell us who was actually leading the men from Gloucester and the 'nearest strongholds' in the passage cited above. The implication is that it was Edward, but Gloucester was a Mercian city, and if there were Mercians forces in the fight, should we consider the possibility that Æthelflæd might have been leading them? This account is contained in the 'A' version of the chronicle, which was composed in Winchester or another part of Wessex. Unlike the Mercian Register it pays her little attention, so it makes sense to assume that if she did play a major role in the engagement of 917 her exploits would not have been mentioned, particularly if she played a decisive role in pursuing and subduing the enemy after the main attack. Such ruthlessness might not sit easily with our picture of Æthelflæd, but as we have seen above, she could be ruthless when she needed to be. She probably did not trust the Vikings when they retreated, nor their promises to never return, and wanted to ensure that they posed no threat to her realm.

The account in the *Anglo-Saxon Chronicle* would explain why Ottir was alive after 914 and went on to participate at Corbridge in 918, where his ally Ragnall was victorious. A final explanation of events is that, while any suggestion that Æthelflæd was involved in that battle is a later myth or confusion of events, what lies behind it might be the fact that she entered a type of coalition with the northern powers. As part of this, they were willing to attack certain targets at her suggestion. It does sound plausible. This coalition would have complemented her chain of fortresses, and would have been useful for assistance and protection. Perhaps Æthelflæd also intended for the combined might of Mercia and the northern kingdoms to take on the Viking kingdom established at York? We will hear more about Æthelflæd's dealings with the kingdom of York later in this chapter.[15] What is clear is that from 916 her military engagements were no longer simply defensive. The following year, 917, she went on the offensive and led her army into Derby.

Derby was one of the so-called Five Boroughs, the name of the region of Danish Mercia comprising Leicester, Derby, Nottingham, Lincoln and Stamford and the surrounding areas. It was created as part of the Danelaw in the 870s after the division of the kingdom under Ceolwulf. There was a Saxon settlement of a different name in Derby before the Danes came, but the present name is of Norse origin, with the common suffix of -by. The name may have meant something like 'deer village', denoting a village or settlement where deer were found; it probably marked it out as a good hunting ground. After nearly forty years under Danish occupation the inhabitants may well have been what we would call second- or third-generation migrants, having probably married into the local population. There is no evidence either way to suggest that that they wanted to be liberated from Danish rule, or sent any invitation. Nevertheless,

Æthelflæd came and brought her army with her. It made perfect strategic sense to attack, considering it was so close to her newly established town at Stafford and the newly restored Tamworth; if the Danes were likely to base an army anywhere, it would have been there. At least, that might have been how she saw the situation, and justified her action. With this in mind, she made a pre-emptive strike.

At Derby, as at Tamworth, we are told that her actions were completed 'with the help of God'. In this case, the divine assistance was particularly needed as, judging from the account in the *Anglo-Saxon Chronicle*, Derby was not easily taken and the fighting was particularly fierce. It is easy to imagine a scenario similar to the one reported in the Irish annals about the siege of Chester eleven years before, in which the defenders threw everything they had at the attackers – quite literally. One passage says that 'four thegns who were very dear to her were slain within the gates', which suggests there was also much close-quarters combat in an area that would have restricted the movements of both sides. The Victorian work *A History of the County of Derby* contained a detailed account of the taking of the city, saying that it involved the storming of the 'castle' and its gates. This attempt was initially unsuccessful but eventually the main gate of the city was burned, allowing the Saxon army to pour in and overrun the place. The same source also mentions that there was a fugitive Welsh prince within the city who had allied himself with the Vikings.[16] There were no castles in Æthelflæd's day, but the account in the *Anglo-Saxon Chronicle* does show that the design and construction of the Viking fort may have been like that of Æthelflæd's own burhs and those of her father and brother. For supposed heathen savages, the Danes were rather good builders, capable of constructing fortified settlements with gates which had to be taken by direct assault. Of course, it is also possible that the Danes may have reused and repaired some part of the Roman fortifications that once existed in Derby and so the fighting may have been at its thickest somewhere near the remains site of the fort of Derventio, or 'Little Chester' as it is sometimes known.

When Æthelflæd achieved victory, one of her first acts seems to have been to secure the relics of St Alkmund, another local saint who had already had a church dedicated to him in Shrewsbury. There is also a church with the same dedication in Derby today, but Æthelflæd chose to rescue him just as she had saved Oswald before him, and is believed to have translated his relics to her foundation in Shrewsbury. Part of what is thought to have been an original sarcophagus of the saint from his original shrine may be viewed in Derby City Museum today. Of course, the taking of Derby should not be read as a religious mission to rescue a saint (that was merely an extra bonus); it was about securing her authority in the region, in this case by conquest (or reconquest, as it was seen). We are told that because of her victory, Derby and all of the surrounding areas which belonged to it submitted to her. It was a decisive and complete submission, without any mention of the exchange of hostages or negotiations. The fact that Derby is less than 30 miles away from Repton, which had been the original base of the Great Heathen Army in the 870s, is something Æthelflæd must have known. The Danish force that had camped there was the same one that had deposed her uncle King Burgred and aunt Æthelswith nearly forty years before.[17]

Now she had avenged them in the most potent way, retaking one of the five most important cities in the Danelaw. But it had come at a cost to her men and, to a certain extent, to her personally. The term used for her fallen men also hints at something of the nature of the relationship that Æthelflæd had with the military men of her kingdom. They were *besorge*, or 'beloved' to her. This term reveals something about the nature of the relationship Æthelflæd established as a female lord with her military retainers and soldiers. The word had 'implications of care and anxiety as well as love and care'. Æthelflæd wanted to be a ruler who not only cherished her people, but cared about her men and genuinely regretted the deaths of those who gave their lives in her cause. Her father had used the word *besorgest* in his translation of Boethius to describe the 'most beloved favourite of a ruler'.[18]

This raises the very real possibility that the men in question were veteran fighters who had served the Lady of the Mercians for many years, and that she knew them well; perhaps they had discussed plans with her in her tent, or attended her on the marches around Mercia. Many thegns and ordinary soldiers must have died in her other military engagements, but that fact that these men's deaths were mentioned in the Mercian Register suggests that their loss was felt keenly by the Lady of the Mercians. As a woman who would almost certainly not have taken any part in the fighting on the front line, but who was the figurehead and leader of the kingdom, Æthelflæd would have had to take the trouble to foster good relationships with her military men – the types of relationships that had been celebrated in heroic literature or historical records of past ages, where men were bound to the lord they called 'beloved' and were prepared to die for him.[19]

Derby had been bought with blood, and Æthelflæd's victory could have put her and her army in a very vulnerable position.

They were now in Danish territory, and were surrounded by the rest of the Five Boroughs, whose leaders could have raised forces against her, as well as the Vikings of Northumbria. Her brother Edward was engaged in his own campaign, during which he captured Tempsford in Essex and conquered East Anglia. Had she been attacked, he may not have been able to respond in time and she would probably have had to retreat back to Mercia or Tamworth. Yet this did not happen. Perhaps the mauling at Tettenhall seven years before meant that the Danes still did not feel strong enough to take on the Lady of the Mercians and risk the wrath of her brother.

Next she turned to another of the Five Boroughs: Leicester. The following year, after the capture of Derby, she took her forces to the city. Remarkably, we are told by the *Anglo-Saxon Chronicle* that 'she peacefully got in control of the stronghold and Leicester, and the most part of the raiding armies that belonged to it were subjected'. Unlike the battle for Derby, the takeover of Leicester was peaceful and apparently bloodless. An action that gets only a cursory mention in the chronicles was, in fact, probably one of the most significant of Æthelflæd's entire career. In her forty-seventh year, it appears that her power and reputation had reached such a zenith that the Vikings and ruling men of Leicester were prepared to submit to her without putting up a fight. Whilst the chronicle's account suggested that her brother struggled to take one city after another, usually by storm, battle or siege, the Lady of the Mercians had simply marched in and her enemies had submitted. Did she strike such terror into their hearts, or command such respect, that her mere presence was enough of a persuasion? Not necessarily. Æthelflæd had been engaging in negotiations with disaffected groups in the region for some time. The pause after

Derby had given her ample time to set up the communication network that she would have needed. Stansbury suggests that Æthelflæd had always been better at pursuing diplomatic and peaceful solutions than her brother. She could, and sometimes did, subdue her opponents by aggressive means when the situation required it, but she seems to have been just as good at winning them over with compromise and negotiation. She had shown this many years before at Chester when, whatever her own opinions may have been, she allowed Ingimund to settle in her kingdom and was happy to allow him and his settlers to live a quiet and peaceful life. If the Irish annals are to be believed, it was the provocation of the attack on Chester that caused her and her husband to act decisively and drive his forces out of the city.[20]

Hence, the submission of Leicester should probably be seen as an arranged handover, resulting from disaffection as well as fear of the Hiberno-Norse Vikings under leaders like Ragnall, who were gaining in strength, and perhaps even the advancing armies of her brother from the south. The inhabitants of Leicester had lost faith in their rulers and, seeing danger closing in from all sides, decided to throw in their lot with the best and most magnanimous ruler they could find – and that happened to be Æthelflæd, the woman who had been undefeated on the battlefield since 911, who had restored the fortunes and honour of her kingdom, who was loved and respected by her people so much that they had chosen her to rule them. More than this, she was prepared to be merciful in victory, accepting a bloodless submission in return for loyalty and obedience to her law and rule. In return, she could offer the kind of stability and protection that she had bought to Mercia. In some way, she must have been greatly relieved at the way the events in Leicester had turned out. No wonder she was described again as succeeding 'with God's help'.[21]

Now approaching her forty-eighth birthday, the Lady of the Mercians had ruled her people for over thirty years, and had shouldered the burden of independent leadership for seven. In that time her career had been fruitful, but with hard and arduous rounds of marching, building, fighting and defending, overseeing and managing smaller details. The joint strategy of her and her brother had resulted in long spells of siege warfare instead of the more traditional battles, and sieges were always hard. The Lady of the Mercians must have given thanks to God that her latest venture had been quick, easy and painless, especially after Derby. War had defined her life and claimed so much, including the life of her husband, the uncle she had barely known, her cousin Æthelwold and so many others she had known and liked. It may well be true that she did not like fighting, especially in her later years, and avoided it except when she deemed it absolutely necessary.[22] Of course, she had her nephew Æthelstan by her side, and he was of age and fully able to lead men in war. The boy, by then really a young man in his early twenties, has been described as 'of middling height, slim build and flaxen hair with piercing blue eyes'. Her relationship to him may well have been so close that she considered him to be her adopted son. His training in battle and at her court prepared him for power, which would become apparent a few years later.[23]

Æthelflæd was at the height of her power, ruling all the land north of London to the borders of Northumbria and the territory of the Scots, from Shrewsbury and the Severn in the west to Leicester in the east. She had recaptured much of the former territory of the old kingdom of Mercia and restored its ancient capital at Tamworth alongside many other ancient cities. She had strengthened the economy, the defensive system, education and religion – in the latter case not only by building great churches but also by restoring some of the historical saints of Mercia, an act which helped to restore ancient pride and dignity. She had, in short, done everything for Mercia that her father had done in Wessex before her. No doubt he and her husband would have been proud of her.

Yet her work was still not entirely done. When her brother captured Nottingham and rebuilt the defences in Stamford, four of the Five Boroughs were effectively back under English control. One kingdom remained, with one of its main centres of power represented by another city that dated back to Roman times. The kingdom of Northumbria had been the first great Christian kingdom of the Anglo-Saxons, and one of its main cities was York. Nearly fifty years before it had been taken by the Danes, and it had been a centre of Danish Northumbria since then. They changed the city's name from the Anglo-Saxon Eoforwic (derived from the Latin Eboracum) to Yorvik, from which the modern name is derived. Archaeology has shown how the city was a wealthy and bustling trading centre at the time, with the various commodities traded including slaves.

Then, in the summer of 918, in the greatest triumph of her career yet, it emerged that Viking York was prepared to submit to the Lady of the Mercians. The submission was driven by a group of Christian Northumbrians who were opposed to paganism and, like their fellows at Leicester, worried about the progress of the pagan Ragnall. They therefore chose to throw in their lot with the pious Christian lady who seemed to have the favour of God, and she chose to receive their submission. The final great bastion of Danish rule in England was about to be reclaimed. The next entry in the Mercian Register recorded the savage irony that prevented forever the Lady of the Mercians from receiving the submission of York in person. It tells us, 'The folk of York promised her ... that they would be at her disposition. But very quickly after they had done that, she departed, twelve days after Midsummer inside Tamworth.' That is, on 12 June 918, Æthelflæd, daughter of Alfred and Lady of the Mercians, died at the age of approximately forty-eight in 'the eighth year that she held control of Mercia in rightful lordship'. She was buried near to her husband 'in the east side chapel of St Peter's church [St Oswald's Priory]'. A passage of just four lines records the death of the greatest female leader of her time.[24]

14

THE LADY AND THE STONE 918–919

Æthelflæd, Lady of the Mercians, was dead at the height of her power. The events of the last few years, the constant marches and campaigning, must have taken their toll. However, the death does seem to have come as a surprise. It is possible it resulted from the sudden onset of a health condition, such as a stroke or even a major disease; we simply do not know. Æthelflæd was taken to her great foundation, St Oswald's, Gloucester, where she was buried near to her husband. Her daughter and nephew, as well as all the great men and women of her kingdom, would have followed as a funeral retinue. Tragically, the former abbey stands in ruins today, a victim of the English Civil War, but by that time it was little more than a parish church. The place had fallen into obscurity many centuries before, with many of its landed endowments taken away and used elsewhere. We do not know how long the tombs of the Lord and Lady of the Mercians survived, but there is nothing left of them today.

Everything about her rise to power had been unprecedented (right down to the Mercian witan choosing a woman to rule over them), and the same would be true of the events following her death. She was the first female ruler to be succeeded by another female of her own blood. Ælfwyn, her only surviving child by Æthelred, became the second Lady of the Mercians. Ælfwyn's brief career is even harder to track than that of her mother. She was chosen to succeed her mother precisely because of who she was: the representative of the alliance between Mercia and Wessex, which had spanned three generations, an alliance forged of necessity but tempered in blood on the battlefield. She clearly had some involvement in the business of government, judging from the way her name appeared in charters from the first two decades of the tenth century, and it is hard to believe she would not have learned anything from her intelligent and capable mother. She grew up in 'an atmosphere which promoted education', probably attending the same court school as her cousin (or shared a tutor), and so was at least as learned as her mother.[1]

Other personal details are not known for certain, even her age. Some historians and writers believe she was born late in her parents' marriage and was little more than a teenager when her mother died, while others maintain that she was born within the first few years and must have been in her late twenties or even early thirties. The latter position is favoured here, but there are some reasons to consider the former, one being that Ælfwyn was not, to the best of our knowledge, ever married. It does seem strange that a thirty-year-old woman of royal blood who had not entered holy orders or taken a vow of chastity would have been unmarried at the time.

It also seems strange that Æthelflæd did not arrange a suitable match for her daughter to continue the line and create possible heirs, but could this have been another aspect of the grand dynastic strategy in which her mother had apparently been involved? We have already seen that having only one child may have been a conscious decision on Æthelflæd's part, using abstinence as birth control to avoid producing a male heir who could thwart attempts to unite Mercia and Wessex. Did she do the same thing with her daughter, never making arrangements to find a suitable husband so that, even if she succeeded her, she would die childless and the unification would become inevitable? Or was there some marriage arranged that simply went unmentioned for some reason? Whatever the case, any plans that Æthelflæd may have had for her daughter's future would be nullified by the events in the months after her death.[2]

Ælfwyn may have been competent in the usual business of ruling, and perhaps her parents had even ensured that she had the education and training to follow them. However, just like when her father had died, the situation on her mother's death would have placed Ælfwyn in a difficult situation. Her mother had achieved so much, and she was expected to step into her shoes. As has already been stated, Æthelflæd had manged to secure a promise of submission for the Vikings at York. As was common with such promises, it did not outlive the ruler to whom it was made. The Vikings were not bound to keep any such promise to the new ruler of Mercia, who was an untried young woman. Perhaps they chose not to keep the promise, but it is more likely that the movers and shakers at York were overtaken by events. Æthelflæd's actions in the north, the two burhs she built on or near the Mersey and the northern borders of her kingdom (Runcorn, Scargeat), had largely been in response to the threat of the Vikings from Ireland.

In the year of Æthelflæd's death Ragnall defeated an army of Scots, Britons and English at the battle of Corbridge, which allowed him to set himself up in the north, and by 919 he was king of York. Æthelflæd's last act had failed, and then her brother came to Tamworth where, we are told, 'all the nation of Mercia which had previously been subject to Æthelflæd submitted to him'. It is hard to know whether this happened before or at the same time that Ælfwyn, after having been in power for less than six months, was 'deprived of all control in Mercia and led into Wessex three weeks before Christmas' by none other than her uncle. This act earned King Edward the condemnation of later chroniclers and observers, but his motivations are worth examining.[3]

Traditionally, it is believed that he took power to stop Mercia from asserting its independence and to bring the kingdom firmly under West Saxon control for good. If the order of events from the *Anglo-Saxon Chronicle* is correct, then the submission of the Mercians to Edward happened before the deposition of Ælfwyn. Did the Mercians hope to keep some measure of independence by retaining their own ruler despite technically submitting to a West Saxon king? Alfred had happily allowed her father to rule Mercia when he was technically the overlord, after all. Edward, it seems, was not so happy with such an arrangement, even when it involved the daughter of his sister and his former comrade-in-arms. Yet it has been suggested that perhaps the Mercians assented to the deposition of Ælfwyn because she did not prove as capable a ruler as her mother, and because she had failed to consolidate her mother's achievements and victories. The sources do not tell us of any Mercian involvement in the struggle against Ragnall during the summer and autumn of 918.

Her mother would have taken action, probably leading her armies again with her brother and her allies to the north, so why did her daughter apparently do nothing? The victory of Ragnall and his seizure of York 'introduced and entirely new dynamic into the political alignment of eastern England' which left young Ælfwyn without the credibility 'to retain the Lordship of Mercia even if she had her uncle's overall authority'. This does bear out the argument above, that she simply wasn't suited to the job and Edward thus took matters into his own hands. This was harsh, but Edward was from a fiercely pragmatic family that had often survived by putting political and military necessity before personal sentiment.[4]

Another suggestion is that Edward feared that without his direct intervention Ælfwyn might have been tempted to join a northern alliance with her mother's old allies in Scotland and Strathclyde, and perhaps even with Ragnall, which would prove detrimental to him. Æthelflæd would hardly have tolerated such an arrangement, which would have torn her family and ancient ties between Mercia and Wessex apart, but can we speak for her daughter? Could she even have considered breaking with tradition and seeking a marriage alliance in one of those regions? It does not seem likely, but considering how Edward sought to consolidate the English position in the north it does seem that he was worried about potential hostilities there.[5]

In the two years following his sister's death, Edward first secured the submission of English Mercia (as mentioned). At the same time, we are told three Welsh kings also 'sought him as their lord'. Then he ordered Nottingham rebuilt, and 'all the people that was settled in the land of Mercia, both English and Danish, turned to him'. The following year he took his forces to Thelwall, and from there he sent another army to see to the fortifications in Manchester and man them. By 919 he had taken charge of the Mercian army, as well as that of Wessex. His most active and successful year in this northern campaign was 920, when he built another fortification in Nottingham on the south side of the river, and then another further south in Bakewell. Then, all at once, the Scots, the Britons of Strathclyde and the rulers of Northumbria, Ragnald and 'Eadwulf's sons' and 'all those who live in Northumbria, both English and Danish and Norwegians and others ... chose him as their father and Lord'. Other manuscripts of the *Anglo-Saxon Chronicle* record this as having happened some years later, but the event is still the same. All the north had submitted to Edward. We are not told in the pro-Wessex 'A' version if the submission resulted from a battle or other hostilities, but it is still impressive. Of course, the submission of Ragnald did not stop him from becoming king of York sometime between 919 and 923, so here was one independent (or semi-independent) ruler that the king of Wessex was prepared to tolerate. It is ironic that York and Leicester had submitted to Æthelflæd to avoid this man, only for him to take power there on Edward's watch.[6]

Edward did not have everything his way, though. Later tradition records that in the year of his death, 924, Edward travelled to Mercia to quell a combined Mercian and Welsh rebellion there. The *Anglo-Saxon Chronicle* does not record this event, only that he was in Mercia when he died. It does seem too late for this rebellion to have been any kind of reaction to the deposition of Ælfwyn, so it has been speculated that this revolt was in fact a reaction to the division of Mercia into shires or just a general response to Edward's heavy-handed tactics. It is known that he had constructed a fort at Rhuddlan three years before. This was after the time of the Welsh submission, so the siting of the fortress there does raise questions. We do not know the result of this rebellion, if there was indeed any, for the next entry records the death of King Edward, which occurred on 17 July 924.[7]

The West Saxon's king's subjection of Mercia was followed by a remarkable twist of fate when Æthelstan, his firstborn illegitimate son, was proclaimed king of Mercia and crowned in Kingston-upon-Thames. Æthelstan is better known than his predecessors for another reason: he was the first acknowledged king of England. This was a remarkable and unexpected occurrence, as he was never even meant to be king of Wessex. Michael Wood has suggested that Edward intended for his firstborn son to be the ruler of Mercia, perhaps a new Lord of the Mercians, and his sister had done her job very well in educating, coaching and preparing him for a position of leadership.

Yet Edward wanted another of his sons to follow him as king of Wessex. This son, a younger half-brother of Æthelstan, was named Ælfweard. A son by Edward's second wife, he did indeed succeed his father but then died within a few weeks of his accession – one source says it was only sixteen days after. Æthelstan had already been accepted in Mercia, as was to be expected considering that he had been raised there for most of his life under their beloved Lord and Lady. Then, the death of his brother opened up an entirely new opportunity: to become king of Wessex, and unite the two remaining great Saxon kingdoms under one ruler. His path to power in Wessex was not a smooth one, however, as sources suggest that the death of his brother created a succession crisis. Many West Saxon nobles did not favour Æthelstan, who seemed more Mercian, and would have preferred to see another son of Edward and brother of the late Ælfweard on the throne. In the end, the winning candidate was the one who was most senior and had the most military experience, gained during the campaigns of his aunt, uncle and father. He was crowned in Wessex a year after his father's death, although there remained some residual opposition to him for most of his reign, and there was even a plot to kidnap and blind him before his coronation. Despite all of it, Æthelstan had finally fulfilled the ambition of his grandfather, father and aunt to unite the kingdoms of Wessex and Mercia under one king, even if he was not the person who everyone would have chosen or expected to fulfil the role. In his fifteen-year reign he brought Northumbria under his authority, finally achieving the status and title not just of king of the Anglo-Saxons like his predecessors, but king of all England.[8] During his lifetime, and for much of the Middle Ages, he was remembered and lauded as a great, warlike, pious and learned king, even more so than his grandfather.

The boy who had been raised and educated under the care of Æthelflæd and her husband succeeded to her kingdom, as well as that ruled by her father and brother. Since so many of his formative years had been spent in Mercia, it is likely Æthelstan had a close affinity with the region, and he was as close as the Mercians could get to another child of their beloved lady. Like her, he was intelligent and much given to scholarly pursuits; a poem described him as 'abundantly endowed with the holy eminence of learning'. From the legacy of his grandfather, and most likely under the tutelage of the men to whom his aunt and uncle had entrusted him, he developed his love of books. Interestingly, he also demonstrated a devotion to the saints and holy men of old, including St Oswald and the seventh-century St Aldhelm, and it is tempting to think he got this from his aunt. He was even to claim later that his half-sister was a direct descendant of the Northumbrian saint-king. There is evidence from Æthelstan's later years that he fondly remembered his surrogate parents, the Lord and Lady of the Mercians. There is a record from the thirteenth century of a charter, supposedly dating from Æthelstan's accession, which granted privileges to St Oswald's priory, and a 'pact of paternal piety which formerly he pledged with Æthelred, ealdorman of the people of the Mercians'. His aunt would no doubt have approved of his tastes, and the care he took to preserve her foundation.[9]

It is interesting to note that Æthelstan never married, and that this was his conscious choice. There have been various explanations suggested, one being that he was a closet homosexual, which seems unlikely; indeed, there is no indication of this in the evidence. Another, more plausible theory is that because of his illegitimate birth he wished to leave the throne to his legitimate brothers and their heirs after his death, a deliberate dynastic strategy with interesting parallels to the one his aunt might have enacted in Mercia before him by not choosing a husband for her daughter and not sleeping with her husband after her birth. By the time he became king of the new realm of England he was in his late twenties, and so he may have already made the decision to marry. Some may wonder why he was not considered a possible suitor for his cousin Ælfwyn. As has already been stated, it was not unknown for first cousins to marry, and such a match may have seemed to make sense in the Mercian court. It is possible that a reforming movement among the clergy brought any proposed match into doubt, but it is also known that the works of Aldhelm were popular with Alfred (and so also possibly in the Mercian court). Aldhelm was yet another seventh-century cleric and saint, once the abbot of Malmesbury and bishop of Sherborne. He had written a treatise called *De Virginate*, unsurprisingly in praise of virginity and chastity. Did works like this influence Æthelstan? He could not become a monk, but he could choose to live a chaste life, effectively taking a vow of virginity to devote himself to God *like* a monk, perhaps reinforcing his decision not to marry for spiritual as well as personal or political reasons.[10] It is said that Alfred regarded Aldhelm as his favourite poet, and his works became very popular during the Benedictine reform period in the tenth century.

One final question remains to be addressed. What happened to Ælfwyn? The twelfth-century chronicler William of Malmesbury, who is one of our main sources for the early life of Æthelstan, believed she was forced to become a nun somewhere in Wessex, and this is the explanation that is usually accepted. It does seem her most likely fate, as she simply disappears from the historical record after 919. There was nothing that Æthelstan could have done to prevent such a thing during his father's reign, and it would have done nothing for his reputation to pull his cousin out of a nunnery afterwards.

Other, darker theories have suggested foul play, but there is no evidence either way and it almost more comforting to believe the traditional explanation. Alternatively, it has been argued that Ælfwyn may have lived for several years in the West Saxon royal court before willingly retiring to a convent. This is based on the identification of one Ælfwyn who is named as a 'royal' woman in a charter of 948. If the lady in question was indeed our Ælfwyn, she would have been well into her sixties by then.

If true it would mean that she did not entirely disappear from the records, but it is equally possible that the woman in question was not her at all. No fewer than eight people called Ælfwyn are listed in the *Prosography of Anglo-Saxon England*, and the woman in question could just as well have been another lady of royal birth, perhaps the wife of one Æthelstan 'half-king', who was an East Anglian ealdorman living in the second quarter of the tenth century. Most likely, Ælfwyn, granddaughter of Alfred, last of a prestigious line and second Lady of the Mercians, spent the rest of her days in obscurity in a West Saxon abbey.[11]

15

'HEROIC ELFLEDE'

Heroic Elflede! great in martial fame,
A man in valour, woman though in name:
Thee warlike hosts, thee, nature too obey'd,
Conqu'ror o'er both, though born by sex a maid.
Chang'd be thy name, such honour triumphs bring.
A queen by title, but in deeds a king.
Heroes before the Mercian heroine quail'd:
Caesar himself to win such glory fail'd

Henry of Huntingdon[1]

In the centuries after her death, the Lady of the Mercians was remembered by her people in many legends that grew up about her. The name Æthelflæd became popular in the tenth and eleventh centuries, when it had been an obscure name before. Although she and her husband were known as the last independent rulers of Mercia, and his predecessor Ceolwulf as the last official king, there did remain in Mercia some residual sense of independence. For instance, some still referred to the 'kingdom' of Mercia long after the last king was gone and it had been subsumed into England. There was even a brief period in the tenth century when King Edgar 'the peaceable', a great-nephew of Æthelflæd, ruled with the title of 'king of the Mercians' from 957 to 959 while his brother Eadwig ruled the southern part of the kingdom. This came to an end, just as in Æthelstan's time, when his brother, who still retained the title of king of England, died the same year.[2]

Less than a century after Æthelflæd's death in 1016, the kingdom of England was conquered by Canute, the son of Svein 'Forkbeard' of Denmark. Ironically, Canute did not take the whole of the kingdom at first; he had agreed to another division whereby Wessex would be taken by his rival, the eldest son of King Æthelred 'the Unready'. That man was Edmund 'Ironside', the aforementioned ancestor of the Empress Matilda and ultimately the Plantagenet kings. This arrangement was also ended by death when Edmund was murdered a short time later. Canute and his Danish countrymen were by then quite firmly Christian, although they still raided the coasts of England and had strong connections with the north country and York. Indeed, the name of the Danelaw persisted in the records a long time after it had ceased to exist as a political entity.

Of course, fifty years after Canute England was conquered once again, this time by the Normans, exactly 148 years after death of the Lady of the Mercians at Tamworth. Much of Anglo-Danish England was swept away in the wake of the Norman Conquest, including many of the great churches. Alfred's New Minster and burial place ended up being re-sited outside the walls of the city (along the royal remains interred there) on the orders of Henry I, and were eventually destroyed following the Dissolution of the Monasteries. Many of the old saints went out of fashion, and dedications of churches were changed. In the generations after the Conquest, however, the interest in the pre-Conquest past increased, bolstered by the marriage of William the Conqueror's son Henry to Matilda (birth name Edith), a woman descended from the West Saxon kings and from Alfred. The clerical writers and chroniclers of eleventh- and twelfth-century England were rather enamoured of Æthelflæd, and although they did not devote very much space to recounting her life and reign, everything they did write about her was positive.

William of Malmesbury called her a 'virago', and he is probably the originator of the story that Æthelflæd chose to renounce physical relations with her husband after the birth of Ælfwyn.[3] A close contemporary, John of Worcester, is said to have had a 'Mercian' perspective and 'optimised' the role of the Mercian royal family in his chronicle. He lauded Æthelflæd's 'prudence and justice' as well as her moral virtue and 'vigorous' rule.[4] Henry of Huntingdon penned the Latin poem quoted at the beginning of this chapter praising her as more renowned than Caesar. Often, her courage and prowess was described in masculine terms. Huntingdon wrote of her as a woman worthy to be called a man and both king *and* queen.

There was also an element of sexual purity in his praise, for she was described twice as 'virgin' (Latin *virgo* or *virago*), an attribute which made her even more holy, and so all the more admirable.[5] His description of her as the daughter of Lord Æthelred was an error, but even for those who correctly described her as his widow it was possible for widows to be virgins dedicated to God, as we saw with the biblical and poetic heroine Judith in chapter 12.[6] These notions of brave women described in male terms, or holy heroines devoted to God, were not uncommon in the works of writers of the eleventh and twelfth centuries. Medieval historians were unashamedly didactic. Unlike today, secular history was written with the purpose of instructing the reader, and events filtered through the norms and expectations of the time.[7] From the late eleventh century onwards came a growing desire for 'role definition', which could provoke stronger reactions to 'behaviour considered unusual for women'.[8]

Two twelfth-century Englishwomen are relevant to this work, and both were known to have been distant relatives of Æthelflæd. One was the Matilda mentioned above, wife of Henry I and daughter of Matilda of Scotland, and the other was her daughter and namesake, a woman known to history as the Empress Maud and Lady of the English. The former was adored by the chroniclers, especially William of Malmesbury, whom she commissioned to write his *Lives of the Kings of England*. Noted for her piety, generosity and learning, she was also recognised for her distinguished lineage. William of Malmesbury traced her descent back to Edmund (Ironside), identified as Edward the Confessor's brother (technically his half-brother). As such she was also a descendant of Alfred the Great and a distant kinswoman of Æthelflæd, and William was certainly aware that she was descended from this 'ancient and illustrious' line of kings.[9]

She is more important to this study as the mother of the Empress Matilda, having transmitted her blood claim to West Saxon descent to her daughter – as well as passing on her love of learning. William of Malmesbury recounted how this distinguished heritage was set out for Queen Matilda in a letter to her daughter. According to this account, Queen Matilda had proudly spoken of her legendary descent from Aldhelm, the saint whom the monks of Malmesbury held in high esteem, upon which she was reminded that Aldhelm, and she, shared the same descent from the ancient Kings of Wessex. At the fascinated Queen's request, a list of Kings was drawn up.[10] So, Empress Matilda was made aware of her heritage (if this had not already been imparted to her by her mother), and she too was a patron of Malmesbury Abbey and of its most famous writer. Hence, figures from the past, such as Æthelflæd, would have been useful moral exemplars for William's patrons, and considering the values and preconceptions by which he filtered his narrative, and judged the figures he wrote about, the 'Lady of the Mercians' may have been a particularly useful and relevant model for the times.

William of Malmesbury believed that the marriage of Henry I to the Empress Matilda's mother fulfilled an ancient prophecy (reported to have been made by Edward the Confessor) by bringing about the restoration of the ancient line of English kings, but also its unification with the line of William of Normandy.[11] After the death of her brother, Matilda remained the sole legitimate heir of King Henry and as such was named his successor. The events of the war following the usurpation of Matilda's cousin Stephen are well documented. For the purposes of this study, William's depiction of the career and characteristics of Matilda and her fellows are of greater importance. To him, an ideal ruler was supposed to be morally upright, virtuous and the upholder of justice in their realm. Not that they were supposed to be *perfect*, as Henry I was well known for having many mistresses and illegitimate children – but he was also noted as a king who upheld justice and a 'peacemaker'.[12] So was Matilda in William's view, despite having fought a war to retake the throne that, in his view and that of other partisans, was rightfully hers.[13] These events were still in the future in 1125 when the *Gesta Regum Anglorum* was being composed, yet there are parallels between the depiction of Æthelflæd in this work and Matilda in the later *Historia Novella*, composed during the period of the war, demonstrating that William may well have been seeking to model one woman on the other. The latter contains a revealing passage that claims the descent from the West Saxon dynasty through Edmund Ironside was 'well known'; apparently in the fifteen years since the writing of the *Gesta Regum* Matilda's heritage had been widely broadcast. Perhaps it served her purposes well, strengthening her claim to the throne.[14]

In the *Gesta Regum* Matilda's predecessor had been described as a 'woman of great determination' who could strike terror into the hearts of the enemy, truly worthy of the epithet 'virago', which was given to her by the chronicler. Despite the aforementioned translation, *virago* did not necessarily mean a virgin – it could refer to a woman who behaved like a man,[15] in the same way Matilda was 'a woman of masculine spirit' who used this spirit to fight for her rights.[16] Also, like her forbear, Matilda was supposed to have been a woman who did not act alone, but relied much on one of her foremost commanders: Robert, Earl of Gloucester, her illegitimate half-brother. When she had first taken the throne, he assisted her by 'speaking affably' to the chief men of the kingdom, who 'looked to her for authority', and brought the opposition around with 'intimidation' or promises.[17] Perhaps here, too, she was seen to be following in the footsteps of her predecessor by being a 'tower of strength' to her friends but a formidable foe to her enemies.[18] Finally, Matilda was according the title of 'Lady of the English', indeed she may have chosen it herself, staking a claim to the heritage of her West Saxon ancestors, and taking the title of her ancestor, Æthelflæd – a title that carried with it all the implications of female rule.[19]

Matilda failed to be crowned and acclaimed by her people, perhaps because she was attempting to deal with the 'implicit contradictions of being a woman and a king'.[20] The *Gesta Stephani* accused her of possessing a haughtiness and arrogance unbecoming of her sex, a charge that was perhaps not entirely unfounded. For it appeared she began to pay no attention to the advice given her by loyal allies such as Robert, and allegedly treated them rudely in public. This behaviour was said by Nesta Pain to have been caused by Matilda's having suddenly obtained a position of real power, and her wish to make this power felt. Elsewhere Marjorie Chibnall asserted that traits which 'may have passed in a man as dignity, resolution and firm control were condemned in her as arrogance, obstinacy and anger'.[21] In other words, there may not have been anything wrong with her change in behaviour; perhaps it only merited attention because Matilda was female, and had strayed outside the contemporary expectations of a woman's behaviour. Malmesbury did not go so far as the author of the *Gesta Stephani*, who accused her of undesirable traits, but he did (alongside the aforementioned) blame the failure of her campaign on overconfidence, or else gave more credit to Robert of Gloucester.[22] She could be seen as strong for having adopted the spirit of a man when it mattered, to give her courage, strength and fortitude. Yet she was also seen to have failed by reason of her gender: she tried to be too much like a man, alienating advisors and some sections of the populace.

Perhaps, then, Matilda failed to emulate her famous ancestor, who, if some chroniclers were to be believed, ranked among the greatest women who ever lived. Possibly the reason for this failure was because, unlike Æthelflæd, the 'lady of the English' failed to fully co-operate with her male compatriots when it mattered most, and unlike her distant ancestor she was not a widow, forced to rule a kingdom on her own whilst maintaining independence from her southern neighbour. In this sense, Matilda and Æthelflæd were not so very much alike after all. Or perhaps Matilda had more in common with the Lady of the Mercians as a real woman fighting for her cause against the odds, rather than as some unattainable ideal of womanhood so prevalent during her time.

CONCLUSION
A HEROINE LOST AND FOUND

Michael Wood recently described Alfred, and the two generations of his descendants after him (his children and grandson Æthelstan), as the greatest royal dynasty in English history. This is probably true. Love or loathe Alfred, it is almost impossible to deny his achievements and extraordinary intellect. He stands out among the kings of Anglo-Saxon England not just as an accomplished warrior but also a patron of learning and a scholar who longed to restore the golden age of learning, when some of the greatest scholars and writers in Europe had been his fellow countrymen.

His daughter's life and career are no less remarkable- even if she did not help translate as many books or fight as many battles. A girl, born to the fifth son of a King, in a small Kingdom situated in the Southernmost part of the British Isles, grew up to restore her Kingdom and become famous across the land of her birth, and far beyond. Nothing about her life was inevitable from the start, she could have died young, like her siblings, could have married a nobleman from the continent and ended up as the

Countess of Flanders like her sister, or even died in childbirth. They could very easily have been no Lady of the Mercians-although the same could be said of many other historical figures. Yet one cannot help thinking that Mercia, and the later Kingdom of England would have been worse off without her.

Æthelflæd comes across as every inch her father's daughter. As a child, she must have soaked up the lessons and examples of leadership from him and his leading nobles. She also inherited her father's thirst for learning and love of 'wisdom' from books. As children do, it is possible that if she learned any Latin, she may have mastered it more quickly than he did, but there was enough literature in her own mother tongue to satisfy her tastes. Did she listen with rapt excitement to heroic poems like *Beowulf* just as those hearing it for the first time might do so today? For the author's part, what makes Æthelflæd so interesting and brings her to life is her humanity. Everyone loves a hero, someone to admire to and put on the pedestal. As was suggested by Tom Holland, Æthelflæd provides girls with a heroine to admire as the life and times of Alfred and his children are rediscovered in schools.

Yet it would be too easy to cast her as an idealised and romanticised figure, as past generations have done for her father. One thing that emerges from this study and the evidence is that while Æthelflæd was an able commander, a strategist and an erstwhile diplomat, she would do whatever was necessary to achieve her ends. Her Christian convictions did not prevent her from deceiving her enemies, as she did with Ingimund at Chester, or even taking her revenge on those who wronged her, as with King Tewdyr. (Of course, she probably would not have seen that act as revenge, more a matter of political necessity and justice.)

It is important to remember that medieval attitudes towards morality were vastly different from those which exist today. Violence and piety were not necessarily considered opposites, and a concept of just war was starting to develop.

Æthelflæd would have seen the necessity of her actions, and probably believed that it was entirely permissible to use underhand tactics to defeat the pagans, whom she saw as oath-breakers, liars, enemies of her God and oppressors of her people. Her enemies would probably have seen things very differently, believing that they needed good land and access to wealth after they had been expelled from Ireland, where they had made their homes. It would be more interesting to know the other side of the story of what happened to Abbot Ecgfrith. Was he totally innocent, or did he do something to offend King Tewdyr? Did the king simply resent yet another attempt by the Mercians to impose their authority and overlordship upon him and his people? The Welshman Asser had called Æthelflæd's husband a tyrant; would they also have considered Æthelflæd a tyrant for building unwelcome burhs on the borders of their territory, marching an army into Wales and burning down the residence of one of their kings?

It is fashionable to promote 'revisionist' interpretations of well-known historical figures, rehabilitating the unpopular ones and questioning the virtues of those held up as heroes. The author is not intending to do this, merely to reveal Æthelflæd as a well-rounded human being who was as capable of acts of anger, spite or harsh political necessity as she was of great feats of heroism, guiding her armies to impressive victories against her enemies. Not everything she did was necessary to defend her country, and it was not always heroic; sometimes she just fought dirty. Such has always been the reality of warfare and politics. It is all too easy for those of us who have never been involved in either to judge past leaders, but it is not always helpful to do so.

For all her faults Æthelflæd still emerges as an inspirational and remarkable figure, a woman in a difficult situation who not only survived, but thrived and emerged victorious. She was not, in the modern sense, a warrior woman who had to swing her sword in combat to prove her worth and her equality with men; indeed, such a concept would have been foreign to the times. Instead, she was born into the highest class, and would have been trained in certain roles and to fulfil certain expectations from birth. Not just to be a wife and mother to kings, but to learn how to run a household, produce fine clothing and be a good hostess at feasts and festivals. From the earliest times, poems, songs and riddles had been a form of entertainment, so it was only natural that royal children of both sexes would have been taught some of these, and we have already seen that Æthelflæd had the same level of education as her eldest brother Edward (though not, perhaps, her younger siblings, who directly benefited from educational reforms). It was useful for royal children to be taught some literacy, at least in their mother tongue, even if it was only so that they could go over administrative documents or look over charters before they were approved, and there was no reason why women could not do that. Æthelflæd was more fortunate than other royal princesses in that, while she married a little before her father started learning Latin and translating books, she was embedded in a literate culture. Bishop Wærferth was her adviser and friend as well as her father's, and Alfred sent copies of some of his works abroad, wanting his nobles to learn to read like he did. We don't know when she got to read the book of Judith, which that later poem was based on, if indeed she did commission it or wish it to be written, but it may well have been during her childhood or youth, when she heard other Bible stories and ancient literary works of her people.

As she grew into an adult, the Viking wars that had defined so much of her life had continued. The wars had nearly swept away her homeland and her father. As the daughter and sister of a king (and the wife of a man who was king in all but name), it was inevitable that the men she loved and cared for would be involved in the wars. In a sense, the events of the 860s and 870s forced Mercia and Wessex to overcome their differences and work together to form and maintain the alliance to which she was so vital because of her marriage. Hers was just one of many political marriages in history, and in the short term did not prove very successful dynastically.

It was only after her father's death, and during her husband's illness, that Æthelflæd's capabilities became apparent. We do not have many details about the day-to-day aspects of her life as the consort to the ruler of Mercia, or how she related to her subjects, but we do know from the surviving charters that she was very much involved in the establishment and restoration of towns and churches like St Peter's, Worcester, and St Oswald's, Gloucester, from an early period. When she did first come onto the scene in an independent capacity, it was to give Ingimund and his exiles from Ireland permission to settle in part of Mercia, a decision which proven to be ill-advised. It was probably quite normal for the deputy of a ruler to be sought out on such matters, although that deputy would not normally have been a woman; we don't know of Ealswith ever having been entrusted with such an important matter when Alfred was ill.

The traditions of Mercia may simply have allowed Æthelflæd more power and influence, although it does seem as though her father had been willing to involve her in meetings her husband attended. This element of trust does come across quite strongly in the sources. From the early tenth century, when she was in her thirties, Æthelflæd was trusted with power by her nobles and apparently her people. So, she must have proved herself capable in the years before that. At the end of her husband's life she was chosen to wield power over her kingdom. From sometime before, she had been consciously emulating her father's methods to defend and strengthen her kingdom, planning and building burhs and cities (and restoring others), boosting the economy and also establishing a school in Worcester and promoting scholarship. In the last four years of her life she showed as much determination and drive as her brother to reconquer the Danelaw as part of their joint effort. This military campaign seems to have been genuinely united, with the brother-and-sister team engaging the same strategy to basically envelope the Danelaw in a pincer movement, united by their bonds of blood, marriage and common purpose, and perhaps also bound by their father's vision of creating a single kingdom of the Anglo-Saxons.

Together, for the four years between 914 and 918, they seemed almost unstoppable. Yet it was Æthelflæd who, in the end, stood poised to take that jewel in the crown of Viking rule in England, York. Even more remarkably, it would have been a bloodless coup, for even though Æthelflæd was a gifted leader who marched with her armies and commanded them on horseback (and was prepared to chase her enemies to the last, if the account of her involvement at Corbridge is true), she was also good at winning hearts and minds. Leicester had already submitted to her shortly after the taking of Derby. It must have seemed as though her progress was inevitable, but it is also entirely possible that Æthelflæd was possessed of a charismatic personality, which allowed her to persuade people to come over to her cause. She was a peace-weaver as well as a shield maiden, fully able and willing to use diplomatic means to serve her ends, making friends and alliances to protect her borders and promoting the benefits of her rule and patronage. Had she not restored and brought peace and prosperity to English Mercia? Could she not offer the same to the men and women of the Danelaw? Of course, diplomacy was always stronger when it had military force behind it, and Æthelflæd was more than willing to utilise force when she had to. In fact, on many occasions negotiations and submissions to Æthelflæd were preceded or followed by a show of force. The Lady of the Mercians had turned out to be a forceful woman who tended to get her way, and she was not easily crossed.

She died at the height of her power and fame, and even though her daughter was deposed she was succeeded in Mercia six years after her death by Æthelstan, the nephew whom she had raised and educated, who had learned how to fight and hunt with her and her thegns. The first king of England held the memory of his aunt dear to him for the rest of his life. She also lived on the memory of her people, her name becoming a common choice for noble parents to bequeath to their daughters, and an anonymous chronicler somewhere in Mercia took great pains to ensure that she was not expunged from the records when he penned the Mercian Register. In the century after her death, chroniclers in Ireland took great pleasure in recording stories and accounts about the brave and renowned queen of the Saxons. Her fame had indeed spread everywhere, and it outlived her by centuries. In the eleventh and twelfth centuries, when a number of European women chose to take up arms and fight for their lands and authority, and the Church was struggling to reconcile their actions with its moral teaching and social expectations, the Lady of the Mercians was taken up as a role model.

Yet in the sixteenth century, when a woman again occupied the throne of England and sought a past heroine to look up to, it was Boudicca and not Æthelflæd whom she chose to honour. The fiery redhead from the Iron Age came to eclipse the 'elf fair maiden' from the tenth century, and still does to this day. What caused the waning of the fame of this great lady? It is hard to say with certainty, but it is likely that the loss of medieval records during the Dissolution of the Monasteries and the renewed interest in all things classical during the sixteenth-century renaissance contributed.

Of course, the silence on Æthelflæd in the West Saxon version of the *Anglo-Saxon Chronicle* did not help. Even when people began to take a renewed interest in Alfred and all things Anglo-Saxon after the Reformation, they could be forgiven for not knowing much about Æthelflæd if this was all they had to use. More recently, the history of the entire Anglo-Saxon period has come to be neglected in many circles. Æthelstan is still one of the least known of all the kings of England, and his aunt, with her obscure and often misspelled name, has also been forgotten too often. Thankfully, in the last century, with the rise of women's history and a renewed interest in the Anglo-Saxon age, Æthelflæd is rising from obscurity to be remembered in the way that she deserves – as a shining example of what a woman of could achieve through her intelligence, resilience, and strength of character in a 'man's world'.

GLOSSARY

Atheling The modern equivalent of the term might be prince/princess, indicating a person of royal birth who was heir to the throne. However, the original meaning is more complicated. The Anglo-Saxons did not use primogeniture, the dominant system in the later Middle Ages whereby a king was usually succeeded by his eldest child (usually son), or brother if he had no children. Instead, kings would be elected by the witan, a type of council of warriors and prominent men of the kingdom. They might choose any candidate of royal blood based on their fitness to rule; this could be a relative of the king, or indeed a relative of a previous king from an entirely different dynasty. Thus, *atheling* really meant something like 'throne-worthy', and indicated a person of royal or noble descent who was capable of laying claim to the throne. In poetry, it meant something like 'a good and noble man', and was used for Christ, and in Latin the equivalent was *filius Regius* or 'son/descendant of the king'.[1]

Burh Technically, a fortification, enclosure or settlement. These ranged in size, and could include prehistoric hillforts, or walled enclosures around the homes of the nobility, as well as the fortified towns that came to be a defining feature of Alfred and his children's campaigns. The world survives in modern place names which end in the suffix -bury or -borough, or prefixes like Bur- or Brough-.

Ealdorman The meaning and significance of this term changes over time. Originally it was the Anglo-Saxon equivalent of Latin terms like *Dux* or *Princeps*, meaning ruler and prince, chief or head respectively. *The Encyclopaedia of Anglo-Saxon England* says, 'Originally it was applied to high-ranking men … including those of royal or quasi-regal status, the basis of whose power and authority was independent of the king.'[2] By Alfred's time, it had come to refer the leader or chief nobleman of a shire, who held power but was subordinate to the king. By the eleventh century it had taken on the meaning of a nobleman who acted at the behest of the king. By that time their duties included presiding over shire courts and levying taxation.[3] Eventually, the term gave rise to the title and noble rank of earl.

Fyrd Technically 'army', but could also mean a royal military expedition. It could also apply to the men who comprised the army itself, so that the entire *fyrd* of Wessex might mean an army composed of all the nobles, retainers and freemen obliged to follow the king or their lord into battle. According the *Encyclopaedia of Anglo-Saxon England*, 'The core of the army was the royal household, which was supplemented by the levies of free landowners who looked to the king as their personal lord. Local forces were raised and led by local reeves and ealdormen.'[7]

Hlaford Literally 'Lord', the equivalent of the Latin *Dominus*. It seems to have originally applied to the head or lord of a household, or the master of servants. It has been suggested that the word originally derives from the word for 'loaf', denoting the person responsible for providing food and provisions for the household.[4] It could also apply to a king or ruler. In poetry, kings were referred to as lords, often accompanied by some adjective to denote the love, loyalty and devotion of their followers, or even spouse. In one poem, a wife pines for her 'dear Lord'. God and Christ were also often referred to by this term, and in the Judith poem the titular character refers to God as 'the dear Lord who made the wind and air'.[5] It became an unofficial title used for Æthelred of Mercia in the records, marking him as a leader of high and almost royal status without using the word king. When he died, his wife came to carry the female equivalent *hlæfdige*, literally translated as 'lady'. It is sometimes believed that she was the first woman to whom the term was applied as a title, but there is some suggestion that the title was also given to the wives of the kings of Wessex as they adopted the tradition of not calling their spouses queens.[6]

Jarl Roughly the Scandinavian equivalent of earl or ealdorman.

Morgengifu Literally 'morning-gift'. Defined as 'the gift made by the husband to the wife the morning after the consummation of the marriage'.[8] The gift could be anything from money to livestock or, for those of the highest status in society, land. The woman was supposed to have full control of her *morgengifu* and could do with it as she pleased.

Theyn/Thegn The literal meaning is 'one who serves', a retainer, a soldier, or a minister.[9] They were of the highest rank of society (although not as high as the ealdormen). 'All thegns were expected to perform military and administrative services … they were the ones with the local power and influence', and they were supposed to be bound to the king by oaths of loyalty. They would hold land, and 'had useful social connections' which made them invaluable to the kings or rulers whom they served. They were not the same as the later knights, but they may be considered the rough equivalent of knights or barons for definition's sake.[10]

Witan The king's council. The literal meaning is 'wise men' or even 'to have knowledge/be aware'. They could appoint or elect the person they chose to be king, but it also seems to have been possible for the king to fall foul of them. Justin Pollard suggests that the Guthrum's attack on Chippenham was preceded by a conspiracy of certain men in the witan, and perhaps even by them de-selecting or deposing him. A witan would consist of the great men of the kingdom, the 'members of the royal household', churchmen, ealdormen and nobles. In some cases, women were even included, such as the queen and abbesses.

NOTES

Introduction: In Search of the Lady of the Mercians

1. Edward 'the elder' is a nickname, which is not contemporary. Surnames were not introduced to England until the Norman Conquest, and did not become hereditary until the fourteenth century. Therefore, historians have often taken to distinguishing the pre-conquest Kings by their nicknames. Edward was simply the elder son of Alfred, and the first of three pre-conquest Kings of Wessex and later England to carry the name. The others were Edward 'the martyr' who was reportedly murdered by his stepmother, and the more famous Edward 'the confessor'.
2. Pauline Stafford,' Political Women in Mercia: Eighth to Early Tenth Centuries' in *Mercia: An Anglo-Saxon Kingdom in Europe* eds. Michelle P. Brown and Carol A. Farr (London, 2005), p. 49.
3. Judith Arnopp, 'Aethelflaed: The Lady of Mercia', *Judith Arnopp, Historical Fiction Author*, 2010, accessed 23rd September 2014. http://www.juditharnopp.com/aethelflaed.htm

4. Unlike that of his brother-in-law, Æthelred's title is the translation of one that was actually given to him at the time. He was never officially recognized by Wessex as King of Mercia (although certain sources from outside England describe him as such), but he was accorded such titles as 'lord' or 'ealdorman' of Mercia.

1 *Sons of the Wolf*

1. Edoardo Albert and Katie Tucker, *In Search of Alfred the Great: The King, The Grave, The Legend,* Amberley (Stroud), 2015, p. 61.
2. *Ibid*, p. 35–6.
3. Pauline Stafford, 'Succession and Inheritance: a gendered perspective on Alfred's family history', Timothy Reuter ed. *Alfred the Great: Papers from the Eleventh Centenary Conferences,* Ashgate (Aldershot), 2003, p. 259.
4. The problem is that the tribe of the Gaini is not mentioned anywhere outside Asser (as far as I can find). It could be a corruption of the name of another old Anglo-Saxon tribe. So the assumption that the town of Gainsborough is named after them may simply be an example of backwards projection because of the names sounds like each other.
5. Stafford, Succession and Inheritance, p. 259.
6. *Ibid*, p. 260.
7. *Ibid*, pp. 260, 264.
8. *The Anglo-Saxon Chronicles* ed. and trans. Michael Swanton, Phoenix Press (London), 2003, p. 70–71.
9. *Ibid*, p. 72–3.
10. Albert, In Search of Alfred, p. 86–7.

2 The Great Heathen Army: 871–December 877

1. All the major biographies of Alfred, as well as the Oxford Dictionary of National Biography article give a date of *circa* 870 for her birth. There are a few, non-academic sources, mostly internet sites, which give an earlier date in the 860s. The History of Tamworth website gives the earliest date of 866, but this does not make sense, as it would mean she was born two years before her parents had married or even met, and so Alfred was not her father. Many of the earlier birth dates have probably been calculated to make sense of the date of her marriage, in the 880s.
2. Simon Keynes and Michael Lapidge, (trans), *Alfred the Great: Asser's* Life of Alfred *and other Contemporary Sources*, Penguin (London), 2004, p. 90.
3. Michael Wood 'King Alfred and the Anglo-Saxons: Episode 2, The Lady of the Mercians', BBC 2, Broadcast 13th August 2013. For the alternative translation see Sally Crawford, *Daily Life in Anglo-Saxon England*, Greenwood World Publishing (Oxford), 2009, p. 70.
4. Don Stansbury, *The Lady Who Fought the Vikings*, Imogen Books (Devon), 1993, p. 13–14.
5. John Haywood, *Northmen: The Viking Saga: 793–1241*, Head of Zeus (London), 2015, p. 57.
6. *Ibid*, p. 15.
7. Benjamin Merkle, *The White Horse King: The Life of Alfred the Great*, Thomas Nelson, (Nashville) 2009, p. 79.
8. Richard Abels, *Alfred the Great: War, Kingship and Culture in Anglo-Saxon England*, Pearson (Essex) 1998, p. 149.
9. Stansbury, p. 20.

10. Sally Crawford, *Childhood in Anglo-Saxon England,* Sutton (Stroud), 1999, p. 132.
11. *Ibid*, p. 122–126.
12. Stansbury, p. 21–22.
13. Merkle, *White Horse King*, p. 85.
14. Derek Gore, 'A Review of Viking Attacks on Western England in the early Tenth Century: Their Responses and Motives', *Danes in Wessex: The Scandinavian Impact on Southern England, c.800–c.1100* ed. Ryan Lavelle and Simon Roffey, Oxbow Books (Oxford) 2016, p. 61.

3 Path of the Exile: January–May 878–880

1. See Ryan Lavelle. *Fortifications in Wessex c.800–1066* including the illustration of a 'typical' West Saxon *burh* page 30, as well as Paul Hill below. Also Stansbury as below p. 183.
2. Don Stansbury, *The Lady Who Fought the Vikings,* Imogen Books (Devon), 1993, p. 12–13.
3. Paul Hill, *The Viking Wars of Alfred the Great*, Pen and Sword (Barnsley), 2008, p. 72.
4. *Ibid*, pp. 72.3.
5. *Ibid.*
6. Edoardo Albert and Katie Tucker, *In Search of Alfred the Great: The King, The Grave, The Legend,* Amberley (Stroud), 2015, p. 13.
7. Simon Keynes and Michael Lapidge, (trans), *Alfred the Great: Asser's* Life of Alfred *and other Contemporary Sources*, Penguin (London), 2004, p. 83.
8. Edoardo Albert and Katie Tucker, *In Search of Alfred the Great: The King, The Grave, The Legend,* Amberley (Stroud), 2015, p. 15.

9. Richard Abels, *Alfred the Great: War, Kingship and Culture in Anglo-Saxon England,* Pearson (Essex) 1998, p. 157
10. Abels, *Ibid* p. 157. Albert,
11. Richard Hamer (ed.) *The Seafarer: A Choice of Anglo-Saxon Verse*, Faber and Faber (London), p. 193.
12. Simon Keynes and Michael Lapidge, (trans), *Alfred the Great: Asser's* Life of Alfred *and other Contemporary Sources*, Penguin (London), 2004, p. 84.
13. *Ibid*, p. 84–5.

4 *Return of the King: May 878*

1. Simon Keynes and Michael Lapidge, (trans), *Alfred the Great: Asser's* Life of Alfred *and other Contemporary Sources*, Penguin (London), 2004, p. 84.
2. Edoardo Albert and Katie Tucker, *In Search of Alfred the Great: The King, The Grave, The Legend,* Amberley (Stroud), 2015, p. 115.
3. *Ibid*, p. 117.
4. *Ibid*, p. 120.
5. *Life of Alfred*, p. 84–5.
6. Albert, *In Search of Alfred*, p. 125.
7. *Ibid*, p. 124.
8. Barbara Yorke, *Alfred the Great: Pocket Giants*, The History Press (Stroud), 2015, p. 48.
9. *The Anglo-Saxon Chronicles* ed. and trans. Michael Swanton, Phoenix Press (London), 2003, p. 73–75.
10. There are two main charters from his reign, S215 and S361, which involve the exchange of property, as well as various matters pertaining to the estates, such as exemptions from dues and rents, with Wearferth Bishop of Worcester. The latter

mentions him selling land to the same man. These are the only charters which survive, there may have been others.

11. '*Annales Cambriae*: The Annals of Wales 447–954', Internet Medieval Sourcebook, Paul Halsall ed. 1998, Fordham University Centre for Medieval Studies, accessed 8th November 2016, http://sourcebooks.fordham.edu/halsall/sbook.asp
12. *Ibid.*
13. Albert, *In Search of Alfred*, p. 130.

5 Daughter of Wessex: 880–886

1. Simon Keynes and Michael Lapidge, (trans), *Alfred the Great: Asser's* Life of Alfred *and other Contemporary Sources*, Penguin (London), 2004, p. 101.
2. Chris Peers, *Offa and the Mercian Wars*, Pen and Sword (Barnsley, 2012), p. 50.
3. Simon Keynes, 'King Alfred and the Mercians', *Kings Currency and Alliances: History and Coinage of Southern England in the Ninth Century* ed. Mark A. S. Blackburn and David M. Dunville, Boydell (Woodbridge), p. 39.
4. Edoardo Albert and Katie Tucker, *In Search of Alfred the Great: The King, The Grave, The Legend,* Amberley (Stroud), 2015, p. 61.
5. Keynes and Lapidge, *Alfred the Great,* p. 75. Justin Pollard suggested that this story does not make sense in context, as it places all the brothers together as young children, when there was probably a quite considerable gap between Alfred and his eldest brother, except for Æthelred. Nevertheless, it is a useful example of how oral recitation and memorization of written texts was regarded as a form

of literacy at the time. See *Alfred the Great: The Man Who Made* England, p. 48–9.

6. 'Dhouda's Advice to her Son' in *Carolingian Civilisation: A Reader* Paul Edward Dutton ed. (Ontario, 1993), p. 369–71.
7. The Maxims I, S. A. J. Bradley ed. and trans. *Anglo-Saxon Poetry*, J. M. Dent and Sons (London), 1982, p. 124.
8. Alan Thacker, 'Hild (614–680)', Oxford Dictionary of National Biography, Oxford University Press, 2004 http://www.oxforddnb.com/view/article/13255, accessed 23 July 2016]. For the letter and writings of Hildegard Von Bingen see Joseph L. Baird, *The Personal Correspondence of Hildegard Von Bingen* (Oxford, 2006), p. 4–5. Also, the Encyclopaedia Britannica article on her, https://www.britannica.com/biography/Saint-Hildegard accessed 4th November 2016.
9. This is discussed in more detail in Chapter Twelve, but most historians accept that Æthelflæd had the same education as her brother, and had at least one of the men involved in Alfred's translation programme by her side, the Bishop of Worcester. Michael Wood has also shown how her nephew Æthelstan was literate and enjoyed the works of Aldhelm.
10. Keynes and Lapidge, *Alfred the Great*, p. 153.
11. American scholar Nancy Marie Brown mentions that copies of Bede's work were being read in monasteries in Italy in the late tenth century, and Charlemagne was acquainted with it. This makes perfect sense, considering that Alcuin oversaw so much of the education system, and had close ties with Northumbria, Bede's home kingdom. The dissemination

of Bede's work is discussed in several passages in her book *The Abacus and the Cross* in relation some of the ideas and methods that people took from Bede, such as the AD dating system, and a method of counting on fingers. See Nancy Marie Brown, *The Abacus and the Cross* (New York, 2010), p. 23, 86–7, 97–8.

12. *The Maxims II*, lines 82–90, p. 348.
13. 'The Husband's Message' in Bradley, *Anglo-Saxon Poetry*, p. 400. See also 'Beowulf' lines 13–19, 20–24.
14. Bede, *The Reckoning of Time*, trans. Faith Wallis, Liverpool University Press (Liverpool), 1991, p. 91. See also *Northmen: The Viking Saga: 793–1241*, Head of Zeus (London), 2015, p. 13 in which the author discusses the Vikings grasp of technology. Michael Pye in his book 'On the Edge of the World' suggested that the 'learned men' of Medieval Europe conceived of the earth as 'a pancake on top of a ball' (presumably the hypothetical ball was cut in half) whereas the Vikings knew the right shape. See Michael Pye, *The Edge of the World: How the North Sea Made Us Who We Are* (London, 2015), p. 81.

    Victoria Whitworth discussed the possibility that the library at York may have owned copies of the works by Ovid and Pliny in the historical note of her novel *Daughter of the Wolf*, p. 594.
15. Kathleen Herbert, *Peace-Weavers and Shield-Maidens: Women in Early English Society*, Anglo-Saxon Books (Milton Keynes), 1997, p. 14.
16. Sally Crawford, *Anglo-Saxon England 400–790*, Shire Publications (Oxford), p. 59–61.

17. Albert, *In Search of Alfred,* p. 14–15. See also Justin Pollard *Alfred the Great: The Man Who Made England*, John Murray (London), 2006, p. 172–3.
18. Herbert, *Peace Weavers,* p. 14–15 for the social and religious connotations of weaving. See also Christine Fell, *Women in Anglo-Saxon England and the Impact of 1066*, British Museum Publications (London), 1984, p. 40–41 about the activity in royal and noble households.
19. *The Anglo-Saxon Chronicles* ed. and trans. Michael Swanton, Phoenix Press (London), 2003, p. 77–78. Asser refers to the same engagement, but only mentions two ships. Much of his record for the events of the 880s seems to be directly copied from the *Anglo-Saxon Chronicle.*
20. Richard Abels, *Alfred the Great. The author is quoting from Æthelweard's Chronicle.* See A. Campbell ed. *The Chronicle of Æthelweard* (London), 1962, p. 44. There are translations of the source from the Victorian period, but this is the most popular modern translation.
21. *Anglo-Saxon Chronicles*, p. 78–9.
22. *Alfred the Great,* p. 97–98. Here again we see Asser copying his information directly from the Chronicle. Sometimes he even uses similar wording.
23. *Anglo-Saxon Chronicles*, p. 80–81.
24. Most authors accept that the marriage took place during or shortly before the official handover of London in 886. However, Tony Sharp and other favour an earlier date for the betrothal and even the marriage when Æthelflæd was in her early, or even pre-teens. These estimates are sometimes based on an earlier presumed date for her birth before 870.

See Sharp, *Chronicles, Treaties and Burghs, Part 4: The Burghal Hudage*, p. 17 and Part *8: Guthrum's Retreat from Wessex in 879*, p. 6.

25. Don Stansbury, *The Lady Who Fought the Vikings*, Imogen Books (Devon), 1993, p. 94.

6 Wild Boar of Mercia

1. Richard Abels, *Alfred the Great: War, Kingship and Culture in Anglo-Saxon England,* Pearson (Harlow), p. 180–1.
2. Paul Hill, *Viking Wars of Alfred the Great*, Pen and Sword (Barnsley), 2008, p. 91.
3. Hill *Ibid.*
4. Jane Wolfe, Æthelflæd: Royal Lady, War Lady, Fenris Press (Chester), p. 23.
5. Parts of Gloucestershire were, at various times subsumed into Wessex, but the Abbey seems to have been outside this area, if it was located near the site of the current St Mary's Church as is widely claimed. See the official website of the church http://www.stmarys-berkeley.co.uk/the-site.html
6. Tony Sharp, 'Chronicles, Treaties and Burghs: The Burghal Hidage and the Mercian Reconquest. Part 1 Section 8, Guthrum's Retreat in 879' Published by the Guidable Manor of Southwark, 2013, p. 4–7. Sharp has made a useful study of all the current theories of what happened during this period in the available sources, and makes his conclusions based on material in the Burghal Hidage and the establishment of the *burhs*. Although I do not agree with all his conclusions, his work is still a very useful resource. It is available for free download from Academia.edu.

7. Simon Keynes, 'King Alfred and the Mercians', *Kings Currency and Alliances: History and Coinage of Southern England in the Ninth Century* ed. Mark A. S. Blackburn and David M. Dunville, Boydell (Woodbridge), p. 27. S219.
8. *Ibid*, p. 28–9.
9. *Ibid*, p. 22.
10. *Ibid*, p. 43.
11. Christine Fell, *Women in Anglo-Saxon England and the Impact of 1066*, British Museum Publications (London, 1984), p. 56–7.

7 Most Needful to Know: 886–992

1. John Harper, 'Herald History: Ethelfleda the Mighty Lady of the Mercians', *Tamworth Herald*, October 27th 2015, http://www.tamworthherald.co.uk Accessed 5th August 2016. The *Herald* article is one of several online articles which reports the story of the attack on the wedding party. It also features in American historian and novelist Rebecca Tingle's 2003 novel about Æthelflæd *The Edge on the Sword*. None mentions the ultimate source of the story, so it seems to be a tradition that has grown up around her.
2. Michael Rank, 'HFM 028:The Most Powerful Women in the Middle Ages, Part 1: Lady Aethelflaed of the Mercians (872–918): The Real-Life Eowyn of Rohan and Viking Slayer', *History in Five Minutes,* August 12th 2013, http://www.michaelrank.net/2013/08/12/hfm. Accessed 12th August 2016. This source gives a more detailed, and slightly different account of the story above, but still provides no references or primary sources.

3. Simon Keynes, 'King Alfred and the Mercians', *Kings Currency and Alliances: History and Coinage of Southern England in the Ninth Century* ed. Mark A. S. Blackburn and David M. Dunville, Boydell (Woodbridge), p. 9–10. The date of his death is given in his entry in the *Prosography of Anglo-Saxon England* database.
4. 'Anglo-Saxon Gloucester: c.680 - 1066." *A History of the County of Gloucester: Volume 4, the City of Gloucester*. Ed. N. M. Herbert. London: Victoria County History, 1988. 5–12. *British History Online*. Web. 29 July 2016. http://www.british-history.ac.uk/vch/glos/vol4/pp5-12. A report that archaeologists had located the palace reached the national media in 2012, although the archaeological report from the year before suggests the results were rather less than conclusive.
5. Keynes, *King Alfred and the Mercians*, p. 30.
6. Don Stansbury, *The Lady Who Fought the Vikings*, Imogen Books (Devon), 1993, p. 97–100.
7. Document 99: Charters and Laws, 'Arrangement about the building of fortifications in Worcester', Dorothy Whitelock, ed. *English Historical Documents, Vol 1: 500–1052*, Eyre Methuen (London), 1979, p. 540–541. (Hereafter cited as 'Worcester Charter' and the book as EHD).
8. Stansbury, p. 152–55. For the possible ancient Welsh connection of the city, see Simon Jenkins, *Wales: Churches, Houses, Castles* Allen Lane (London), 2008 p. 245. Jenkins asserts that is was the ancient capital of Powys, but gives few other details.
9. Simon Keynes and Michael Lapidge, (trans), *Alfred the Great: Asser's* Life of Alfred *and other Contemporary Sources*, Penguin (London), 2004, p. 92.

10. *Ibid*, p. 109–10.
11. *Ibid*, p. 93.
12. 'From the Translation of Gregory's Pastoral Care', Simon Keynes and Michael Lapidge, (trans), *Alfred the Great: Asser's* Life of Alfred *and other Contemporary Sources*, Penguin (London), 2004, p. 124–5.
13. F. T. Wainwright, 'Æthelflæd, Lady of the Mercians' in *Scandinavian England: Collected Papers by F. T. Wainwright* ed. H. P. R Finberg (Chichester, 1975), p. 306.
14. Janina Ramirez, *The Private Lives of the Saints: Power, Passion and Politics in Anglo-Saxon England*, WH Allen (London), 2016, p. 259–60.

8 The Heathens Rage: 892–899

1. *The Anglo-Saxon Chronicles* ed. and trans. Michael Swanton, Phoenix Press (London), 2003, p. 84.5.
2. *Ibid*, p. 84.
3. *Ibid*.
4. *Ibid*. p. 86.
5. Edoardo Albert and Katie Tucker, *In Search of Alfred the Great: The King, The Grave, The Legend,* Amberley (Stroud), 2015, p. 186.
6. A. Campbell ed. *The Chronicle of Æthelweard*, Thomas Nelson (London), 1962, p. 49.
7. Albert, p. 189.
8. *Ibid*, p. 190.
9. *Anglo-Saxon Chronicles*, p. 88. Other sources like Æthelweard say many thousands. Possibly this is result of dramatic exaggeration or mistranslation.

10. *Ibid*, p. 87. This is one of the passages in the *Chronicle* in which the role of Æthelred is mentioned. Edward's role at Farnham was largely ignored. Æthelweard's account is almost identical and so he may have been taking it directly form the version of the *Chronicle* that he had access to.
11. T. M. Charles Edwards, *Wales and the Britons: 350–1064*, Oxford University Press (Oxford), 2012, p. 507–9.
12. *Ibid*. See also the *Anglo-Saxon Chronicles* edition cited, p. 87.
13. 'Ælfwyn 2', Prosography of Anglo-Saxon England, http://www.pase.ac.uk, Accessed 28th August 2016. The charter itself is S367, and is a fairly standard renewal of a land grant of an estate in Risborough, Buckinghamshire.
14. *William of Malmesbury, Gesta Regum Anglorum*, p. 199. See abbreviations section for full details.
15. Kathleen Herbert, *Peace Weavers and Shield Maidens: Women in Early English Society*, Anglo-Saxon Books, (Milton Keynes), 1997, p. 23–25.
16. Don Stansbury, *The Lady Who Fought the Vikings*, Imogen Books (Devon), 1993, p. 93. See Helen Caster *She Wolves: The Women Who Ruled England Before Elizabeth*, Faber and Faber (London), 2010. This title contains much useful discussion of the nature of power exercised by medieval and early modern queens, and the responses to it by contemporaries. Queens such as Margaret of Anjou, Isabella of France and the Empress Matilda were all subject to sometimes vitriolic criticism by their contemporaries and later observers for assuming traditionally male roles in leadership and war.
17. *Anglo-Saxon Chronicles*, p. 89. Richard Abels discussed the significance and possible Frankish origins of the tactic of

building the double burh on opposite sides of the river. See Richard Abels, *Alfred the Great: War Kingship and Culture in Anglo-Saxon England*, Pearson (Harlow), 1998, p. 302.

18. *Anglo-Saxon Chronicles,* p. 89. See also Abels, p. 303 in which he discusses the changing political situation. Ealdorman Æthelnoth's visit to York is mentioned in Æthelweard's chronicle.
19. *Anglo-Saxon Chronicles*, Ibid. Abels, *Ibid.* See also Albert, p. 196–7.
20. The *Anglo-Saxon Chronicle*s contain the account of the naval engagement of 896 (see pages 90–91 of the Swanton edition), the same passage also remarks on the size of Alfred's ships. The design flaw would show up in the later part of the account, when Alfred's larger and longer ships got stuck at low tide. See Yorke, *Alfred the Great*, p. 94 for the Anglo-Saxons use of ships before Alfred
21. *Anglo-Saxon Chronicle, Ibid.* This passage in the *Chronicle* also mentions Frisian soldiers in Alfred's army, ancient Frisia included parts of modern day Northern Holland and a small area of Germany bordering Denmark. See Abels p 306 for a more detailed discussion of the problems faced by Alfred's ships.
22. Alfred's treatment of the Danes caught after the sea battle does seem rather ruthless considering his previous record for mercy. It must be asked, though, if the sources over-emphasised that particular aspect of his character. See Abels, p. 307 for a mention of how Alfred might have considered the pirates.
23. See Albert, p. 199 for the mention of Alfred pursuing his lifelong pleasure for hunting. There are a considerable number

of images from manuscripts or tapestries from the late Middle Ages that depict women hunting, or taking a role in hunting. The earliest examples I could find date from the 1300s. Sometimes they are shown wielding bows, with hunting dogs, or with birds of prey. What is notable is that they were almost always shown with other women. See the illustrations section for some specific examples. It could be argued that this does not prove women in Æthelflæd's day were encouraged to hunt, but there is less surviving secular art from this time, and we should not assume that a pleasurable activity common to her successors was closed to women at her time.

24. Keynes and Lapidge, *Alfred the Great*, p. 108–9.
25. 'The Will of King Alfred' in Keynes and Lapidge, *Alfred the Great* p. 174–5.
26. Abels, p. 314–15. See Barbara Yorke p. 102 for the note on Alfred's tendency to micromanagement, and his desire to resolve any problems that came his way.

9 *The King of the Pagans: October 899–902*

1. Barbara Yorke, *Alfred The Great: Pocket Giants*, The History Press (Stroud), 2015, p. 77–8. See also Richard Abels, *Alfred the Great: War, Kingship and Culture in Anglo-Saxon England*, Pearson (Harlow), p. 178–80.
2. *The Anglo-Saxon Chronicles* ed. and trans. Michael Swanton, Phoenix Press (London), 2003, p. 92–3.
3. Jeffrey James, *An Onslaught of Spears: The Danish Conquest of England*, The History Press (Stroud), 2013, p. 43–4.
4. *Ibid*, p. 44.
5. Marios Costambeys, 'Ealhswith (*d.* 902)', *Oxford Dictionary of National Biography*, Oxford University

Press, 2004 http://www.oxforddnb.com/view/article/39226, accessed 17 Sept 2016]

6. Martyn Whittock and Hannah Whittock, *The Viking Blitzkrieg, AD 789–1098*, The History Press (Stroud), p. 133–4
7. *Anglo-Saxon Chronicles*, p. 92–3.
8. Whittock, *Ibid*, p. 134.
9. *Anglo-Saxon Chronicles*, p. 94–5.
10. *Ibid.*
11. Whittock, p. 134–5. Also, James Campbell, 'What is not known about reign of Edward the Elder' in *Edward the Elder: 899–924* ed. N. J. Higham and D. H. Hill, Routledge (London), 2001, p. 21–3 for more discussion on the Mercian athelings and what the result of an victory for Æthelwold might have been.
12. Fragmentary Annals of Ireland: Annal Fragment 401, University College Cork, Corpus of Electronic Texts Edition (CELT), p. 169–171, http://www.ucc.ie/celt/published/T100017/

10 *Scourge of the Heathens: 902–911*

1. S221. The same charter also granted the church 10 hides of land, but the gift of the chalice seems more personal than the usual grant of land. Perhaps the royal couple had worshipped there when they had travelled in Shropshire, or had just learned about the Saint it was devoted to.
2. John Blair, 'Mildburg (*d.* in or after 716)', *Oxford Dictionary of National Biography*, Oxford University Press, 2004 http://www.oxforddnb.com/view/article/18693, accessed 18 Sept 2016]. See also 'Diocese of Shrewsbury', *Saints and Martyrs: Saint Milburga* http://www.dioceseofshrewsbury.org/about-us/

saints-and-martyrs/st-milburga, Accessed 16th September 2016. for information on the Saxon Minster where she was originally buried.

3. *The Anglo-Saxon Chronicles* ed. and trans. Michael Swanton, Phoenix Press (London), 2003, p. 94–5.
4. F. T. Wainwright, 'Æthelflæd, Lady of the Mercians' in *Scandinavian England: Collected Papers by F. T. Wainwright* ed. H. P. R. Finberg (Chichester, 1975), p. 309. The mention of Æthelstan hunting in the Forest of Dean comes from the third episode of his documentary 'King Alfred and the Anglo-Saxons', which was devoted to Æthelstan. It makes sense to assume that this would have been the region in which he lived and played in his early youth and teens, because Æthelred's capital was based in Gloucester. See the bibliography for the full reference to the television programme.
5. Fragmentary Annals of Ireland: Annal Fragment 401, University College Cork, Corpus of Electronic Texts Edition (CELT), p. 169–171, http://www.ucc.ie/celt/published/T100017/
6. *Ibid*, p. 171–3.
7. *Ibid.*
8. *Ibid.*
9. *Ibid.*
10. For the tradition regarding the translation of St Werburg's relics see the website of St Werberg's Parish and Church, http://www.stwerburghchester.co.uk/. No independent citations are given on this page, but other sources say that the translation happened c.875, and draw upon the writings of the thirteenth century Chronicler Ranulf of Higden.

11. Martyn Whittock and Hannah Whittock, *The Viking Blitzkrieg, AD 789–1098*, The History Press (Stroud), p. 137. The quote about the sumptuous decoration of the church comes from Geoffrey Hindley, *A Brief History of the Anglo-Saxons* (London, 2006), p. 118–19.

    Max Adams is amongst those who suggests that Æthelflæd may have been personally behind the operation to recover the relics, and suggests that she and her husband may in fact have several churches dedicated to St Oswald, and calls Æthelflæd one in a succession of royal body snatchers. See *The King in the North: The Life and Times of Oswald of Northumbria*, p. 368.
12. A. Campbell ed. *The Chronicles of Æthelweard* (London), 1962, p. 52–3. The same section also mentions that the attack was made whilst the Danes were 'still engaged in crossing' the bridge over the Severn.
13. *Anglo-Saxon Chronicle* p. 94–6. The passages in question do mention the 'English' which traditionally included the West Saxons as well as the Mercians, and anyone else who spoke the English tongue, or was of 'English' blood, including those who might have lived in the Danelaw.
14. Æthelweard, p. 53. The actual phrase used is 'hastened to the hall of the Infernal One' but the quote is a commonly used alternative rendering.

11 Lady of the Mercians: 911–916

1. See, *The Anglo-Saxon Chronicles* ed. and trans. Michael Swanton, Phoenix Press (London), 2003, p. 95–98. It is later Chroniclers, including Æthelweard who mention that he

was buried at St Oswald's, Gloucester, rather than St Peter's Worcester, where he and his wife had made provision for religious services. The following entries suggest his death was early the year after Tetenhall- 911. See *The Viking Blitzkrieg* p. 137 and Campbell ed. *The Chronicles of Æthelweard*, p. 53. It is 'later authors' who suggest that he was wounded at the battle, according to Kathleen Herbert, *Peace Weavers and Shield Maidens*, p. 22.

2. Martyn Whittock and Hannah Whittock, *The Viking Blitzkrieg, AD 789–1098*, The History Press (Stroud), p. 136–7. See also Jeffrey James, *An Onslaught of Spears: The Danish Conquest of England,* The History Press (Stroud), 2013, p. 41.
3. The reference to Cynethryth and the extent of her control is from Pauline Stafford, 'Political Women in Mercia, Eighth to Early Tenth Centuries' in in *Mercia: An Anglo-Saxon Kingdom in Europe* eds. Michelle P. Brown and Carol A. Farr (London, 2005), p. 39–43.
4. The titles used for Æthelflæd come from various charters, which are listed in the Bibliography. These are in the Sawyer collection S221, S225, S1282. The nature and origin of the Anglo-Saxon term for Lady of the Mercians as a feminine form of 'Lord' or *hlaford* has been well discussed in Herbert. See *Peace Weavers and Shield Maidens* p. 17.
5. Don Stansbury suggested that the seizure of the two cities actually took place because Edward was not entirely happy about what had taken place, and how easily she had taken power, almost as a way of punishing Mercia. An example of sibling jealousy? Perhaps. See *The Lady Who Fought the Vikings* p. 179.

6. The charter is S224, and the term used is one reasonably common in some of Æthelflæd's charters 'meo fidelo amico' or 'my faithful friend'. It is nice to think this was a term she reserved for advisors of officials who had perhaps served her well, or with whom she had a close relationship, however, it could simply have been a form of political flattery.
7. Æthelweard gives the most detailed account of the position of the armies at Tettenhall, and helps us to understand not only how the battle may have been won, but also why Æthelflæd built her burh where she did. It also proves my theory, that they were attacked whilst crossing the bridge correct. The account is in Campbell's edition of Æthelweard p. 53.
8. Donald Stansbury, *The Lady Who Fought the Vikings* (Devon, 1993), p. 186. The silver penny coin can be seen in the images section.
9. Chris Peers, *Offa and the Mercian Wars* (Barnsley, 2012), p. 172. Peers explains how the once great state of the Mercian capital had been reduced. The state of the church of St Agatha is quoted on the official website for the church its publications. See *The Collegiate and Parish Church of St Editha, Tamworth: Our History,* The Parish of Tamworth, Accessed 15th October 2016,
10. Jim Gould, *The Early History of Tamworth and the Lower Tame Valley,* (Staffordshire County Council, 1974), p. 7, 12–20. This is a useful little booklet by a local history expert and archaeologist, copies can be found in Tamworth and Lichfield libraries. See Stansbury, *The Lady Who Fought the Vikings*, p. 187 for the more detailed descriptions of the fortifications including the reported walkways.

11. Gould, *Ibid*, p. 16–17 for the position for the discussion of Danish settlements. See *The Anglo-Saxon Chronicles* p. 97, for the official account of the building of the town.
12. Martin Carver, *The Birth of a Borough: An Archaeological Study of Anglo-Saxon Stafford* (Woodbridge, 2010), p. 74, 99–100.
13. *Annals of Ireland*, Annal Fragment 459, Corpus of Electronic Texts Edition (CELT), University College Ulster, p. 181–3, http://www.ucc.ie/celt/published/T100017/
14. For the possible meaning of *Scargeat* see Tony Sharp, 'Chronicles, Treaties and Burhs: The Burghal Hidage and he Mercian Reconquest, Part 1 Section 4, The Burghal Hidage, p. 19 and 'Part 2: Identifying the Forts of the Mercian Reconquest', Published by Guildable Manor of Southwark, 2013. For a discussion of the possible order of building. This is a short abstract in the publication, which is free self-published document available for download from the author's page on Academia.edu.
15. Martin Carver, *Birth of a Borough*, p. 143–5.
16. Tom Holland, *Athelstan: The Birth of England* (London, 2016), Caption Figure 6 is where the author actually uses the term 'urban regeneration'.

12 *Daughter of God*

1. Alfred's preface to St Gregory's *Pastoral Care* can be read in Simon Keynes and Michael Lapidge ed. and trans. *Alfred the Great: Asser's Life of Alfred and Other Contemporary Sources*, p. 124–5 and notes. Michael Wood also discussed the text in the first episode of his documentary *King Alfred and the Anglo-Saxons* (BBC 2, 29TH August 2014).

2. See Keynes and Lapidge above, p. 128–9. This is from extracts from the text itself instead of just the better known preface.
3. See the 'Worcester Charter' in EHD, p. 540–41.
4. Pauline Stafford, *Queens, Concubines and Dowagers: The King's Wife in the Early Middle Ages* (London, 1998), p. 26. See also *Longman Anthology of Old English, Old Icelandic and Anglo-Norman Literatures,* ed. Richard North et al. (Abingdon, 2011), p. 402.
5. 'Judith', *The Apocrypha KJV*, (Iowa, 1996), Chapters 1–8, p. 53–9.
6. *Judith*, p. 141, lines 1–25.
7. *Judith*, p. 141–3, Lines 29–36.
8. *Judith*, p. 145–147, Lines 67–109
9. Elizabeth Shaughnessy, "Judith's Necessary Androgyny: Representations of Gender in the Old English Judith." *Emergence: A Journal of Undergraduate Literary Criticism and Creative Research* 3 (2012), p. 4.
10. See the *Anglo-Saxon Chronicles* and the CELT version of the *Annals of Ireland* p. 181–3 for these remarks, showing how observers believed Æthelflæd succeeded by her own cunning and wit and sometimes by divine favour.
11. *Judith,* lines 131–197.
12. Stafford, *Queens, Concubines and Dowagers*, p. 26–7.

13 Shield Maiden: 916–June 918

1. Judith Jesch, *Women in the Viking Age* (Woodbridge, 2001), p. 5, p. 65, p. 79–83, p. 190–208.
2. See James Illston, 'An Entirely Masculine Activity'? Women and War in the High and Late Middle Ages Reconsidered',

MA Thesis (University of Canterbury, 2009), p. 57–8. Also See Robert Bartlett, *The Making of Europe: Conquest, Colonization and Cultural Change 950–1350* (London, 1993), p. 244 and The Encyclopaedia Britannica entry on Matilda. https://www.britannica.com/biography/Matilda-of-Canossa. There is also a useful e-book on Matilda edited by Marian Ebrahim and Aldo Terrebruno which is part of a series on Women and Power in Medieval Italy. Unfortunately, like most ebooks it does not use actual page numbers, so can only be cited by title. Ebrahim and Torrehundo ed. *Matilda of Canossa: Women and Power in Medieval Italy Book Two,* English Edition (Milan, 2003), Kindle Edition.

The quote from William of Malmesbury comes from his *Gesta Regum Anglorum* or History of the Kings of Britain, abbreviated here to WM, GRA, p. 613. See the abbreviations section for the full citation.

3. *Ibid,* p. 58. See also Christine de Pisan, Sarah Lawson (tr.), *The Treasure of the City of the Ladies* (London, 2003), p. 109–11 for the passage advising women to familiarize themselves with the use of weapons.
4. Anna Comnena, *The Alexiad of Anna Comnena*, trans. E. R. A. Sewter (Harmondsworth, 1969), p. 121.
5. Susan M. Johns, *Noblewoman, Aristocracy and Power in the Twelfth-Century Anglo-Norman Realm* (Manchester, 2003), p. 14.
6. Pauline Stafford, *Queens, Concubines and Dowagers: The King's Wife in the Early Middle Ages* (London, 1998), p. 117–118.

7. See Geoffrey Hindley, *A Brief History of the Anglo-Saxons* (London, 2006), for the note about Æthelflæd commanding her army on horseback. Bede mentioned that from the earliest period, even pagan priests were not supposed to ride a stallion or use a spear, which is exactly what Coifi, a priest during the reign of the seventh century King Edwin of Northumbria did to desecrate a pagan shrine. See *The Ecclesiastical History, p. 68. (Following the Oxford edition used in the Bibliography*
8. *The Anglo-Saxon Chronicles*, p. 100.
9. The charter is S425. See also Kari Maund, *The Welsh Kings: The Medieval Rulers of Wales* (Stroud, 2000), p. 36 for the discussion of the alternative identity of the obscure Tewdyr.
10. *Annals of Ireland,* Fragment 459, p. 183.
11. *Ibid.*
12. M916.14, *Annals of the Four Masters,* Corpus of Electronic Texts Edition (CELT), University College Cork, http://www.ucc.ie/research/celt/published/T100005B/index.html
13. U918.4, The Annals of Ulster', *ed. & tr. Seán Mac Airt and Gearóid Mac Niocaill (Dublin, 1983),* p. 369. *CELT, Corpus of Electronic Texts Edition, University College Cork*, 2000.
14. *Anglo-Saxon Chronicles,* p. 97–8.
15. See Stansbury, *The Lady who fought the Vikings,* p. 205–6. For the mention of the coalition between Æthelflæd and the rulers of Strathclyde and Scotland see Wainwright, 'Lady of the Mercians' p. 319–20.
16. Thomas Noble (ed.), Stephen Glover, *The History, Gazetteer and Directory of the County of Derby* (Derby, 1829) p. 349. I could not identify the Welsh Prince in question, supposedly named Hughan.

17. The Roman remains of 'Little Chester' have been considered the most likely location of the Battle. Stephen Glover's volume above, referred to the battle taking place at a 'Castle' but there is no castle in the city today, and as has already been mentioned, there would not have been any in Æthelflæd's day. Thus it seems likely that the 'Castle' refers to a stone structure, for which the re-used remains of the Roman fort seem a likely candidate.
18. The reference to the death of Æthelflæd's 'beloved' retainers in the *Anglo-Saxon Chronicles*, p. 101. Victoria Thompson discussed the meaning of the word in a feminine context in her book *Death and Dying in Anglo-Saxon England* (Woodbridge, 2011), p. 11.

    A more detailed discussion of the meaning and use of the word can be found in the very useful Bosworth Toller Anglo-Saxon dictionary, which is available online. Bosworth, Joseph. "An Anglo-Saxon Dictionary Online." *Be-sorg*. Ed. Thomas Northcote Toller and Others. Comp. Sean Christ and Ondřej Tichý. Faculty of Arts, Charles University in Prague, 21 Mar. 2010, Accessed 31 Aug. 2014. <http://bosworth.ff.cuni.cz/003969>.
19. See Ryan Lavelle, *Alfred's Wars: Sources and Interpretations of Anglo-Saxon Warfare in the Viking Age* (Woodbridge, 2010), p. 13–14 and 19–20 for a discussion of what the passage about the death of the thegns can tell us about Æthelflæd's relationship with her warband.

    He relates a passage in the *Anglo-Saxon Chronicle* in which the retainers of Cyneheard, an eighth century King of Wessex chose to die rather than abandon their sworn allegiance to their murdered King. It did not matter to them that the murder was actually part of a particularly nasty blood feud. See *ASC* p. 47–8.

20. *Anglo-Saxon Chronicles,* p. 105.
21. *ASC,* p. 105. See also Stansbury, p. 210–11.
22. *ASC,* ibid. Stansbury suggested that Æthelflæd may well have had a strong personal dislike for fighting, and for this reason avoided direct conflict as much as she could and sought to impose her authority by diplomatic, legal and economic means instead. Considering her background and circumstances, this is not impossible. See *The Lady who fought the Vikings* p. 200–2, 208–11.
23. See Geoffrey Hindley, *A Brief History of the Anglo-Saxons,* p. 268.
24. Her death is one of the few details which is recorded in almost every version of the *Anglo-Saxon Chronicles*, but it also gets a mention in other sources when those of her relatives do not. See the Swanton version of *The Anglo-Saxon Chronicles* (the one used throughout this work), p. 103–5.

14 *The Lady and the Stone: 918–919*

1. In total, her name only crops up in three charters, and in two of those she is only mentioned as a subject. She only acted as a witness in one of them, so it is possible to question the level of her actual involvement in politics. This was charter S225, regarding a grant of land which had been destroyed in a fire. Maggie Bailey proposed another charter S367 may have been signed by her as well, eliminating several other candidates. See Maggie 'Ælfwyn: Second Lady of the Mercians', in

Edward the Elder: 899–924 ed. N. J. Higham and D. H. Hill, Routledge (London), 2001, p. 118–120.

2. Bailey estimates a date of birth sometime in the late 880s, and this is the most commonly accepted supposition. Some have posited a much later date (Victoria Whitworth hints at it in one of her novels-although this may a literary embellishment) probably to account for the fact that she was unmarried in 918. See Kathleen Herbert, *Peace Weavers and Shield Maidens*, p. 25.n for a discussion of what Æthelflæd's reaction might have been to the event. Maggie Bailey and Jane Wolfe suggest her mother may have been fostering her to follow in her footsteps by entrusting her with land.
3. *ASC*, p. 105.
4. Sarah Foot, *Athelstan: The First King of England*, (London, 2011), p. 14–15.
5. See Jane Wolfe, Æthelflæd: Royal Lady, War Lady (Chester, 2001), p. 17–19.
6. *Anglo-Saxon Chronicles*, p. 104, see also Sean Miller, 'Edward the Elder (870s?–924)', *Oxford Dictionary of National Biography*, Oxford University Press, 2004; online edn, Sept 2011 http://www.oxforddnb.com/view/article/8514, accessed 3 Nov 2016]
7. Sean Miller, 'Edward the Elder. (870s?–924)', *Oxford Dictionary of National Biography*, Oxford University Press, 2004; online edn, Sept 2011. See Also the *Anglo-Saxon Chronicles* p. 104–5. The identification with the fortress in Rhuddlan is made in note 14 on page 104.
8. Sarah Foot, 'Æthelstan (893/4–939)', Oxford Dictionary of National Biography, Oxford University Press, 2004; online

edn, Sept 2011 http://www.oxforddnb.com/view/article/833, accessed 3 Nov 2016].

9. Sarah Foot, *Athelstan: The First King of England*, (London, 2011), p. 36–7, p. 206–7. The latter passage contains the reference to the 'pact of paternal piety'.
10. Janina Ramirez tells us that the works of Aldhelm were popular throughout the tenth century and the late Saxon period. See *The Private Lives of the Saints*, p. 274–5.
11. See Maggie Bailey, 'Ælfwyn, Second Lady of the Mercians', N. J. Higham & D. H. Hil ed. *Edward the Elder: 899–924* (London, 2001), p. 124. The charter in question is S534. For the alternative suggestion of who the mysterious Ælfwyn might have been see Shashi Jayakumar, 'Eadwig and Edgar: Politics, Propaganda, Faction' in Donald Scragg, *Edgar, King of the English, 959–975* (Woodbridge, 2008), p. 94.

15 'Heroic Elflede'

1. Poem is from *The Chronicle of Henry of Huntingdon, Trans. Thomas Forester* (London, 1853), p168.
2. Ann Williams, 'Edgar (943/4–975)', Oxford Dictionary of National Biography, Oxford University Press, 2004; online edn, Jan 2014 http://www.oxforddnb.com/view/article/8463, accessed 11 Nov 2016]
3. WM, *GRA*, p. 199.
4. JW: vol. 2, p. 381 and Higham, *Edward the Elder*, p. 3.
5. HH, p309. The definition of 'virago' is open to debate. A meaning other than 'virgin' is discussed later in this chapter. It can also mean a woman who acts like a man.

6. HH, p. 307. See also *Bede*, p. 202–5 for the account of Æthelthryth, the Queen supposedly remained a virgin for the twelve years of her marriage.
7. Björn Weiler,"William of Malmesbury on Kingship." *History* 90.297 (2005): p. 5.
8. McLaughlin, M., 'The woman warrior: gender, warfare and society in medieval Europe' in *Women's Studies: An Interdisciplinary Journal* 17.3–4 (1990), p. 195.
9. William of Malmesbury, p. 755. In a letter to Empress Matilda, contained at the beginning of the work, William recounts how the brothers of his house had told her mother, Queen Matilda of her West Saxon descent when she had boasted of descent from Aldhelm, and drawn up a list of Kings at her request. Considering his own affinity for Æthelstan, it seems highly unlikely he could have been unaware that the West Saxon line included Alfred and Æthelflæd.
10. WM, *GRA*, p. 9.
11. In the *Historia Novella* written c1140, William of Malmesbury asserted that the descent of Matilda from Edmund Ironside was a 'well known' fact. This work was composed some 15 years after the *Historia Regia Angorum,* so it would appear that in the interval, the knowledge of Matilda's lineage seems to have become more widely known and disseminated from the time that the brothers of Malmesbury had to create a King list for her mother.
12. WM, *GRA*, p. 759.
13. WM, HN, p. 54.
14. WM, HN, p. 4.

15. WM, GRA, p. 199. Christine Fell, *Women in Saxon England,* p.187.
16. WM, *HN*, p. 24.
17. WM, *HN*, p. 56.
18. WM, GRA, p. 199.
19. WM, GRA, p. 54. See also Jane Wolfe, Æthelflæd: Royal Lady, War Lady (Chester, 2001) p. 19.
20. Helen Castor, *She Wolves: The Women who ruled England before Elizabeth* (London, 2010), p. 104.
21. Nesta Pain, *Empress Matilda: Uncrowned Queen of England* (London, 1978), p. 103. Chibnall is quoted in James Illston, *Women and War,* p. 22.
22. *Ibid*, p. 63.

Glossary and Back Matter

1. See Michael Lapidge et al. *The Blackwell Encyclopaedia of Anglo-Saxon England* (Oxford, 1999), p. 13–14.
2. *Ibid,* p. 152–3.
3. *Ibid.*
4. Bosworth, Joseph. "An Anglo-Saxon Dictionary Online." *Hláford*. Ed. Thomas Northcote Toller and Others. Comp. Sean Christ and Ondřej Tichý. Faculty of Arts, Charles University in Prague, 21 Mar. 2010. Web. 6 Nov. 2016. For the connection to 'loaf' see Kathleen Hebert, *Peace Weavers and Shield Maidens*, (Milton Keynes, 1997), p. 17.
5. See 'The Wife's Lament', in Richard Hamer ed. *A Choice of Anglo-Saxon Verse* (London, 1970), p. 73, line 46. Also *Judith* in the same book, p. 161.
6. Bosworth, Joseph. "An Anglo-Saxon Dictionary Online." *Hlæfdige*. Ed. Thomas Northcote Toller and Others. Comp.

Sean Christ and Ondřej Tichý. Faculty of Arts, Charles University in Prague, 21 Mar. 2010. Web. 6 Nov. 2016.

7. *Blackwell Encyclopaedia*, p. 47.
8. Bosworth, Joseph. "An Anglo-Saxon Dictionary Online." *Morgen-gifu*. Ed. Thomas Northcote Toller and Others. Comp. Sean Christ and Ondřej Tichý. Faculty of Arts, Charles University in Prague, 21 Mar. 2010. Web. 6 Nov. 2016
9. Bosworth, Joseph. "An Anglo-Saxon Dictionary Online." *þegen*. Ed. Thomas Northcote Toller and Others. Comp. Sean Christ and Ondřej Tichý. Faculty of Arts, Charles University in Prague, 14 Aug. 2011. Web. 6 Nov. 2016.
10. Quote from *Blackwell Encyclopaedia* p. 443.

BIBLIOGRAPHY

Primary Sources

A Choice of Anglo-Saxon Verse, Introduction and trans. Richard Hamer (Faber: London, 1970).

Alfred the Great, Asser's Life of King Alfred and other Contemporary Sources, ed. and trans. S. D. Keynes and M. Lapidge (Penguin: London, 1983).

'Annales Cambriae: The Annals of Wales 447-954', ed. Paul Halsall 1998, Internet Medieval Sourcebook, Fordham University Centre for Medieval Studies, http://sourcebooks.fordham.edu/halsall/sbook.asp

'Annals of the Four Masters', ed. and tr. John O'Donovan (Dublin, 1856), CELT, Corpus of Electronic Texts Edition, University College Cork, 2002, 2008.

Anglo-Saxon Poetry, ed. and trans. S. A. J. Bradley (J. M. Dent and Sons: London, 1982).

Amt, Emilie ed. *Women's Lives in Medieval Europe: A Sourcebook* (Routledge: London, 1993).

Anna Comnena, *The Alexiad of Anna Comnena*, trans. E. R. A. Sewter (Penguin: London, 1969).

The Apocrypha: King James Version (World Bible Publishers: Iowa, 1996).

Bede, *The Ecclesiastical History of the English People,* ed. and trans. Judith McClure and Roger Collins (Oxford University Press: Oxford, 1994).

Bede, *The Reckoning of Time,* trans. Faith Wallis, (Liverpool University Press: Liverpool, 1991).

Dutton, Paul Edward ed. *Carolingian Civilisation: A Reader* (Broadview Press: Essex, 1997).

'Fragmentary Annals of Ireland', ed. and tr. by Joan Radner (Dublin, 1978), *CELT: Corpus of Electronic Texts Edition, University College Cork*, 2004, 2008, http://www.ucc.ie/celt

Henry of Huntingdon, *Historia Anglorum: The History of the English People*, ed. and trans. Diana Greenway (Clarendon Press: Oxford, 1996).

The Chronicle of Æthelweard, ed. A. Campbell (Thomas Nelson and Sons: London, 1962).

The Chronicle of Fabius Ethelwerd: From the Beginning of the World to the Year of our Lord 975, ed. and trans. J. A. Giles (London, 1848).

The Chronicle of John of Worcester: Volume II: The Annals 450-1066, ed. and trans. R. R. Darlington and P. McGurk (Clarendon Press: Oxford, 1995).

The Anglo-Saxon Chronicles: New Edition, ed. and trans. Michael Swanton (Phoenix Press: London, 2000).

The Anglo-Saxon World: An Anthology, introduction and trans. Crossley-Holland, K (Oxford University Press: Oxford, 1982).

'The Annals of Ulster', *ed. & tr. Seán Mac Airt and Gearóid Mac Niocaill (Dublin, 1983), CELT, Corpus of Electronic Texts Edition, University College Cork*, 2000.

William of Malmesbury, *Gesta Regum Anglorum: The History of the English Kings, Volume 1*, ed. and trans. RA. B. Mynors, R. M. Thomson and M. Winterbottom (Clarendon Press, Oxford, 1998).

William of Malmesbury *The Historia Novella*: *The New History*, trans. K. R. Potter (Thomas Nelson and Sons: London, 1955).

Whitelock, Dorothy (ed.), *English Historical Documents, Vol 1: 500-1052* (Eyre Methuen: London, 1972).

Charters

All charters are categorized by their name, page, or number in the collection in which they are contained or transcribed today. Those beginning with the letter S are from the E-Sawyer catalogue, which is an online database of the Anglo-Saxon charters adapted from the book *Anglo-Saxon Charters: An Annotated List and Bibliography* by Peter Sawyer, which was published by the Royal Historical Society in 1968.

S1201

S1280

S1282

S215

S221

S224

S225

S361

S367

S525

Secondary Sources

Abels, R., *Alfred the Great: War. Kingship and Culture in Anglo-Saxon England* (Longman: Harlow, 1998).

Albert, Edoardo, and Tucker, Katie, *In Search of Alfred the Great*, (Amberley: Stroud, 2014.)

Adams, Max, *The King in the North: The Life and Times of Oswald of Northumbria* (Head of Zeus, London, 2013).

Astell, Ann W., 'Holofernes's head: tacen and teaching in the Old English Judith' in *Anglo-Saxon England* 18 (Cambridge, 1989), p117-133.

'Alfred 8', Prosopography of Anglo-Saxon England, http://pase.ac.uk, Accessed 29th July 2016.

'Ælfwyn 2', Prosopography of Anglo-Saxon England, http://www.pase.ac.uk, Accessed 28th August 2016.

'Æthelflæd 4', Prosopography of Anglo-Saxon England, http://pase.ac.uk, Accessed 28th August 2016.

'Æthelred 1', Prosopography of Anglo-Saxon England, http://pase.ac.uk, Accessed 28th August 2016.

Bailey, Maggie, 'Ælfwyn, Second Lady of the Mercians', N. J. Higham & D.H. Hill ed. *Edward the Elder: 899-924* (Pearson: London, 2001),

Baird, Joseph L., *The Personal Correspondence of Hildegard Von Bingen* (Oxford University Press: Oxford, 2006).

Bartlett, R, *The Making of Europe: Conquest, Colonization and Cultural Change 950-1350* (Penguin: London, 1993).

Bassett, S., 'Divide and rule? The military infrastructure of eighth- and ninth-century Mercia' *Early Medieval Europe* 15.1 (2007) p53-85.

Blair, John 'Mildburg (*d.* in or after 716)', *Oxford Dictionary of National Biography*, 2004-16, www.oxforddnb.com

Bosworth, Joseph, "An Anglo-Saxon Dictionary Online." Ed. Thomas Northcote Toller and Others. Comp. Sean Christ and

Ondřej Tichý. Faculty of Arts, Charles University in Prague, 21 Mar. 2010.

Brown, Nancy Marie, *The Abacus and the Cross: The Story of the Pope who bought the Light of Science to the Dark Ages* (Basic Books: New York, 2010).

Campbell, J., 'What is not known about the reign of Edward the Elder', Higham, N.J. and Hill, D.H. (eds.), *Edward the Elder, 899-924* (Routledge: London, 2001).

Castor, H., *She Wolves: The Women Who Ruled England Before Elizabeth* (Faber: London, 2010).

Carver, Martin, *The Birth of a Borough: An Archaeological Study of Anglo-Saxon Stafford* (Boydell Press: Woodbridge, 2010).

Clayton, M., 'Ælfric's Judith: manipulative or manipulated?' in *Anglo-Saxon England* 23 (Cambridge, 1994) p215-227.

Costambeys, Marios, 'Ealhswith (*d.* 902)', *Oxford Dictionary of National Biography*, 2004-16, www.oxforddnb.com

Costambeys, Marios, 'Æthelred (*d.* 911)', *Oxford Dictionary of National Biography*, Oxford University Press, 2004-2016, www.oxforddnb.com

Costambeys, Marios, 'Æthelflæd (*d.* 918)', *Oxford Dictionary of National Biography*,2004-2016, www.oxforddnb.com

Crawford, S., *Childhood in Anglo-Saxon England* (Sutton Publishing: Stroud, 1999).

Crawford, S., *Daily Life in Anglo-Saxon England* (Greenwood: Oxford, 2008)

Cumberledge, Nicola, "Reading Between the Lines: The Place of Mercia Within an Expanding Wessex." *Midland History* 27.1 (2002), p1-15.

Dalton, Paul, 'The Topical Concerns of Geoffrey of Monmouth's Historia Regum Britannie: History, Prophecy, Peacemaking and English Identity in the Twelfth Century' in *Journal of British Studies,* Vol. 44, No. 4 (October 2005), p688-712.

Downham, C., *Viking Kings of Britain and Ireland: The Dynasty of Ívarr to A.D.1014* (Dunedin Academic Press: Edinburgh, 2007).

Fell, C., *Women in Anglo-Saxon England and the impact of 1066* (British Museum Press: London, 1984).

Fenton, K. A., *Gender, Nation and Conquest in the Works of William of Malmesbury* (Boydell Press: Woodbridge, 2008).

Ferguson, Robert, *The Hammer and the Cross: A New History of the Vikings* (Penguin: London, 2009).

Foot, Sarah, 'Æthelstan (893/4–939)', *Oxford Dictionary of National Biography*, 2004-2016, www.oxforddnb.com

Foot, S., *Æthelstan: The First King of England* (Yale University Press: London, 2011).

Gies, F. and Gies, J., *Women in the Middle Ages* (Harper Collins: New York, 1978).

Gould, Jim, *The Early History of Tamworth and the Lower Tame Valley* (Staffordshire County Council: Stafford, 1974).

Harper, John, 'Herald History: Ethelfleda the Mighty Lady of the Mercians', *Tamworth Herald*, October 27th 2015, http://www.tamworthherald.co.uk

Haywood, John, *Northmen: The Viking Saga, 793-1241* (Head of Zeus: London, 2015).

Herbert, K., *Peace Weavers and Shield Maidens: Women in Early English Society* (Anglo-Saxon Books: Milton Keynes, 1997).

Herbert, N. M. ed. 'Anglo-Saxon Gloucester: c.680 - 1066', in *A History of the County of Gloucester: Volume 4, the City of Gloucester* (London, 1988), pp. 5-12. *British History Online* http://www.british-history.ac.uk/vch/glos/vol4/pp5-12.

Hindley, Geoffrey, *A Brief History of the Anglo-Saxons* (Robinson: London, 2006).

Holland, Tom, *Athelstan: The Making of England* (Allen Lane: London, 2016).

Higham, N., 'Edward the Elder's Reputation: An Introduction', Higham, N. J. and Hill, D. H. (eds), *Edward the Elder, 899-924* (Pearson: London, 2001).

Higham, N. J. and Ryan, M. J., *The Anglo-Saxon World* (Yale University Press: New Haven, 2013).

Hinton, D. A., *Gold & Gilt, Pots & Pins: Possessions and People in Medieval Britain* (Oxford University Press: Oxford, 2005).

Illston, J. M., "An Entirely Masculine Activity?': Women and War in the High and Late Middle Ages Reconsidered", MA Thesis (University of Canterbury, 2009).

Jayakumar, Shashi, 'Eadwig and Edgar: Politics, Propaganda, Faction' in Donald Scragg, *Edgar, King of the English, 959–975* (Boydell Press: Woodbridge, 2008).

James, Jeffrey, *An Onslaught of Spears: The Danish Conquest of England* (The History Press: Stroud, 2013).

Jesch, Judith, *Women in the Viking Age* (Boydell Press: Woodbridge, 1991).

Keynes, S., 'Mercia and Wessex in the Ninth Century', in *Mercia: An Anglo-Saxon Kingdom in Europe* ed. Michelle P. Brown and Carol A. Farr (Continuum: London, 2005) p310-328.

Keynes, S., 'Edward, King of the Anglo-Saxons', N. J. Higham & D. H. Hill ed. *Edward the Elder: 899-924* (Pearson: London, 2001).

Lapidge, M., Blair, J., Keynes, S. and Scragg, D. (eds), *The Blackwell Encyclopaedia of Anglo-Saxon England* (Blackwell Publishers: Oxford, 1999).

Lapidge, M., 'Aldhelm [St Aldhelm] (*d.* 709/10)', *Oxford Dictionary of National Biography* 2004-2016, www.oxforddnb.com

Lavelle, R., *Fortifications in Wessex c. 800-1066*, (Osprey: Oxford, 2003).

Lavelle, R. *Alfred's Wars: Sources and Interpretations of Anglo-Saxon Warfare in the Viking Age* (Boydell: Woodbridge, 2010).

Lavelle, R. and S. Roffey (ed). *Danes in Wessex: The Scandinavian Impact Upon Southern England, c.800- c. 1100* (Oxbow Books: Oxford, 2016).

Marren, Peter, *Battles of the Dark Ages: British Battlefields AD 410-1065* (Pen and Sword Books: Barnsley, 2006).

McLaughlin, M., 'The woman warrior: gender, warfare and society in medieval Europe' *Women's Studies: An Interdisciplinary Journal* 17.3-4 (1990), p 193-209.

Merkle, Benjamin, *The White Horse King: The Life of Alfred the Great*, (Thomas Nelson: Nashville, 2009).

Miller, Sean, 'Edward [Edward the Elder] (870s?–924)', *Oxford Dictionary of National Biography*, 2004-2016, www.oxforddnb.com

Nelson, J. L., 'Wealth and Wisdom: The Politics of Alfred the Great' in *Rulers and Ruling Families in Early Medieval Europe: Alfred, Charles the Bald and others* (Routledge: Aldershot, 1999), p31-52.

Nicholson, H., *Medieval Warfare, Theory and Practice of Warfare in Europe, 300-1500* (Palgrave Macmillan: Basingstoke, 2003).

Pain, Nesta, *Empress Matilda: Uncrowned Queen of England* (Weidenfeld and Nicolson: London, 1978).

Partner, N. F., *Serious Entertainments: The Writing of History in Twelfth- Century England* (University of Chicago Press: Chicago, 1977).

Pollard, J., *Alfred the Great: The Man Who Made England* (John Murray: London, 2005).

Rank, Michael, 'HFM 028 – The Most Powerful Women in the Middle Ages, Part 1: Lady Aethelflaed of the Mercians (872-918): The Real-Life Eowyn of Rohan and Viking Slayer', *History in Five Minutes,* August 12th 2013.

Ramirez, Janina, *Private Lives of the Saints: Passion, Politics and Power in Anglo-Saxon England* (Allen Lane: London, 2015).

Sharp, Tony, 'Chronicles, Treaties and Burhs: Part 1 Section 4, The Burghal Hidage', Guildable Manor of Southwark, 2013.

Sharp, Tony, 'Chronicles, Treaties and Burhs: Part One Section 8, Guthrum's Retreat in 879, Guildable Manor of Southwark, 2013.

Sharp, Tony, 'The Mercian Reconquest: Part 2.

Shaughnessy, E., 'Judith's Necessary Androgyny: Representations of Gender in the Old English Judith.' *Emergence: A Journal of Undergraduate Literary Criticism and Creative Research* 3 (2012), p1-8.

Stafford, P., *Queens, Concubines and Dowagers: The King's Wife in the Early Middle Ages* (Leicester University Press: Leicester, 1983).

Stafford, P., *Unification and Conquest: A Political and Social History of England in the Tenth and Eleventh Centuries* (Edward Arnold: London, 1989).

Stafford, P., 'Succession and Inheritance: A Gendered Perspective on Alfred's Family History', in *Alfred the Great: Papers from the Eleventh Centenary Conferences* ed. Timothy Reuter (Routledge: Aldershot, 2003), p251-264.

Stafford, P., 'Political Women in Mercia: Eighth to Early Tenth Centuries' in *Mercia: An Anglo-Saxon Kingdom in Europe* ed. Michelle P. Brown and Carol A. Farr (Continuum: London, 2005), p35-49.

Stafford, P., "The Annals of Æthelflæd': Annals History and Politics in Early Tenth-Century England', in *Myth, Rulership, Church and Charters: Essays in Honour of Nicholas Brooks,* ed. Barrow. J. and Wareham. A. (Routledge: Aldershot, 2008), p101-116.

Stansbury, Donald, *The Lady Who Fought the Vikings* (Imogen Books: Devon, 2003).

Thacker, Alan, 'Hild (614–680)', *Oxford Dictionary of National Biography*, 2004-16, www.oxforddnb.com

Thompson, V., *Death and Dying in Later Anglo-Saxon England* (Boydell Press: Woodbridge, 2004).

Wainwright, F. T., 'Æthelflæd, Lady of the Mercians', in *Scandinavian England* ed. H.P.R. Finberg (Phillimore and Co: Chichester, 1975), p305-324.

Weiler, Björn, 'William of Malmesbury on Kingship' *History* 90.297 (2005), p 3-22.

Williams, G., 'Military Institutions and Royal Power' *Mercia: An Anglo-Saxon Kingdom in Europe* ed. Michelle P. Brown and Carol A. Farr (Continuum: London, 2005), p296-309.

Walker, I. W., *Mercia and the Making of England* (Sutton: Stroud, 2000).

Wall, Martin, *The Anglo-Saxon Age: The Birth of England* (Amberley Publishing: Stroud, 2015)

Wall, Martin, *The Anglo-Saxons in 100 Facts* (Amberley Publishing: Stroud, 2016).

Whittock, Martyn and Whittock, Hannah, *The Viking Blitzkrieg, AD 789-1098* (The History Press: Stroud, 2013).

Wolfe, J., *Æthelflæd: Royal Lady, War Lady* (Fenris Press: Chester, 2001).

Woolf, A., 'A View from the West: An Irish Perspective on West Saxon dynastic practice', Higham, N. J. and Hill, D. H. (eds.), *Edward the Elder, 899-924* (Routledge: London, 2001).

Wood, Michael, *In Search of the Dark Ages* (BBC Books: London, 1981).

Wood, Michael, *In Search of England: Journeys into the English Past* (Penguin: London, 1999).

Wood, Michael, 'King Alfred and the Anglo-Saxons: Episode 2, The Lady of the Mercians', BBC 2, Broadcast 13th August 2013.

Wood, Michael, 'King Alfred and the Anglo-Saxons, Episode 1: Alfred of Wessex', BBC 2, Broadcast 8th August 2013.

Wood, Michael, 'King Alfred and the Anglo-Saxons, Episode 3: Athelstan', BBC 2, Broadcast 22nd August 2013.

Yorke, Barbara, *Alfred the Great: Pocket Giants* (The History Press: Stroud, 2015).

Yorke, Barbara, *Kings and Kingdoms of Early Anglo-Saxon England* (Trafalgar Square: London, 1990).

Works of Fiction

Cornwell, Bernard, *Sword Song* (Harper: London, 2007).

Cornwell, Bernard, *The Burning Land* (Harper: London, 2009).

Grieser, Marjory A., *King Alfred's Daughter: The Lady of the Mercians* (Dog Ear Publishing: Indianapolis, 2010).

Tingle, Rebecca, *The Edge on the Sword,* (Speak: New York, 2001).

Wall, Martin, *Ismere: A Story of the Lady of the Mercians*, Lulu.com, 2013.

Whitehead, Annie, *To Be a Queen*, Amazon Publishing, 2013.

Whitworth, W. M., *The Bone Thief* (Ebury Press: London, 2012).

Whitworth, W. M., *The Traitor's Pit* (Ebury Press: London, 2013).

Whitworth, Victoria, *Daughter of the Wolf* (Head of Zeus: London, 2016).

ACKNOWLEDGEMENTS

Grateful thanks to the lovely people at Tamworth Castle & Heritage trust, and High House, Stafford for their help, advice, and pointing me to so many useful books. Also, to the person whose name sadly escapes me, who led me on an impromptu tour around St Edith's church Tamworth with so many useful details about its history. I am heartily glad that Æthelflæd is better known up in Staffordshire. Hopefully, I have done justice to your Great Lady.

Thanks are due also to Edoardo Albert for his useful advice and encouragement as a 'publisher buddy', Tom Holland for letting me use the image of the Chester Coin (his precious) featured in the pictures section, and to Professor Simon Keynes for permission to use the maps. Also, I must extend my thanks to fellow Amberley author Sara Hanna Black for letting me use her images of St Oswald's Priory.

Finally, I'm grateful to my family for tolerating my transformation into a hermit for days on end when I was working on this book.

INDEX

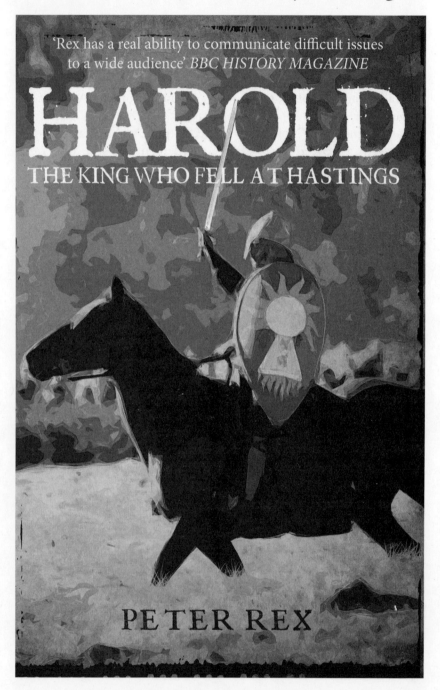

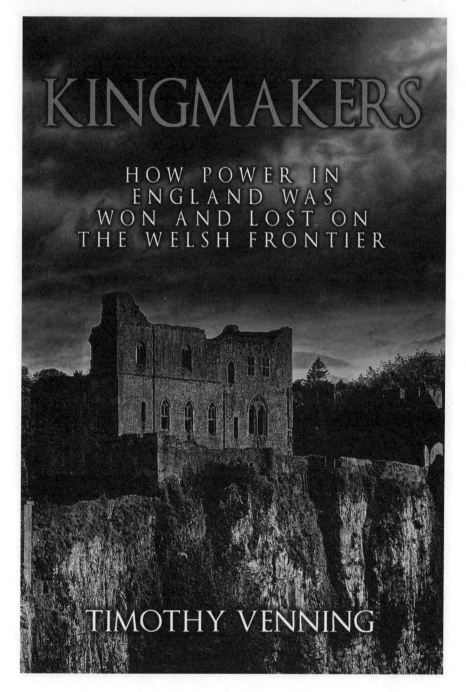